"High-profile folks like Marian Carey and Henry Kissinger rely on Bash, the trainer who can turn the most problematic pooch into a model canine."                                                —W

"Bash did a great job in training Sally, our Border Collie, and in return, she absolutely adores him. That, to me, seems like the best endorsement of his training philosophy."        —Matthew Broderick

"Bash not only trains dogs, but he truly loves them. And they love him too."                                     —Sarah Jessica Parker

"There's nobody quite like Bash when it comes to dogs!"
                                          —Barbara Taylor Bradford

"Bash Dibra has such a cult following among Manhattan pet owners that he is known simply as Bash, like a rock star. . . . To clients like Alec Baldwin, he's 'top dog' among personal pet trainers."
                                               —*The New York Times*

"Perhaps you are thinking of buying or adopting a dog. Or you may already have one, but there are still some things you wish he didn't do. Either way, Bashkim Dibra is the man with the answers."
                                                      —*Woman's Day*

### *Dog Training by Bash*

"A great book."                    —*Los Angeles Times Book Review*

"A helpful, easy-to-follow, complete guide."              —*Booklist*

"Great fun to read . . . well-written, accurate, informative, and entertaining."                                    —*Library Journal*

# BASH DIBRA

### WITH ELIZABETH RANDOLPH AND KITTY BROWN

## Your
## DREAM DOG

### A GUIDE TO CHOOSING THE RIGHT BREED FOR YOU

NEW AMERICAN LIBRARY

New American Library
Published by New American Library, a division of
Penguin Group (USA) Inc., 375 Hudson Street,
New York, New York 10014, U.S.A.
Penguin Books Ltd, 80 Strand,
London WC2R 0RL, England
Penguin Books Australia Ltd, 250 Camberwell Road,
Camberwell, Victoria 3124, Australia
Penguin Books Canada Ltd, 10 Alcorn Avenue,
Toronto, Ontario, Canada M4V 3B2
Penguin Books (N.Z.) Ltd, Cnr Rosedale and Airborne Roads,
Albany, Auckland 1310, New Zealand

Penguin Books Ltd, Registered Offices:
80 Strand, London WC2R 0RL, England

Published by New American Library, a division of Penguin Group (USA) Inc.
Previously published in a New American Library hardcover edition.

First New American Library Hardcover Printing, June 2003
First New American Library Trade Paperback Printing, June 2004
10  9  8  7  6  5  4  3  2  1

Kelpie photo copyright © Pet Profiles—Isabelle Francais
Plott Hound photo copyright © United Kennel Club
All other breed photos by Tara Darling

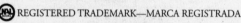 REGISTERED TRADEMARK—MARCA REGISTRADA

New American Library Trade Paperback ISBN: 0-451-21201-0
The Library of Congress has catalogued the hardcover edition of this book as follows:

Dibra, Bashkim.
Your dream dog : a guide to choosing the right breed for you / Bash Dibra with
Elizabeth Randolph and Kitty Brown ; breed photos by Tara Darling.
p.  cm.
1. Dogs.  2. Dogs—Selection.  3. Dog breeds.  I. Randolph, Elizabeth.
II. Brown, Kitty.  III. Title.
SF426 .D52 2003
636.7'1—dc21          2002040961

Set in Adobe Garamond
Designed by Ginger Legato

Printed in the United States of America

To all dog owners who appreciate
the unconditional love and joy a dog brings to their lives

# ACKNOWLEDGMENTS

There is no way to express gratitude to all those people whose patience and understanding support a writer through the writing of a book. Without the support of family and friends, such a project would not be possible.

Bash wishes especially to thank his sister Meruet, who took over all business matters while he was "otherwise occupied"; his sister Hope, who always is there for him; and Mary Ann Crenshaw for her support during the writing of this book. And he gives special thanks to all his loyal clients, who care for and love the dogs he has trained.

Elizabeth and Kitty both wish to thank their families, who understood that lives are put "on hold" during the writing of a book.

And all three of us thank our editor, Ellen Edwards, for her ongoing guidance.

# CONTENTS

# INTRODUCTION

As a dog trainer, I consider myself the luckiest man in the world. I'm doing the work I've always dreamed of, and a large and gratifying part of that job is ensuring that other people's dreams come true, as well. Every day I have the opportunity of doing the work I love with the creatures I love—dogs. I also get to meet their owners, from average people to CEOs of *Fortune* 500 companies, heads of state and some of the world's most celebrated superstars. I've trained Sarah Jessica Parker and Matthew Broderick's Border Collie, Sally; Mariah Carey's Yorkshire Terrier and Jack Russell (which add up to a handful!); Martin Scorsese's Bichon Frise; and Jennifer Lopez's Chihuahua. Even Henry Kissinger, who could solve the world's problems, needed help with his Labrador Retriever, Amelia. As you can see, the stars, just like all dog lovers, run the gamut of breed types and sizes with their choices, and each of these dogs has its own personality and characteristics. When owner and dog are a perfect match, it's a dream come true. When they are out of sync, it can be a nightmare for both parties. That's where I come in. Making the right choice, picking the dream dog for you, is crucial in the owner-dog relationship.

My lifelong affinity for dogs began when I was a small child in a Yugoslavian internment camp, where my family was detained after fleeing Albania. We were confined behind barbed wire, guarded by armed men and guard dogs—snarling, fearsome creatures that did a very good job of intimidating people. But for some inexplicable reason, I wasn't afraid of them. Much to the horror of the guards, I stuck my hand through the fence—and was rewarded with a warm lick. The

German Shepherd became my first dog friend, and I've had a soft spot for the breed ever since.

Later, when my family was finally freed, we traveled throughout Europe, where we worked for the landed gentry. These were some of the world's wealthiest people, owning thousands of acres of land, with stables and kennels. I had my first taste of working with dogs, and the passion has never left me.

During these years, I apprenticed with some of the most renowned trainers and kennel masters in Europe, and worked in kennels devoted to developing and breeding show-quality dogs. This experience gave me the unique opportunity to get to know almost every breed of dog and to learn the important qualities that differentiate a best-of-breed dog from one that is just mediocre. For instance, I learned that to breed an ideal hunting dog, one needs to watch for many things: a good nose; a willing, easy-to-please temperament; steadiness (calmness) in the face of gunfire; the ability to focus; and a good soft mouth for retrieving game. In other words, all the qualities needed to serve its master well on a hunt.

In addition to temperament and talent, the dog must be bred for beauty, to match what we in the profession call *standards*. These are different for each breed, depending on the breed's performance goals. Selective breeding—breeding the best to the best—results in dogs designed for a specific purpose. For instance, Dachshunds are long and low because they have been bred to crawl into the holes of badgers and foxes. Greyhounds are bred for speed, with long legs, a lean aerodynamic body and a small head. Labrador Retrievers have gentle mouths (the better for bringing game home unscathed), a water-resistant coat (to protect them when retrieving from lakes and ponds), while Border Collies are masters of the "stare" game, with an extraordinarily penetrating focus that lets them—with just a look—make the sheep go wherever the dog wants.

My experience with these remarkable kennel masters in my youth convinced me that working with dogs was what I wanted to do with my life. When my family moved to America, my path was already clear. I vowed to follow my dream of becoming a breeder and trainer of championship dogs. I would use my knowledge of breed standards to create the best possible hunting dogs. I wanted to enter my dogs in field trials for their talents, shows for their confirmation, and obedience trials for their intelligence. I aimed to create a Triple Crown champion, one that would be the hunting dog at its most perfect.

My breed of choice was the German Shorthaired Pointer. As it turned out, I couldn't have made a better choice. My dogs won championship after championship, while I became expert at showing them and, of course, training them. I used these same techniques to help breeders train their own show dogs of other breeds, rounding out my experience of all breeds and teaching me the quirks and idiosyncrasies that are peculiar to each.

I gained recognition as an expert trainer, and before I knew it, I was becoming the trainer of choice for the film and entertainment industries. They needed perfectly trained dogs as performers—dogs that could stack up against the famous German Shepherd and first dog star, Rin Tin Tin, or the unforgettable Collie, Lassie. But nothing in my experience prepared me for the event that would change my life forever. The producers of what would become a landmark in children's educational television—*The Boy Who Cried Wolf*—asked me to raise and train a wolf.

I was overwhelmed, exhilarated, and intimidated by the challenge. Who could know how a wolf might react to living in a house and being raised as a household pet? As I pondered that question, I had an epiphany: it was not just what I could teach the wolf, but what the wolf—the ancestor of the dog—could teach me, as well.

Mariah became my best friend, my loving companion, and the muse who inspired me. She helped me understand, with amazing clarity, that all dogs are created equal in the wolf. When, by selective breeding, we remove some of the primeval characteristics and reinforce others, we develop breeds designed for specific purposes, with specific characteristics from which prospective owners can pick.

Don't misunderstand me. There is no such thing as a "wrong dog." But if, for example, you live in a studio apartment in a crowded city, with no yard and no room for a dog to run, you wouldn't want to select a high-energy hunting dog as your canine companion. Both you and the dog would be far happier if you select a small breed like the Bichon Frise, who is always happy just being where you are. On the other hand, if you live on a hundred-acre farm and you want a dog that will keep watch over the place when you're not around, then a Briard or Great Pyrenees would be an excellent choice. Jennifer Lopez takes her Chihuahua, Raya, everywhere with her, which is pretty easy because the dog weighs only three pounds!

Excluding a breed that does not fit into your lifestyle isn't discrimination. Your choice cannot depend solely on whether you like or dislike a breed. If you're dreaming of cuddling up with a dog and a good book in a cozy nook, and you pick a dog that, unbeknownst to you, is dreaming of heading upstream after dark and treeing a raccoon—well, obviously, this match would not be a dream come true for either one of you.

Finding your dream dog takes a little bit of work, and you need to make intelligent decisions. The way to do this is not only to research what is "out there"—but also to determine what is within you. For whether your dream dog is going to be a "one-man dog" or a family pet, it is a very personal decision that will affect—and should enhance—the lives of all concerned. This is a relationship that should last a (dog's) lifetime—hopefully either side of a full and happy fourteen years. So it is important to understand the evolving relationship that you will be embarking on with the puppy of your choice—how it all began, where you're going, and what the future will hold.

With my wolf, Mariah, as a guide to the dog's ancestral heritage, this book will arm you with invaluable insights in choosing your dream dog. It will detail both the generic and breed-specific origins of our dogs and show how their unique instincts, natures, temperaments, and abilities have been finely tuned, through our stewardship, to preserve, protect, and enhance their lives and breeds, and their special places in our lives and our world.

Then, with a solid knowledge of what's out there, it's time to get up close and personal, both with yourself and your potential dream dog. I'll have you do a lot of soul searching (and ask you to be ruthlessly realistic) about your aim and purpose in acquiring a dog. Your specific personality, lifestyle, hopes, and dreams may establish just what dog will enhance your life and fulfill those dreams. Quite frankly, you will have to scrutinize yourself as much as you have scrutinized your dream dog candidates to find the perfect match.

Once you've narrowed the field of potential dream dogs down to a handful of breeds, I'll take you to the next level of choosing your dream dog, which is talking with the various professionals in the dog world who can be invaluable in making your dreams become reality. But these people—breeders, veterinarians and health care professionals—are only as valuable as their accessibility, and I'll give you an insider's primer on how to find these professionals, talk to them, understand them, and fit into their inner circle. Admittedly, entering this world can be a little daunting to first-timers—indeed, one client of mine, a corporate powerhouse in the international business world, likened this to learning political business lingo and networking up the corporate ladder! But I'll take you every step of the way, and you'll not only find your dream dog (along with the help of a special "hands-on" test I've devised to help you choose the absolute *right* puppy from a litter of seemingly equally adorable puppies), but you'll also find that these professionals will become an extended family in your dog's health and well-being.

And when it's time to bring your new dog home, I'll show you how, in practical terms, to make your dream dog fit into your household. In fact, I'll provide you with a blueprint of just what you need to do *before* the puppy comes home to ensure a safe and happy welcome and to avoid any unexpected pitfalls. I'll also point out the puppy's first tentative "baby steps" in learning the ABC's of living in your household (everything from helping you to understand his "baby talk" and meet his special needs to showing you how to make him understand housebreaking and other household rules).

As wonderful as puppyhood is—and it's certainly an adventure in itself—once your dog grows up, his horizons can widen, and so can your dreams. Indeed, there is a veritable kaleidoscope of adventures in canine companionship for you and your dream dog to embark on. From out-and-out fun and sporting adventures in the fields of the great outdoors to adventures in the fields of therapy and education— which will enrich not only the life you and your dog share, but also the lives of others—this book will show you the varied vistas waiting to be explored by you and your dog.

This book also provides a manual with markers of basic veterinary care and a glossary of terminology to help facilitate effective communication between you and your dog's veterinarian. Among the many ways in which you and your dog will bond and enrich one another's lives, your most important role is safeguarding his health and well-being. With this handbook, I try to reinforce that most vital of roles and illustrate how you and your dog can become partners in ensuring the health and well-being of future generations of both dogs and their people.

And finally, I've listed a directory of dog organizations, resources that may help you and your dog to explore further dream adventures on your own.

It has always been—and continues to be—my dream to help make the shared dreams of people and dogs come true. In my day-to-day life I'm able to give one-on-one hands-on care. Although I can't be there in person for you, I hope that by sharing my personal and professional experiences, I can help you find your dream dog and make your shared dreams come true for you and your pet.

Part I

# HOW TO CHOOSE YOUR DREAM DOG

Psychologists tell us that dreams stem from our subconscious desires struggling to come to the surface. *Para*psychologists, on the other hand, believe that dreams emanate from an unseen metaphysical world, where hidden forces foretell our future. As an animal behaviorist and dog trainer, I often use a little of both. I need to divine what a well-intended but misguided client is trying to articulate about the kind of dog he wants—and then I need to predict what the best dog will be for him. Hopefully, both client and dog will share a rosy future together.

Walt Disney's "Cinderella" sang: "A dream is a wish your heart makes," and my mission is to show that there is a dream dog—just waiting to be discovered—for everyone. How do you make that dream come true? I think all dogs are wonderful, but believe me, not every dog is the right dog for you. When the wrong one moves in with you, nobody—including the dog—is happy.

## HOW TO CHOOSE THE RIGHT BREED

Your dog needs to be the right match for your lifestyle, your surroundings, your living space, and the amount of time you have to spend with your new pet. Getting a dog on impulse can have sad consequences. Just read what happened to a person referred to me . . . and how we saved her from a terribly wrong choice and helped her to choose the perfect companion.

I got a call one day from a client asking me to counsel a friend of hers about what dog to get. When I called the friend, she said, "Too late, Bash. My daughter and I went to the pet store, and she fell in love with the cutest little white dog—a Samoyed. We're supposed to pick him up tomorrow."

Knowing that she lived in a high-rise apartment in New York City, with no garden or space for exercise, I was concerned. I asked her if she had any idea how big a Samoyed grows to be. She admitted she didn't, and when I told her that a full-grown Samoyed can weigh from forty to seventy-five pounds, she was shocked. "But what will I tell my daughter?" she wailed. "She'll be so upset." I suggested that we make a quick trip to a breeder of Samoyeds I knew, and the next day the three of us set out.

When my new client and her daughter confronted a pen filled with large, romping, cavorting, muscular, and furry Samoyeds, they gasped. They'd had no idea that the cute little white puppy they'd chosen would grow into a dog like these. By the time the breeder had explained the needs of Samoyeds—enormous amounts of exercise (these are sled dogs, after all), regular brushing (they shed seasonally), constant grooming, and very cool weather (hot New York City streets would make them miserable)—even the daughter realized that this wasn't the dog for them. Her mother now clearly understood the importance of researching a breed before bringing it into her home.

She asked if I would help them find a more suitable dog. I suggested we attend a dog show that was taking place that very weekend. There they had the opportunity to examine a variety of breeds. We selected a few that answered the "little cuddly white dog" description—the Bichon Frise, Papillon, Maltese, and Miniature Poodle—and chatted with the breeders about each. I also wanted them to meet the dog they might be buying. You should always get up close and personal, since the right chemistry between dog and owner is crucial to a good relationship over the long haul.

Finally, after hours of looking, mother and daughter decided on a Havanese (see chapter 3), a wonderful little dog that resembles both a Bichon Frise and Maltese. The trio went home to their high-rise apartment to live happily ever after, the little dog reveling in love, luxury, and just the right fit with his family.

This is a perfect example of why you should do your research before buying a dog. Impulse buying of a dog is just asking for trouble, and too many perfect matches await you out there for anyone to end up with a wrong choice. Sometimes, though, the right choice has more to do with the prospective owners than with the dog.

First of all, family members have to agree on what they want. At times I feel more like a marriage counselor than a dog trainer. Here's an example of what I mean. One new client called me with a problem. She and her husband desperately wanted a dog—they both loved dogs and each had owned a dog as a child. But they couldn't, for all they discussed the issue, agree on a breed. She wanted a Poodle, a small dog she could take almost anywhere. Her husband said, "No way! I'm not going to walk a Poodle!" He had his heart set on a Labrador Retriever. The problem was that she was allergic to any dog that shed. To make them both happy, I suggested a Portuguese Water Dog, a wonderful breed that has characteristics of both a retriever and a Poodle. It's hypoallergenic, with the curly coat and happy disposition of a Poodle and the athleticism of the Labrador Retriever. Portuguese Water Dogs are wonderful, playful dogs, somewhat clownish and comical, and they are great swimmers, which delighted the husband. Mission accomplished, marriage saved, dog and owners happy.

Obviously, choosing the dream dog for you involves far more than finding one you think is cute. You also need to be realistic about what sort of a dog you can accommodate into your lifestyle. There are more than 160 registered dog breeds to choose from, making the choice even more difficult. Narrow it down by first asking yourself some important questions—and answering them *honestly*.

For example, what size dog are you looking for? If the answer is "a big strong dog," are you absolutely sure your studio apartment will be suitable? I had a client who lived in a tiny Manhattan studio and who, without consulting me, purchased a Great Pyrenees, a huge dog originally bred, as its name suggests, for mountainous living. This breed was bred to rescue victims of avalanches and to guard people and property. They're wonderfully gentle, good-natured, hardworking dogs, and great with kids. But in a tiny Manhattan studio?

Nevertheless, I worked with the owner to make the dog, Thor, as well behaved as possible. He learned to heel, to sit, to stay, and to be completely obedient to his owner. He grew into a big, white, over-grown 125 pounds of sweetness who loved everybody, and everybody loved him in return. But as his owner soon discovered, Thor had a hard time fitting into the studio apartment. For one thing, he needed room. In addition, Thor shed and shed and shed. Pretty soon white hair covered the owner's beautiful suede sofas. Also, Thor wasn't getting nearly enough exercise. His owner had a high-pressure Wall Street job, worked long hours, and even though he hired a dog walker to take Thor out several times a day, the dog wasn't getting as much exercise as the breed requires. Luckily, this story has a happy ending. Thor's owner met a wonderful woman, fell in love, and got married. Now there were three in that tiny apartment, which was too small for two! Something had to change. They either had to give up Thor or move to bigger quarters. Since the new bride adored the dog as much as her husband did, the decision was easy. They moved to a new house in the country just thirty minutes from Wall Street. Thor could roam the grounds to his heart's content, then retreat to his elegant new dog-house. Fortunately, the woman's taste ran more to chintz than suede, so the sofas were saved. And they all lived happily ever after.

Unquestionably, *size* matters, so when you begin to make your list of potential dogs, a very good starting point is considering whether you want small, medium, or large.

The activity level of a breed is another vital consideration. You shouldn't pick a high-energy dog that requires a minimum of one hour's exercise a day just to stay healthy if your job keeps you away from home all day or if you have a physical condition that prohibits heavy-duty exercise. Put all such dogs out of the running, and con-sider instead one of the Toy breeds—the kind once called lapdogs—such as Cavalier King Charles Spaniels, Miniature Poodles, Maltese, or Chihuahuas. That narrows the list considerably.

Equally important is temperament. Some dogs are people dogs—they love cuddling up to their owners, delivering extravagant kisses and exorbitant displays of affection. Others are bred to protect, and they react aggressively to the approach of any unknown person or an-imal. This trait is useful for someone living alone on a large country property, or in an apartment where break-ins are common. However, it can be a distinct disadvantage in a more suburban neighborhood, where the person your dog perceives as a threat may be your next door neighbor or his dog. Only you can assess your needs in the temperament department. Reading the listings for each breed in chapter 3 will tell you how to weigh this question.

Finally, decide what you would like to do with your dog. Actor Matthew Broderick knew right from the start that he wanted an active dog that could go inline skating with him and join him on bike rides. He made a very good choice with his Border Collie, Sally. Border Collies are herding dogs, a high-energy breed with a surplus of personality and keen intelligence. They're extremely adept at learning, which is why they're easy to train. Once trained, their skills are astonishing, and if you've ever watched a lone dog control a large herd of sheep, you'll understand why they're invaluable to sheep farmers. Matthew, of course, had no interest in herding, but he did want his dog to catch a Frisbee. We worked together with Sally, who became an expert at the game—so much so that she was a featured star in my dog training video *Teach Your Dog to Behave.* Matthew loved to take Sally with him on film sets, where she would entertain cast and crew with her amazing feats. But we didn't stop there. Knowing the extraordinary talents of the Border Collie, I suggested giving Sally agility lessons (jumping hurdles, crawling through tunnels, climbing ladders, maneuvering across seesaws and down slides), and soon she was running agility courses like a pro.

## HOW TO CHOOSE THE RIGHT DOG

When Matthew and Sarah Jessica Parker became a couple, the family expanded to three. This presented a brand-new experience for Sarah Jessica, who never had owned a dog. But she, too, fell for Sally's charms and soon was as doting an owner as Matthew. She even discovered an unanticipated benefit of owning a dog. She was scheduled to appear in an off-Broadway play, *Sylvia,* in which she played—guess what?—a dog. Sarah Jessica spent weeks studying Sally's movements, facial expressions, and body language. The play opened to rave reviews, and critics bestowed overwhelming praise on the star, saying she seemingly had transformed herself into a dog. Let's just say Sarah had a great acting coach in Sally!

What did Sally teach Sarah Jessica? Body language, facial expressions, and vocalization. How can these qualities, which helped Sarah Jessica to portray a dog, help you choose your dog? Here's a checklist I've devised to help you recognize your potential dream dog:

- Observe the expression. If a dog has a lively, alert, and happy expression, chances are good that he's a happy, intelligent dog. If he looks slightly cowed, doesn't want to make eye contact, and is reluctant to interact with you, he's probably timid and fearful.
- Watch the ears. Ears that lift (or prick up) at the slightest noise or motion tell you that you have a very alert and aware dog. That's a plus. Ears held low and drooping (this also applies to droopy-eared dogs, such as spaniels) are indicators of apprehension or fear and may be a signal that this is a frightened or timid dog.
- Look into the eyes. Just as with people, bright, wide-open eyes are indicative of intelligence, alertness, and curiosity. An eager expression in her eyes is a good sign that she's open or playful. If the dog avoids eye contact or slightly lowers his lids, that shows a fearful, timid disposition.
- Check the body language. An upright body posture, with head held high, ears pricked, and tail up and wagging, shows a positive, extroverted personality. A cowering body, with tail held between the legs, ears low and drooping, and eyes averted is a sign of a scared and possibly problematic dog.
- Listen to the voice. By nature, all dogs have a spectrum of sound: whine, whimper, yip, bark, and growl. Whining and whimpering indicate anxiety or fear. A yip indicates excitement, eagerness, or curiosity. A bark is generally for attention or to alert to danger, and a growl is a warning of aggression and dominance.

## FIVE-POINT TEMPERAMENT TEST

Now that you have this checklist, here's how to make it work for you. Take my client, Alice, for example. She and her family wanted a

Wheaten Terrier. Through their local veterinarian, Alice was directed to a breeder who had eight puppies available. All the puppies were adorable and seemingly indistinguishable. The family was in a quandary. How could they possibly choose? Which puppy was right for them?

That's where I stepped in. You know the old saying, "That's an accident just waiting to happen!" (All the signs signal trouble ahead, but you just don't see it.) Here's a little test I devised to help you read the signals, avoid the pitfalls, and choose the right dog.

I took everybody—Alice, her family, and all eight of the pups—into a small room with few distractions. Then I began to weed the puppies out into categories. First, I clapped my hands. Three of the puppies barked, snarled, or growled. I tied red ribbons onto their collars. But two of the dogs had simply looked up at me curiously, to see what was coming next—they got green ribbons. The other three ran off and tried to make themselves as small as possible—yellow ribbons for them.

If you haven't guessed by now, the ribbons worked like traffic lights. The puppies who exhibited aggressive behavior "earned" red flags—Stop! An aggressive dog is truly an accident waiting to happen. The yellow ribbons—like the yellow traffic light—mean proceed with Caution. The behavior exhibited by the yellow-ribboned puppies was not ideal, but with time, patience, and perseverance it could improve. The behavior of the green-ribboned puppies—neither aggressive nor timid, but inquisitive, bold, and positive—was a green light, a Go.

So now Alice was down to five potential puppies, three yellow and two green. For the next test I picked up each pup and turned her on her back in my arms, cradling her. If the puppy struggled and nipped to get free, she was red-ribboned because of aggressive qualities. Next, I touched the puppy's ears and toes. If he pulled away—and especially if he growled—he was also red-lighted. Finally, I threw a couple of squeaky toys on the floor. The puppy that picked up the toy and displayed possession and aggression earned another red ribbon. But the puppy that picked up the toy, played with it, and responded to Alice's encouragement to return to her was green-lighted all the way. That puppy was the dream dog for Alice and her family.

This is an example of the Five-Point Temperament Test you can use to choose *your* dream dog:

1. Carefully observe the interaction of the litter. You'll see in a flash that some pups have either dominant or submissive personalities. The dog that bullies the others, hovering over them or pushing them away from the food, is too aggressive. This pup will be hard to handle and rebellious, testing your authority on a daily basis. The submissive dog, the one that stays in a corner apart from the others, rarely interacting, and, in extreme cases, cowering and shivering in fear, is also not the right dog. He's timid, standoffish, and afraid of confrontation. He may be so panicky that he'll have a hard time focusing on future training. Neither the bully nor the fearful dog is a good choice. The perfect pup is the one that interacts in a calm, alert, sociable, and playful way, taking your presence in stride.

2. Clap your hands sharply, and observe the reaction. Some puppies will look up inquisitively (the ideal response), others will run for cover (too nervous), and some will growl or bark and run toward you (overly aggressive). If the dog doesn't show any response to a clap, it's a good bet the dog is deaf. A bark could be a simple alert signal, but growling when you approach is a clear warning that the pup has an aggression problem.

3. Pick up each pup, one at a time, cradle it in your arms, and see how each responds to being held. If the pup is quiet and relaxed, and accepts being handled in stride, that's a sign that she already has trust in you. A struggle against being handled may indicate either an overly dominant or overly fearful dog. The fearful pup may tremble or revert to an age-old protective instinct and freeze. Any dog this nervous will prove to be problematic. A pup that growls while you hold it is far too aggressive. The dream dog is one that's confident, relaxed, and friendly, reveling in your attention.

4. To test further the pup's response to handling, gently touch its ears and its toes, softly massaging its body. What you're doing is reproducing the mother's reassuring touch, her nuzzling, her licking. It's an experience most pups will love. But if the puppy shivers and whimpers (too fearful) or growls and snaps (too aggressive), it's not a dog you want. Your goal is a pup that remains happy, playful, and positive, no matter what the challenge.

5. To test inquisitive behavior and alertness, toss a squeaky toy or any other noisy object into the pups' pen. If a dog is curious, picks up the object, and plays with it, that indicates she has a healthy interest in everything around her. She's alert, attentive, and playful. Her ears are up, her eyes focused on the newfound object. But if the pup runs away from the object, that indicates a nervous, fearful disposition—a drawback that doesn't improve with age. Working with each dog individually, roll the toy along the ground. If she picks up the toy and plays with it, you have a relaxed, playful pup. And if she brings it back to you, that shows a born retriever and a high degree of intelligence.

Sometimes, however, you don't fall in love with the dog that makes the perfect A grade. You like the dog that falls into the yellow, cautionary zone. This doesn't mean you shouldn't have the dog. It just means you will have to work harder to understand and train the dog.

I can't emphasize strongly enough that owners should decide, right up front, what they really want in a dog. Big or little, cuddly or athletic, affectionate or reserved, docile or aggressive? Only the owners know whether they have the physical strength to match that of, say a Shar-Pei or an Akita, the space for a Great Dane, the budget for the grooming of a high-maintenance breed such as the Poodle, or the time for the mile-long daily run a Labrador really needs. (Note the number of overweight dogs around and you'll realize that most owners don't give this factor enough thought.) If your dog's personality is a poor match for yours, the relationship is doomed from the start.

I always urge my clients to consider all the points of a breed before making the final choice. Above all, remember that whether you choose a gargantuan Saint Bernard or an affectionate little Affenpinscher as your newest family member, that dog's closest relative is the *wolf*—who may pop up for an unexpected visit every now and then! That is why it is so important to understand the origins of the many breeds that have evolved from the wolf to the dog of today. Let's take a closer look at that genetic inheritance in the next chapter and determine how it affects your choice of the right dog for you.

# FROM WOLF TO DOG: THE ORIGIN OF THE BREEDS

Not too long ago, I was conducting my annual STARPET Theatrical Workshop for Broadway-bound hounds. We were housed in a historic rehearsal studio in the shadow of Times Square, a stone's throw away from another historic studio where my wolf, Mariah, and I had worked in television. That same theater had also launched a much-talked-about Broadway hit, *Six Degrees of Separation,* which put forth the intriguing theory that everyone is separated from everyone else by no more than six people. From socialites to scientists, in salons and subways, rose the buzz about how we—New Yorkers who hail from every race, nationality, culture, and religious background—are really so intimately related. It occurred to me that I might have a real blockbuster on my hands if my STARPET clients put on a *canine* version of the show: *From Wolf to Dog—1 Percent of Separation.* After all, dogs, from the tiniest Chihuahua to the mammoth Great Dane, are separated from the ancestral wolf by only 1 percent in their genetic makeup.

While the dog is our proverbial best friend, the wolf may be our oldest friend. Discoveries of dog and human fossils together date back fourteen thousand years, but commingled wolf and early human fossils date back to over four hundred thousand years. Recent scientific evidence suggests that man first began domesticating the wolf about 135,000 years ago.

It has taken science many years to confirm what a wise man told me when I was a young boy in that Yugoslavian internment camp. My family had fled the tyranny of communism that plagued our homeland, Albania, and our days were filled with unrelenting hardship and despair. However, as a five-year-old boy, I was drawn to the snarling, growling guard dogs. When one of them licked my hand, this holy man took me aside and told me a story. That story lives with me to this day, and it reflects my own feelings about the bond wolves and dogs share with each other, as well as with us.

"You are very lucky, Bash," he told me, "that you have had this amazing experience with animals. The relationship that we have with dogs—this bond we feel—is a gift from God. And it comes from a time in the far, far past, when man lived in the Garden of Eden, and it was a very beautiful world. Man and nature were in unison in this very special place, where man and animals lived harmoniously, and could talk together, each in his own language. All understood one another perfectly, and life was beautiful. It was nothing at all like this camp.

"But one day man broke God's rules, and God was very, very angry. He gathered all the animals in the garden and told them that because man had broken the rules, he would have to leave the garden. However, being a merciful God, he asked that one animal remain by man's side. The world outside the garden was a frightening and lonely place, and God wouldn't be there to protect man, who would need a friend. All the animals looked at one another and not one said a word. Finally, a wolf stepped forward and stood next to the man. And when the man and the wolf stepped through the gate of the garden into the wide world outside, the wolf was transformed into a dog. Man and dog have been best friends ever since."

Did nomadic man follow the wolves, or did the wolves follow man? Either way, their symbiosis fulfilled intrinsic, lifesaving needs. The famous mythological twins, Remus and Romulus, are a perfect example. According to legend, Romulus, the son of Mars, was the founder and first king of Rome. But as an infant, he and his brother, Remus, were abandoned and left to die in the Tiber River. Amazingly, a mother wolf happened upon them and took them in as her own, nursing them and raising them to boyhood.

While this sounds improbable, anthropologists throughout the world have consistently reported seemingly real-life instances of wolves tending children. Almost every culture throughout time has its own variation of the theme. In 1758, the great naturalist Linnaeus produced the first scientific treatise on feral children. In the tenth edition of his acclaimed *Systema Naturae,* he described three defining traits witnessed in these "wolf children." First, they were *tetrapus,* or "four-footed," habitually gamboling about on hands and feet (or knees). Second, they were *mutus,* mute except for the language of yips, barks, growls, and howls—all trademark wolf vocalizations. Third, they were *hirsutus*—exceptionally hairy for a human, but entirely well suited for a person living naked outdoors year-round. In the next century, Maj. Gen. Sir W. H. Sleeman published reports of six so-called wolf children he had personally observed. Right into the twentieth century, several countries, especially India, reported numerous accounts of wolf children. The most famous of these were Amala and Kamala, supposedly a pair of sisters who were discovered by a missionary in Midnapore. As the story goes, the children, although filthy and malnourished, were found living peacefully in a den with a she-wolf and her litter of pups.

Rudyard Kipling comes closest to capturing the ancient human-wolf bond. In *The Jungle Book,* the hero Mowgli is an endearing young orphan boy, raised by wolves and living in harmony with all the animals in the jungle.

Having spent as much time as I could with the guard dogs at the internment camp, I felt a kinship with them in the same way the fictional Mowgli, the "Man Cub," bonded with his wolf family. And as I look back on my early days raising Mariah when she was just a wolf pup, I believe Kipling aptly captured the beginnings of the intrinsic symbiotic nature of the ancient man-wolf bond with these lines from his *Just So Stories for Little Children:*

> Then the Woman picked up a roasted mutton-bone and threw it to Wild Dog, and said, "Wild Thing out of the Wild Woods, taste and try." Wild Dog gnawed the bone and it was more delicious than anything he had ever tasted, and he said, "O my Enemy and Wife of my Enemy, give me another."
>
> The Woman said, "Wild Thing out of the Wild Woods, help my Man to hunt through the day and guard this Cave at night, and I will give you as many roast bones as you need."

Since food is integral to the survival of any species—and our ancient relationship with the wolf was probably instrumental to the survival of both species—guarding our food is an equally strong, inborn self-protective instinct of any species, especially a wolf. From a very early age, a young wolf has to guard its food from everyone else, including its litter mates, until it has eaten its fill—or else it will soon go hungry.

The strength of this drive was readily apparent in my observations of my wolf, Mariah. I had bottle-raised her since infancy, and I was quickly and firmly imprinted on her as her pack leader. Nevertheless, when I switched her from bottle feeding to solid food in a dish, her primal food-guarding instinct immediately manifested itself. I overcame this—much like the Woman in Rudyard Kipling's *Just So Stories* who shared mutton bones with the Wild Thing—by hand-feeding Mariah every morsel of her food.

Because a wolf's senses and reactions are just like a dog's, only many times more intense, my experience raising, teaching, and working with Mariah gave me the key to understanding the inherent nature of canine behavior. Basic to this understanding is the fact that domestic dogs, like wolves, are pack animals by nature, and all their behavior is based on various aspects of pack structure and instinctive pack mentality. Even though they have been domesticated for centuries, dogs still remain wolves "under the skin."

## MARIAH THE WOLF

The story of Mariah provides a number of illustrations of the traits shared by dogs and wolves. Understanding the basis for so many things dogs do will help in your selection process. So let's take a closer look at what Mariah taught me about canine behavior.

Mariah was an exquisite creature, both inside and out. I discovered her—only days old—at a wolf sanctuary in Maine, where a group of biologists were breeding wolves in captivity for various purposes. Some were bred to be reintroduced into the wild to replenish depleted populations, others for educational purposes and to restock zoos and wildlife parks.

Because wolves can be so difficult to work with, I wanted to choose "my" wolf carefully. I knew I wanted a female cub because through my work with dogs, I'd found that males of any breed tend to be more aggressive and dominant than females. This is especially true of wolves, because in the pack hierarchy, a male must constantly fight in order to retain his alpha, or "top dog" position. I was particularly drawn to one family of wolves. Mariah's mother had been born in captivity, and the more time she spent with me, the more she trusted me to handle the young pups in her litter. The pup I chose would not only have to be young enough to imprint—that is, to bond—with me, but would also have to have the temperament that would allow me to train it. I chose Mariah exactly how I would choose any domestic dog pup: by observing the interactions of the pups within the litter, as well as their reactions to sudden noises and movements. I also picked up each pup and held her in my arms. The pup that would relax in my arms would indicate she possessed just the right amount of submissiveness. Mariah passed these tests with flying colors.

The next part was trickier. It is extremely important for a wolf cub, as with a domestic dog puppy, to spend sufficient time with its mother and littermates to develop socially and behaviorally. However, our case was unique, as it was equally important that she share this time with *me*. She needed to bond to me. She would be my pup; I would be her alpha male (the leader she would look up to). So while Mariah remained with her wolf family for the first six weeks of her life during that critical and delicate developmental stage, I had to be intimately involved, so she would imprint to me and come to regard me as her family, as well. This was crucial not only because of our future life together and the film training we had ahead of us, but also because wolves, with their strong pack behavior, have such deep affection and loyalty toward their families that it can be traumatizing for them to be separated, and I wouldn't allow that to happen to Mariah. To facilitate the process, I spent as much time as I could with her. I wanted to accustom her to my presence and my scent. As she was being weaned, I bottle-fed her daily, and once she was ready for solid food, I prepared her meals and gave them to her myself, sometimes from a bowl, sometimes by hand.

After six weeks, Mariah and I had succeeded in becoming a pack of two, with me as the alpha leader. She was totally dependent on me, and I was solely responsible for her. It was the relationship that, genetically, as a wolf she needed and expected—an unbreakable bond, identical to the one that develops between dog and dog owner.

We packed our belongings and headed back to New York. I was determined to preserve all that was wolf in her (which is why the producers wanted a real wolf, with the striking visage, carriage, and distinctive demeanor that is unmistakably wolf, and not just a wolfish-looking German Shepherd or Husky-Shepherd mix). Nevertheless, Mariah still had to make the transition from wolf cub to house pup before we could even think of transforming her into a film star. Just as I had worked with Mariah's wolf family, Mariah needed—even more so—to assimilate into my "pack" at home: ten very diverse but definitely domestic dogs.

At first Mariah and I spent five days as just an intimate pack of two. I wanted her to get used to her new "den" and surrounding environs before she met her new "littermates." Finally, I presented each dog to Mariah individually. Because wolf puppies are always subordinate to all the adults in the pack, I put my dogs in a down or stay position so Mariah wouldn't feel overwhelmed and could approach and sniff them. And, because Mariah would lie on her back—belly up, in a traditional submission posture—I occasionally instructed my dogs to lie on their sides, to telegraph to Mariah their acceptance of her, and she got the message. It was wonderful to see her happily interact with her new pack. My young adult German Shepherd, Orph (short for Orphan), became Mariah's special friend and guide. They developed a unique bond, perhaps because a Shepherd's and a wolf's physique and temperament are closely related. Orph's firm but gentle guidance seemed to calm Mariah and give her confidence, and he became my "teaching assistant." I often took Orph with Mariah and me on her early training sessions, and his presence was invaluable.

I soon found that even though I did not want to squelch Mariah's innate wolf behavior, I did have to suppress aggression tendencies toward unfamiliar animals, and I had to curb some other behavioral traits, as well—such as the extreme flight behavior that would surface whenever she was confronted with unknown people, different surroundings, or new or unusual experiences. Harnessing these unbridled wolf behavioral traits was paramount both for her happiness and safety, and for the safety and well-being of others.

Yet I didn't want Mariah caught between two worlds, belonging in neither. I wanted to give Mariah a kind of dual citizenship. I hoped to do more than just train her and pay passing homage to her wolf heritage. I wanted Mariah to retain her species' birthright and yet function happily within *my* species' confines. To do this, I knew I would have to work with the wolf traits, not against them. No amount of human companionship or socialization can override a wolf's genetic makeup. I would have to train Mariah from within her deeply imprinted code. I would somehow have to merge the wolf behavior she was born to exhibit with behavior that was socially acceptable in a civilized world.

Mariah not only thrived, but she flourished as well. Along with her many acting roles, she was an original "supermodel"—winning the coveted "cover girl" spot for Revlon's Gypsy Gold. But Mariah was definitely not a diva. She seemed to understand that fate had thrust her into a position to foster interspecies understanding and to promote humane education and pet-facilitated therapy. Dr. Marlin Perkins, creator and host of Mutual of Omaha's award-winning *Wild Kingdom,* the longest-running animal show on television, tapped Mariah and me to go on tour to benefit the Wolf Canid Survival and Research Center. The tour was a great success in contributing to the public understanding of wildlife in general, and wolves in particular. In fact, soon after, Mariah was selected by the International Olympic Committee to serve as the official mascot and goodwill ambassador of the 1984 Winter Olympics in Sarajevo, Yugoslavia. Ever the pro, Mariah traveled to Sarajevo for the opening ceremonies, unfazed by the lights and cameras, and always ready for the action.

Back on our own home shores, Mariah continued to spread goodwill. She was asked to participate in Capitol Hill's First Annual Celebrity Dog Parade in Washington, D.C., given for the benefit of the Children's Museum. Dozens of members of Congress and the diplomatic corps came with their dogs, but Mariah made a point of remaining at the side of then White House Press Secretary James "The Bear" Brady. It was Mr. Brady's first outing since he had been paralyzed in the assassination attempt of President Reagan, and perhaps

Mariah sensed this. Mr. Brady's family and doctors were so pleased with his response to Mariah that they decided on the spot that a dog would be a wonderful addition to his life. Soon after, he acquired a beautiful Labrador Retriever, and his renewed interest in animals led to his pioneering and ongoing participation in horseback riding therapy, which has proved so beneficial that there has been a proliferation of pet therapy and riding programs. I like to think Mr. Brady's meeting with Mariah was instrumental in reawakening his childhood love for animals. It certainly reconfirmed my lifelong belief in the importance of animals to the spirit and well-being of people—and it reaffirmed my resolve to continue this work with Mariah. When Mariah was about twelve years old, I felt it was time for her to slow down and retire from her sometimes hectic public life. She lived for three more idyllic years on our country property in upstate New York and died peacefully, of natural causes, in her sleep.

In our fourteen years together, I found in Mariah the Rosetta stone I needed to help me decode the fourteen thousand years of genetic evolution cloaked within the dog of today. To understand the complex behavioral makeup of the dog, one must understand that the dog's innate behavior is composed of nine key drives inherited from the wolf.

## NINE INNER DRIVES OF DOGS

Ever since the modern movie classic *Dances with Wolves* captured the public's fancy, I find that my clients—from pet people in public parks to power brokers in penthouses—all want to discover the wolf within their dogs! To give them an easy analogy, I often point to the famous scene in the film where Kevin Costner's character catches the wolf's eye, and the two begin to engage in playlike "dance." As any dance aficionado will tell you, all the complicated choreography of the most beautiful ballets are drawn, unbelievably, from only five basic positions—so, too, all the engaging, endearing, incomprehensible behavioral traits that your dog exhibits spring from just nine basic wolf-inherited behavioral traits. Try to imagine your dog's behavior as an incredible canine choreography—with the wolf the master choreographer.

In fact, that popular scene in *Dances with Wolves* illustrates quite nicely the following list's third basic behavioral trait, which is *socialization*. So, before we look at the nine recognized groups of dogs today (comprising more than 160 breeds), let's examine the nine behavioral traits these dogs—from the largest Newfoundland to the tiniest Australian Terrier—all share. When you can identify and understand these nine basic behavioral traits from which all "canine choreography" flourishes, you and your dog will truly be in sync.

## 1. Pack Behavior

Mariah's need to follow a pack leader was deeply ingrained, and I was the leader she chose to follow. I vividly remember that when she was a pup, her need of social confidence and security was crucial to her well-being. One day I received a call from an advertising agency that handled the Revlon cosmetics account, wanting Mariah to be the "cover girl" for Revlon's newest perfume, Gypsy Gold. The ad would be shot at a studio on Madison Avenue in Manhattan. I knew Mariah and I had our work cut out for us. I brought Mariah into Manhattan, but before hitting Madison Avenue, I detoured first to Central Park, where I walked her around to build her confidence. To a wolf, the hustle and bustle of Madison Avenue—with crowds of people on the move and with cars and buses racing with horns blaring—can be an unnerving, if not altogether frightening, place. It can readily trigger another drive we will discuss later—*flight*—which could endanger her. By first walking in Central Park, she gained a sense of security and was comforted by having me, her pack leader, lead the way and show her around. This enabled Mariah to walk Madison Avenue like she had been doing it for years. Because I was with her, she exuded a confident and calm demeanor and was very responsive to my commands. All this made for an ideal photo shoot.

Watching Mariah easily navigate the crowded streets and handle the photo shoot like a seasoned pro impressed upon me how a pack leader or owner of a dog can instill confidence and stability in a dog faced with an unfamiliar environment. Dogs of today look for the alpha in their owner to guide them, to give them the security of knowing that they have a leader and they are part of a pack.

All dogs have inherited the social pack behavior of the wolf. Specific, complex relationships exist within a pack of wolves. When you understand pack behavior, you realize how important it is for you to form a close relationship with your dog early in the dog's life and become, once and forever, the dog's leader.

A wolf pack consists of a multitiered hierarchy. At the top is always a dominant male and female, known as the alpha pair. All of the other wolves in the pack are submissive to the alpha pair. In turn, there are several tiers within the pack below the alpha pair, with the wolves on each tier in a position of dominance over the wolves in the tiers below.

Wolves by nature band together, have strong family loyalty, and often establish strong bonds with other wolves. They bond together to facilitate hunting for food, protection, raising pups, and for company. If a wolf is somehow separated from the pack, he will suffer from separation anxiety. A "lone" wolf is a distressed wolf. Because your dog, Fido, is also a pack animal, Fido feels the same anxiety when you go out, leaving him alone. Because he feels lonely, rejected, and anxious, he will often take his feelings out on your furniture and anything else he can find in the house to destroy. It is very important for you to establish yourself as the dog's leader.

To do this, you need to be kind, firm, consistent, and affectionate all at the same time in your handling of your dog. Do that and your dog will quickly come to accept you as his leader. Again, you need to be affectionate and kind, yet strong and uncompromising so that your dog will not get mixed signals and will look up to you.

## 2. Dominant and Submissive

When I was raising Mariah, it was very enlightening to observe how she interacted with my other dogs. Orph, a huge German Shepherd, was the reigning alpha male of my pack of dogs. Mariah recognized that he was the alpha male, and she was submissive to him. In encountering Orph, Mariah would first go down on the ground with her head and ears back, tail down. She would then slowly turn over on her back and expose her belly and neck to him, a submissive and vulnerable position announcing that she wished to be accepted into this pack. Not only was she accepted, but as time went on, Mariah grew, and she became the alpha female of the pack.

Mariah presented herself to my other animals through body language proclaiming her status as the alpha female. To appreciate this, just imagine what the other dogs saw and what she was telling them. She stood tall with her tail held high, her ears completely straight, her eyes bright and open, her body radiating confidence, in essence saying "Here I am. I am the alpha."

As the alpha of your family of animals (whether you have one animal or ten), you need to reinforce your leadership role on a regular basis and never allow your dog to prevail in a challenge to your authority. Within a wolf pack there is a continuing struggle for dominance. This means that you have to constantly reinforce your leadership role.

A submissive wolf always lowers his body when he meets a more dominant animal. Bear this in mind when you meet a strange dog. If you crouch down in front of him, he may try to dominate you by showing aggression.

### 3. Socialization

The most engaging and endearing trait of the wolf behavior is their socialization. When I lived with my animals in upstate New York, I would often let Mariah, along with all my dogs, play freely within the safe confines of my fenced-in property. This was our special family time, where we played and socialized. Invariably, with the dogs running around in the fields, out of the corner of my eye I'd see Mariah hiding. I would pretend that I did not see her, and she, in turn thinking I was unaware of her presence, would run up and playfully hurl her body against me like a hockey player throwing a body check. This was a very affectionate game that wolves in packs play. It can best be described as a kind of combination of the children's games of tag and hide-and-seek. Wolves always take time to play, making it an essential part of pack life and their social structure. Dogs today, just like their wolf ancestors, love to play, but they also *need* to play. Indeed, any dog who is kept isolated from canine or human companionship—who never enjoys a game of toss the ball or tug the bone, or experiences the joy of a playful relationship with its owners—will be an unhappy dog. This unhappiness can manifest itself in behavioral problems. For instance, excessive barking or aggression are signs of boredom and discontent. Therefore, interaction with others is crucial.

So you, without even realizing it, are part of this centuries-old wolf pack social structure. In these deceptively ordinary moments—where for example, you play hide-and-seek with your dog—you accommodate your dog's innate drive to socialize. It is through such games that you and your dog truly bond.

## 4. Aggression

Socialization is fun to experience and observe. Other drives are less endearing, such as the one Mariah exhibited in establishing her position as the alpha female of the pack. I must say that observing her aggression was upsetting to me. I had in my family of dogs a female Doberman Pinscher named Sweetpea. When Sweetpea went into heat (estrus), Mariah viewed this as a challenge to her. Within a wolf pack, only the alpha female is allowed to breed. Mariah instinctively became very aggressive to ensure that Sweetpea would be an outcast and not a threat to Mariah's position as the alpha female and to her relationship with Orph, the alpha male. In trying to rectify the problem, I could not alter Mariah's ingrained aggressive instinct. Therefore, I had to remove the challenge she perceived by removing her need to respond to it. The solution was simple: I had to spay Sweetpea.

Still, aggression, as unsettling as it may appear to us, is necessary for a wolf's survival. It helps pack members establish their territory, maintain their rank in the pack hierarchy, protect their food supply, and drive away would-be predators. It is a deeply ingrained instinct. In both wolves and dogs, it is triggered by various causes, such as threats to their territory, food, offspring, and, perhaps most often, fear. But in our socialized world, aggression is unacceptable behavior, and there is absolutely no place for it in the life of a domestic dog. Thus we need to remove the causes that trigger aggression.

## 5. Territorial

Mariah really took this behavioral trait to an extreme level. This was most evident when I would have all the dogs out for a group playtime in upstate New York. The males would routinely inspect the perimeters of the property—which, with all the fields and woodlands, harbored lots of interesting scents, I'm sure—and mark their territory by urinating, as would the females. Mariah, in order to make sure that everyone understood she was the alpha, would go and mark every spot previously marked by the dogs. She had to have the last word, and that word was "I am in charge, and these are the boundaries of my territories."

This aspect of pack life—the need to define and protect territory within which to live, raise pups, or hunt—is very important. In the wild, each wolf must establish its own territory. To survive, the wolves give clear warning to other packs: "This is home—you stay out!" A dog urinates to mark its proprietorship of a neighborhood. In fact, the dog's sense of smell is so acute, it can distinguish one drop of urine in ten thousand gallons of water. (Yet they still stick their heads into the toilet bowl, just to make sure their noses do not deceive them!)

Territorial behavior is also displayed by barking to alert others in the pack that there are intruders, and by using aggression to keep intruders at bay. Sound familiar? A dog exhibits this behavior each time it barks when a stranger approaches its property, or growls if another dog approaches its master or the boundaries of its home territory.

As wolf packs travel through or around their territory, previously laid scents provide them with a detailed set of clues. It's like reading a newspaper. They can immediately tell which individuals have been there before and in what direction other pack members have traveled. They can also detect the presence of a stranger who may have intruded within their borders. Dogs today leave scents so other dogs will smell them and read their messages. Often an owner out walking his dog may be annoyed and frustrated when he sees something off in the distance or is heading to a destination that he thinks his dog will find interesting, but the dog is insisting on sniffing in every nook and cranny. Don't be annoyed, and don't get frustrated. Your dog's sense of sight is so much less powerful than her extraordinary sense of smell. You find your dog's obsession with sidewalk smells boring, but for your dog, this is the chance to "read" the neighborhood gossip sheet. And don't forget, each new day brings a new edition of the *The Territorial Tattler.*

## 6. Food Guarding

Normally, the wolf's nature is to protect the food they have. They will growl or display aggression to keep an interloper away from the food. In the beginning, whenever my dogs would go near Mariah while she was eating, she would growl and bark into the dish and warn them not to go near it. This was not acceptable to me. So, I modified Mariah's behavior by feeding her by hand to convince her that it's not necessary to guard the food. I was there to feed her, and I would never take the food away from her. This gave Mariah a strong sense of security that her food would never be taken away. Eventually, through this behavior modification training, all the animals, including Mariah, respected each other's territories to the point that when they finished eating, they could check one another's food bowls without an aggressive confrontation. With dogs, you must establish a positive atmosphere early on, so the need to guard food never develops.

## 7. Chase

Mariah and I would frequently go off on long, solitary walks together without my dogs. We enjoyed the companionship, although she would walk a few yards ahead of me. Often, when we were startled by the presence of a rabbit, Mariah would stop dead in her tracks, as would I. Invariably, the rabbit would panic and start running. This flight would trigger in Mariah chase behavior—it automatically kicks in—and instinctively she would take chase after the rabbit. At full speed she would bound, zigzagging through the field after the rabbit, stopping only after the rabbit leaped into a rabbit hole, safely beyond Mariah's reach.

The instinct in wolves and dogs is to chase and pursue anything that runs from it. That is why you should not attempt to run from a strange dog or one you're not sure of, as you may unwittingly be encouraging the dog to chase you. If you stand still, you stop the chase behavior from kicking in. Similarly, a pet dog that is being chased by an unknown person or dog will naturally flee.

## 8. Flight

One scary moment occurred when Mariah and I were walking in the woods, never imagining that strangers would be there hunting in the off-season. When they began firing their rifles, I was frightened that they might see Mariah, panic, and shoot her. Fortunately, her natural instinct for self-preservation kicked in, and she took flight. It was a case of flight or fight (for survival) and in this case, flight prevailed. You've probably observed this behavior in your dog responding to firecrackers or other loud noises. When a dog is startled by the backfire of a passing car, the first thing he does is try to flee. That is why, no matter how well trained your dog is, it is imperative to keep your dog on a leash when cars are nearby. Even the best-trained dog may panic and flee right into an oncoming car.

## 9. Vocalization

To my mind, a truly awesome behavior characteristic of wolves that Mariah demonstrated is howling. People always think that wolves only howl at the moon. In reality, the wolf is howling to call and locate the members of its social pack. That is why Jack London's book was called *The Call of the Wild* and not *Howling at the Moon.* The lone wolf is howling "Where are *yoouuu?*" and the pack howls back to the lone wolf "Here we *aaarrree!*"

I find this to be one of the most endearing and amusing behavior characteristics of wolves. Upstate where Mariah and I lived, most people had crowing roosters waking them up. I had a howling wolf. Mariah was my alarm clock. Her howl was the most beautiful sound you could ever imagine. It was her way of communicating to me that she wanted to start her day. Where was I, she wanted to know. Although I didn't return a corresponding howl, I did go to her, assure her of my presence, tell her what a good girl she was, and then begin our morning ritual. I would let her loose, and together we would walk in the woods. This gave her social contact, a chance to play and to partake of our pack ritual. I have often seen this behavior in dogs. When left alone they will howl, telling you to come back and socialize with them. It is instinctive for dogs to want to communicate with other dogs. Dogs that are left alone outside, in particular, may find the need to find another canine to "talk" to, or just to vocalize, "Here I am. . . . Where are you? I'm all alone!"

Dogs, like people, are socially oriented. Both our ancestors—wolves and primitive nomadic tribes—began to learn from one another and to rely on one another. With their strong survival instincts, these two very social species moved beyond *competition* to survive to *cooperation* to survive. By understanding how early man came to understand the wolf, we can gain insights into how the wolf evolved into the many modern breeds of dogs today.

Once nomadic tribes and wolf packs lived and hunted in close proximity, their territorial boundaries began to fade. These tribes were of a hunting-and-gathering culture, and they began to follow the wolf packs and their prey in quest of their own game. In turn, wolves often followed the nomads, scavenging food from the tribes' discarded carcasses. As primitive man began to understand the wolf, he also began to understand how the wolf could help him. These nomadic tribes are thought to have raided wolf dens, capturing pups and then raising the ones that showed the greatest promise of being tamed. Soon man came to realize that by breeding certain wolves that shared similar traits, those traits could be improved upon and put to the service of man. Some were bred to guard the dens of early man, others to chase game for hunting, and still others to herd. Eventually, through generations of rudimentary selective breeding, linebreeding, and inbreeding of the wolf, the modern dog breeds began to take shape.

All over the world, different clans and kingdoms bred dogs for myriad specific needs, which aided and improved the lives of these early civilizations. As these cultures began to flourish, so also did their class distinctions. Dogs were no longer kept just to serve man, but also as companions to man. A well-bred and blue-blooded nobleman especially wanted an equally well-bred and blue-blooded dog! The sport of the hunt, of course, was a very important part of the life of the gentry, and the quest for the best hunting dog became as competitive as the sport itself. Contests and competitions to show the finer points and skills of these dogs became popular. Soon the aristocracy had championship events to demonstrate the abilities of their guarding, herding, and working dogs. While kings and noblemen competed with their magnificent Deerhounds and Wolfhounds, the queens and gentlewomen watched the competitions with refined little dogs on their laps. These small dogs were as much status symbols as the giant hounds competing in the shows. They were bred to be lapdogs for nobility—a sign that royalty did not have to work, and neither did their dogs. Living in the "lap of luxury" meant having an elegant little dog sharing your throne with you.

These events created an early kind of sporting club, which soon evolved into kennel clubs. A championship dog was a prized asset for a nobleman, bringing both status and wealth. People naturally wanted to breed the best with the best—champions—and this linebreeding developed the high gene standards that are continued in the breeds of the twenty-first century.

## NINE GROUPS OF DOGS, PLUS ONE

Today, the American Kennel Club divides dogs into nine groups. They are the Sporting, Hound, Working, Herding, Terrier, Non-Sporting, Toy, Miscellaneous, and Rare Breed Groups.

### 1. Sporting

Dogs in this group have been bred to hunt and run. They require a lot of exercise and are ideal for families that enjoy outdoor activity, as well as for people who like to hunt and compete in field trials. These dogs tend to be quiet (they bark very little)—but the restraint they show in barking they more than make up for in running. When they run, they run far afield. They love to be up early and go-go-go—life is one big adventure to them. Every morning—the earlier the better—is a new day. This rambunctious group includes Pointers and Setters, which point game for the hunters; retrievers, which retrieve the game and bring it back to the hunters; and spaniels, which both flush and retrieve. For these dogs, pointing, retrieving, and flushing are not work; they are play. Sporting dogs love to romp, chase, and retrieve. Plus, this breed loves to swim. Be prepared that some of these dogs will seek out any pond or swimming hole to dive into, or even a city sidewalk mud puddle! In fact, in New York City and other large metropolises, boarding kennels, doggie gyms and day-care centers are beginning to offer hydrotherapy and swim times. Indeed, these dogs' paws are actually webbed to aid them, ducklike, in swimming. From the laid-back, lumbering Clumber Spaniels to the cuddly Cockers and happy-go-lucky Labs, these dogs like nothing more than to share their world with you.

I used to breed and show German Shorthaired Pointers, and they are a perfect example of the Sporting Group. I especially admired their ability to run in the fields, find a bird, and freeze with nose and tail straight out from their bodies. If an owner is a hunter and shoots a bird, this group of dogs will bring the bird back to the owner undamaged. I never liked to hunt, but I really loved to watch these dogs at work. Their particular traits manifested themselves vividly in my dog Eli.

Companionable, smart, and easy to train—not to mention beautiful—Eli was a natural for television commercials and magazine print ads. One day we were in New York City to work on two separate print advertisements. With serious time constraints, we were rushing down Madison Avenue to make our second photo shoot when Eli stopped to point out an entirely different sort of shoot. At that moment, in the middle of the madness that is Madison Avenue, Eli stopped—literally "froze"—to point out her "game": the notorious New York City pigeon. It was amusing to see this quality of the breed, which is genetically inherited, transported into modern-day New York. Evidently, everyone else thought so, as well, because soon Eli and I were surrounded by an admiring audience of usually unflappable New Yorkers. As Eli stood there, still as a statue, the pedestrian traffic around her also "froze." I had to smile because it occurred to me that these jaded, "been there, done that" New Yorkers were unwittingly doing just what fellow sporting dogs would do for Eli—they were, in AKC terms, "honoring the point." But I also realized that if they didn't move, and Eli didn't move, then the pigeon wouldn't move and we would never make the shoot on time. I had to help Eli flush out the pigeon by shooing it away and up into the air. Only then was Eli satisfied that he had accomplished the job he was bred to do, and we were able to make my shoot—the photo shoot—and accomplish the job Eli was contracted to do.

## 2. Hound

Similarly, the Hound Group has been bred to help man hunt, and is happiest when actively pursuing game. But if hunting is not your thing, hounds are just as happy to play any game you choose, whether it's a rough-and-tumble game of Frisbee or endless hide-and-seek. This classification may not look like one group to the uninitiated, because it is made up of seemingly unrelated dogs—they come in diverse shapes and sizes. But one trait they have in common is that they enjoy reveling in their "wolf" within by indulging in a little howling or baying now and then just to remind you of their origin.

The Hound Group is composed of two subgroups: the Sighthounds and the Scenthounds. Sighthounds, also called gaze hounds, have keen visual sensitivity and are very quick. They hunt independently, not needing commands from their masters. Nowadays, Sighthounds are rarely used for hunting. Professionally, they are confined to a racetrack or course, where they follow a lure that is pulled ahead of them. The Greyhound, Scottish Deerhound, Borzoi, Basenji, and Afghan are representative of this group. These dogs have great speed and grace and enjoy lots of outdoor time and vigorous activity. Be aware of their keen eye and love of the chase, and be prepared to hold on to the leash if you're playing in a busy park with lots of squirrels, joggers, and cyclists.

Scenthounds, on the other hand, are stimulated by their incredibly sensitive noses. The Beagle, Dachshund, Basset, and Bloodhound are members of this group. These dogs are also very good with children, and their strong sense of play combined with their sense of smell can make them enduring companions for children. These pets love nothing more than to roust a newly discovered playmate hiding out under the bedcovers! Extremely loyal, hounds are friendly, dedicated, and determined to please their people. This makes them, especially the Bassets and Bloodhounds, very good at finding lost children.

A wonderful story about a Scenthound involves a client of mine whose three-year-old child had wandered off. Naturally, everyone was frantic. The parents called the police, who responded with a Bloodhound named Duke. They gave Duke a piece of the child's worn clothing to sniff. He immediately put his nose to the ground and started pulling and tugging on his harness. (Scent dogs always wear a harness instead of a collar, so that they can pull without discomfort.) We waited at the house for about two hours, until Duke appeared with a tired-looking child holding on to his harness. One wonderful thing about Duke, as well as all Bloodhounds, is that his appearance is not at all threatening. Instead, the dogs are funny and endearing, so children are not at all afraid of them.

## 3. Working

This group is another known for its diversity. These dogs are happiest when they are working, and their work is as diverse as the breeds themselves. From the Saint Bernard rescuing errant skiers and trapped mountain climbers high up in the Alps to the Newfoundland bounding into the briny seas to rescue capsized seafarers to a "draft" dog or sled dog—whether a Samoyed, an Alaskan Malamute, a Bernese Mountain Dog, or a Siberian Husky—pulling a snow sled for endless miles over deep and treacherous snowy terrain, dogs of the working group have hearts as big as their brawn, and their exploits are the stuff of legends.

However, when one thinks of working dogs, it is the police guard and protection dogs, Dobermans, Boxers, Akitas and Rottweilers, that most readily come to mind. These dogs are powerfully built and extremely strong. They are very territorial and bred for aggression, which make them ideally suited for guard and patrol work. They are as strong willed as they are strong. Therefore, these strong dogs are best with an equally strong minded and physically strong person. Although these dogs, when properly socialized and trained, can be the most loyal and gentle of dogs, they need a strong alpha leader to take charge. Otherwise, they will take charge.

The Rottweiler is by nature fiercely loyal and protective. I remember one time when my sister was working in her grooming shop, that a person came in, acting very suspiciously. Apparently he thought she was alone. My sister called for her Rottweiler to come to her, and Cora responded immediately. By sniffing the air containing body chemicals which this man was exuding and by observing his body language, Cora quickly sensed he presented a danger to my sister. Cora took protective measures. She stationed herself between my sister and the man and bared her fangs in an unmistakable challenge to him. At my sister's command Cora lay down, but never took her eyes off the man, who got the message and vamoosed. Sometimes a little "smile" showing some pearly whites (especially on a Rottweiler) goes a long way.

### 4. Herding

Herding dogs were bred to have natural herding instincts and the ability to make decisions about when and where to lead their charges. Over the years certain breeds of dogs were developed to herd specific animals. In the Herding Group we see most clearly the ancestral wolf.

Whether it's a Shetland Sheepdog herding miniature sheep and horses along a wind- and rain-swept Scottish moor or the hardy Australian Cattle Dog maneuvering wild steer in the high temperatures of the barren outback, you'll see them crouching, watching, and moving their charges just as a wolf would when stalking its prey. These dogs are invaluable aides to ranchers and farmers, and since the interaction between handler and dog is vital, herding dogs have been bred to be extremely alert and responsive to commands. All these dogs, from the imposing German Shepherd to the almost comical Corgi, are intelligent, agile, athletic, and remarkably attuned to their masters. These dogs can work on command, but they find their greatest happiness in being with you, following your commands, working with you—some Border Collies never seem to take their eyes off you. These dogs provide both action and interaction. And they don't thrive only on herding; any work that is challenging and stimulating will do. Frisbee and agility courses are ideal for these dogs.

Here's an ideal "rainy day" indoor game I devised for training Dudley, a wonderful Bearded Collie. I used to practice herding with him by scattering all his toys around the house, then sitting down in a living room chair, and saying, "Dudley, get your toys." Off he'd run, gathering one toy at a time and laying it gently by my feet, until all the toys were collected. When his master and mistress had a baby, Dudley immediately recognized and accepted the child as part of the family. When the baby became a toddler and played in a padded play area, Dudley kept careful watch. If the child wandered away from the play area, Dudley would gently nudge him back. Soon, when playmates came over, he would do the same to keep them safely in the prescribed part of the house. As the children got older and played in the backyard with their friends, Dudley continued to be a super-nanny, much to the delight of the adults. If things got out of hand, he would bark until an adult would come to help. When the children were good and playing peacefully in place, Dudley would lie down and watch.

## 5. Terrier

There are many kinds of terriers, and most are feisty, noisy, playful, and fearless—much like exuberant children. Like children—especially those in the terrible twos or difficult teen years—these dogs are inquisitive and tenacious, always bustling about. They are also strong willed, scrappy, determined, and courageous. These dogs make loyal, playful, friendly pets, but they can also be stubborn and domineering at times. They make excellent watchdogs despite their relatively diminutive size. Nor are they traditional lapdogs. They have a mind of their own and may not always want to be cuddled. They are very affectionate, but they will let you know when they have had enough.

The Terrier's name is derived from the Latin word for "earth," *terra*, which describes the job it was bred to do: rout out small animals from their burrows. The Cairn Terrier, for example, was specifically bred to root out small rodents from the stone walls (called cairns) bordering farmers' fields in England, Scotland, and Wales. The Terrier Group includes some of our most beloved breeds, the West Highland Terrier, the Cairn Terrier, and the Wheaten Terriers. Feisty and territorial, these little guys are also very ingratiating and engaging. So even though dyed-in-the-wool Terrier people facetiously refer to their dogs as "little terrors," they wouldn't dream of leaving home without them. In fact, these hardy and adaptable little dogs can successfully call any place on earth home. Wherever you hang his leash, that's home for the tenacious and territorial Terrier.

One client of mine, Don Brown, was an air force man. He had a wife and two young daughters who adored dogs, but they had no idea what kind of dog to get, because they constantly moved from one base to the next. My client flew C-130s, a small but hardy and versatile transport plane that the air force dispatched around the world for a variety of missions. From Germany to Japan, my client never knew where they would end up next. How could you acquire a dog to romp in the open fields with you when, two years later, you could be stationed at a densely populated urban area?

The solution: I enlisted the Cairn Terrier—a small, hardy, and versatile little trouper—to join the Brown troop on its world travels. Playful, curious, and tenacious, Christopher adapted so well to air force life that the Browns acquired a second Cairn, MacDuff. All within one compact, inquisitive, protective, and playful little bundle, the Cairn Terrier is a mother's helper, investigative reporter, and security system—portable and ready to go anywhere at the drop of a carrying case. Plus, when the Browns were transferred to Guam and lived in a small fishing village, Mrs. Brown found she had an on-site furry exterminator. Christopher and MacDuff—doing what Cairns were bred to do—had a great time rooting the vermin out of the nearby seawall.

## 6. Non-Sporting

The Non-Sporting Group covers an extremely wide range of types, making it impossible to generalize. This diverse group evolved basically as a kind of catchall group for breeds that have outlived their original purpose, such as Dalmatians, which were once coach dogs, but now have no coaches to follow (although they were adopted by the firehouses), and Bulldogs, which, thankfully, are no longer used in the cruel "sport" of bull-baiting. Varying widely in size, coats, ears, tails and temperament—unalike in everything, with the exception of the two different sizes of Poodles—they bear little resemblance to one another. The Non-Sporting Group includes small dogs, big dogs, hound types, lapdogs, even—surprise—Boston Terriers, which are members not of the Terrier Group but of the Non-Sporting Group.

I guess it's not surprising, then, that one of my best all-time animal actors was Muffin, my Tibetan Terrier. Being a member of this catchall, can-do-anything, be-anything group is probably what made him such an in-demand member of my STARPET Animal Talent Agency. Muffin reminded me of the actors who at auditions are asked if they can do something they really can't do, like dance or ride a horse. They confidently say yes and then take a crash course to try to learn to do it (or at least fake it). You need a soulful stray for a TV show? Muffin could portray him. A commercial required a lovable shaggy dog? Muffin filled the bill. Desperate to find a Benji look-alike? No problem! A little dye and a little trim and *voilà*, Muffin to the rescue. When *The Edge of Night* needed a scruffy-looking mixed breed to play an abandoned dog, Muffin garnered the recurring role. As they say in show biz, Muffin's acting had range. And talking about range—like home on the range—Chuck Wagon dog food needs an all-American shaggy dog for a commercial, and who do you think saves the day? That's right, Muffin! In fact, his repertoire was so diverse that in his many show business roles, only once did he portray his own breed, a Tibetan Terrier, and that was in a Friendly's Ice Cream commercial with the tag line, "Get friendly with someone you love!" How fitting for Muffin, who was always friendly and loved by all, even if they never quite knew for sure his specific breed.

## 7. Toy

When the uninitiated envision the Toy Group, they usually imagine what many of the breeds in this group were meant for—to be cuddled and snuggled, to have our furrowed brows smoothed by these furry breeds, to have these tiny angels tame the savage beasts within us. Many of them do just that. In ancient Greek and Roman times, both physicians and philosophers (including Pliny) would often prescribe that a person suffering from depression or anxiety carry a small dog with him at all times. If a patient had a stomachache, the prescription was again a small dog, to be held against the abdomen for the medicinal "hot water bottle" effect—hence the term *lapdog*. The nickname also aptly described a second, entirely different job for the cuddly little toy dog. These early physicians often placed them in cribs to act as wet nurses. Later on, of course, these same "lap" dogs became the fancy of privileged ladies, to be fussed and fawned over—appealing little bundles of unconditional love. Nowadays, these breeds, such as the Papillon, Maltese, King Charles Spaniel, Italian Greyhound, and Toy Poodle, are ideal dogs for older people and people with disabilities because they are easily paper-trained and therefore do not have to be walked outside. Their size and disposition make these dogs perfect for pet-facilitated therapy.

Still, although born cute, not all breeds from this diminutive group were born to be cuddled. The twenty-one breeds classified as Toy are all quite different from one another. Many, such as the Italian Greyhound and Toy Poodle, are diminutive versions of their larger relatives, giving you a great dog in a manageable size.

Many toy breeds are powerhouses with Napoleon complexes. They either view themselves as big dogs, or (being acutely aware of their small size and feeling vulnerable) they try to make up for a small body with a large attitude. Just watch any little Chihuahua fearlessly take a preemptive strike at a quizzical Rottweiler.

Many of the Toy breeds, such as the Pomeranian and Shih Tzu, were used in ancient times as portable personal guard dogs. The cute little Pekingese was often kept nestled and hidden in the voluminous sleeves of a Chinese emperor's kimono, just in case an assassin should elude the palace guards and slip into the emperor's personal quarters. Nowadays, these small dogs continue to be great watchdogs. Even law enforcement officials in high-crime areas maintain that these small noisy dogs will deter an intruder, sight unseen.

The Toys are also ideal for first-time dog owners, as any training or behavioral problem that may arise seems less daunting with an eight-pound dog rather than with an eighty-pound one. Toy dogs are also great for the indefatigable traveler who wants to carry her dog every-where with her. Toy dogs are ideal for a family that has limited room, but still wants several dogs. Please remember that while these dogs can be great for children (they are certainly less intimidating than a large breed), they can be fragile, and children have to understand that, de-spite the group's size, these dogs are definitely not toys.

Above all, these dogs are devoted to their owners. Because of their diminutive size and sense of vulnerability, and from being held a great deal, these dogs acquire a sense of dependence that strengthens the dog-owner bond. They require a lot of attention, admiration, fondling, and love, and, of course, they give the same in return—with a free hot water bottle thrown in, to boot.

I had a friend who owned King Charles Spaniels. He was a real out-doorsman, and lived in a house with no heat. He was one of those people who loved to sleep with the windows open to allow in the cool night air. But when the temperatures really dropped, he was no fool. You've heard of Three Dog Night? Well, he had fifteen dogs to help him through any visit from old man winter. When the cold Canadian winds blustered through, all fifteen dogs slept on the bed with him, their body warmth keeping him—and the dogs—snug as bugs in a rug. My friend didn't tell the temperature by degrees but by dogs. We used to joke about whether it was a one-dog night or three-dog night, and so on . . .

## 8. Miscellaneous

Big dogs and small dogs, shorthairs and longhairs, make up the Mis-cellaneous Group. These are dogs who don't fit into any other existing categories, but AKC authorities acknowledge that throughout the world are distinct breeds of purebred dogs that the AKC does not officially recognize. Still, the AKC provides for a regular path of development for a new breed, which can then result in the breed's receiving full recognition and appearance as an official AKC recognized breed. The requirement for admission is clear and categorical proof that a substantial, sustained nationwide interest and activity in the breed exists. This includes an active parent club, with serious and expanding breed activity in a wide geographical area. When the AKC accepts a breed, it is admitted to this Miscellaneous Group, and is then eligible to compete and earn titles in AKC-sanctioned obedience, tracking, and agility events. They can even compete in conformation shows, but are limited to competition in the Miscellaneous Group only, and thus are not eligible for championship points.

Finally, if the AKC is satisfied that a breed is continuing a healthy, dynamic growth in the Miscellaneous class, it may earn the opportunity to be admitted to one of the seven groups and the opportunity to compete in regular classes. Currently, these Miscellaneous breeds are the Beauceron, Black Russian Terrier, German Pinscher, Glen of Imaal Terrier, Neapolitan Mastiff, Plott Hound, Polish Lowland Sheepdog, Toy Fox Terrier, Redbone Coonhound, and Nova Scotia Duck Tolling Retriever.

I have a client who owns this last breed, named Tizzie, who is small and energetic, loves the water, and is an excellent retriever. She is also a great watchdog. Because of her drive as a retriever, she will constantly remind you to throw the ball so she can retrieve it. She loves to play games that test her native skill. You have to fake the toss, then hide the ball somewhere, forcing her to search diligently for the ball. This game gives her ample opportunity—and endless hours of delight—to fulfill her unquenchable retrieving appetite.

### 9. Rare

This group is also very large and widely diverse, and one step further removed from full AKC recognition than the Miscellaneous Group. These dogs don't get any recognition at all. Indeed, the average reaction on the street—if one is *lucky* enough to see one of these rarities on the street—is confusion. Take the Leonberger, for example.

One time a client called me to train her dog, but she was at a loss to explain what it was. A German Shepherd? "No . . ." A Saint Bernard? "Not really . . ." My client was totally perplexed. She wasn't hesitant about keeping the dog—she wasn't sure what it was. The dog had been given to her as a present, but she hadn't yet received the dog's papers. She had no idea exactly *what* she was the proud owner of. I had to go see the dog for myself. When I arrived at my client's home, I was pleased to discover a Leonberger. These are wonderful German water rescue dogs. As we trained her for housebreaking and obedience, she was extremely calm and responsive, and grew up to be a fine example of this very loyal and protective breed.

Many of the Rare Group would like to join the AKC Miscellaneous Group, and some of these breeds are already members of kennel clubs around the world, such as the United Kennel Club, the Canadian Kennel Club, and the Fédération Cynologique (FCI).

### 10. Mixed Breeds

Although obviously not recognized by the AKC, to a large and loyal following of people, the all-American mutt rates a resounding 10. So, for sentimental reasons (some of my best dogs, too, have been mixed breeds), we'll refer to mixed breeds as the tenth group. For even though the mutt (or "Heinz 57") is not recognized by the AKC, these dogs are the silent majority of dogdom, and available or found in shelters all across the country. So large and beloved a group should not be ignored.

Mike is an example of just such a dog who went from rags to riches. My friend and client, a New York City actress, found poor Mike abandoned on the streets of Long Island. He was emaciated and dirty, an all too common case of abandonment. My friend didn't know what kind of dog he was, what breed or background. Undaunted, she took the dog in and nurtured him back to health. Bathing and grooming the dog revealed, to our surprise, a cute shaggy, scruffy, black-and-white dog. A true all-American mutt. After a little training, we realized the dog had great potential. We decided to put him in commercials. He had the looks and the ability, he loved to please, and he loved applause for a well-done trick. Today, his credits include over four thousand movies, commercials, and print advertisements. His commercials include spots for Burger King, Wrigley's Chewing Gum, and

Cheerios. He also appeared on the highly acclaimed NBC TV series *Law & Order*.

This just goes to show what wonderful pets abandoned dogs can make. True to his roots, Mike filmed many public service commercials as a "spokes-dog" for the North Shore Animal League, contributing mightily for the adoption of these wonderful dogs.

If you find your dream dog, whatever the group, you will come to believe that your dream dog is the best dog. Everybody believes that about their dream dog.

And you know what? Everybody is right!

Part II

# BASIC GUIDE TO DOG BREEDS

Now that you have an understanding of how all the different breeds are related to each other, it's time to think of how these dogs might fit into your life. The best way to discover your dream dog is to indulge in a little daydreaming, and I obviously can't do that for you.

Here you'll find a basic guide to the vast number of varied breeds, as well as your own Dream Dog Notebook. As you read this guide, imagine each dog with you, in your home. Record which qualities of which breeds seem to realistically fit your lifestyle. With over 160 breeds to choose from, it's unlikely you'll choose just one. You'll be lucky if you can winnow your favorites to a mere handful.

## MY DREAM DOG NOTEBOOK

As you envision your dream dog, check the characteristics that appeal to you. This will help you profile the many breeds and help select several dream dog candidates for you.

If your dream dog is going to be a family pet, please share this with your children. Letting them participate in the choice will add to the fun and help promote responsible pet ownership.

## PHYSICAL CHARACTERISTICS
Size
   Giant____ Large____ Medium____ Small____ Tiny____
Sex
   Male____Female____
Color

   _____

Coat
   Thick, fluffy____ Long, silky____ Short, smooth____
Ears
   Erect____ Floppy____
Tail
   Long____ Short or cropped____

## PHYSICAL CARE REQUIRED
Stamina
   Sturdy, robust____ Delicate, sensitive____
   Primarily an outdoor dog____ Primarily indoor____
Coat Care
   Easy or little care____ Daily care____
   Regular professional care____
Shedding
   Little, if any____ Heavy seasonal shedding____
   Heavy year-round shedding____
Exercise
   Little____ Moderate ____ Heavy daily____
Space needs
   Little space needed/happy indoors____
   Happy indoors with sufficient daily time outdoors____
   Lots of space/happiest outdoors____

## BEHAVIOR/TEMPERAMENT
Activity level
   Very calm____ Calm indoors when properly exercised____

Very active/lively_____
Playful_____ Vigorous, rough_____ Gentle, affectionate_____
Sociability level
Very good with children_____ Loves everyone_____
Reserved with strangers_____
Noise level
Quiet, rarely barks_____ Barks a lot_____
Good watchdog_____
Very intelligent, can learn tricks_____
Very loyal, obedient_____
Allergic Concerns*
Asthma _____ Pet dander _____

## OTHER QUALITIES I FEEL ARE IMPORTANT:

_____
_____
_____
_____
_____
_____

## MY DREAM DOG CANDIDATES (list your chosen breeds):

_____
_____
_____
_____
_____
_____

* The *Journal of the American Medical Association* has reported that studies show that families with pets have significantly lower instances of asthma and fewer allergic reactions. In fact, the exposure of infants to cats or dogs in the first year of life not only reduces their risks of asthma and pet allergies by 50 percent, but also appears to protect against other common allergens such as mold and grass. Physicians theorize this early exposure is helpful by causing the immune system to produce antibodies without allergic sensitization.

# AFFENPINSCHER (Monkey Dog)

**Size/Group:** Tiny/Toy
**Breed History:** Europe
**Height:** 9 to 12 inches
**Weight:** 7 to 8 pounds
**Life Expectancy:** 12 to 14 years
**Daily Exercise:** 30 minutes
**Behavior Problems:** Independence, house-breaking problems, house soiling, possessiveness of toys

The Affenpinscher is very loyal and loving to family, but tends to be aloof with strangers. Despite a tiny, frail appearance, he is a very good watchdog (but not a good guard dog, because of his size). He may be aggressive toward strangers because he is so possessive of family members. He is also very possessive of "his" belongings, such as his toys and bed.

Also known as a Monkey Dog, he can be stubborn and difficult to train, but at the same time is alert and intelligent—his personality is somewhat terrier-like. This dog is very good with children, but care must be taken that he is not stepped on during boisterous play. Can be very persistent in demanding affection, which may be annoying.

His bristly coat comes in various shades of black, black and tan, or reddish, and he requires little grooming—a good weekly brushing and trimming every two months or so are all that are needed. The Affenpinscher makes an extremely good apartment pet.

Although not especially prone toward congenital diseases and disorders, Affens can develop Legg-Perthes disease (degeneration of the hip joint, leading to lameness), patellar luxation (dislocation of the kneecap), kidney problems, heart murmurs, hypothyroidism, and open fontanel (cranial bones). See Appendix I for more details about these diseases and disorders.

# AFGHAN HOUND

**Size/Group:** Large/Hound
**Breed History:** Afghanistan
**Height:** 25 to 29 inches
**Weight:** 50 to 70 pounds
**Life Expectancy:** 12 years
**Daily Exercise:** 1 hour
**Behavior Problems:** Aloofness and shyness, house soiling, finicky eating, destructiveness, snappish with children, dominance over owner, possessiveness and territoriality, aggression with other dogs

An ancient breed, Afghan Hounds are mentioned in early Egyptian documents and depicted in northern Afghanistan caves. They were developed to chase and hunt gazelles, leopards, and hares. Therefore, they require a great deal of daily outdoor exercise. But they are relatively calm indoors and can be excellent apartment dwellers, as long as they have long walks several times a day and an occasional chance to run free in the park or the country. They have good stamina and are very agile.

Shyness may lead to fear-biting, and they are often overprotective of possessions and family. They are often pampered by their owners, and are therefore undersocialized, which leads to timidity and shyness. They are aloof with strangers and other animals, but require regular affection and attention from their owners. Anxious to please, they make quiet companion dogs.

Their beautiful, long, silky coats require quite a lot of care. They should be brushed at least three hours a week, and even with extensive grooming, they tend to shed. They can be any color, but white markings are not desired.

Possible health problems include hip dysplasia, cataracts, hypothyroidism, and autoimmune diseases. Read more about these conditions in Appendix I.

# AIREDALE TERRIER

**Size/Group:** Large/Terrier
**Breed History:** England, about 100 years ago
**Height:** 22 to 24 inches
**Weight:** 45 to 70 pounds
**Life Expectancy:** 13 years
**Daily Exercise:** 1 hour
**Behavior Problems:** Excessive barking, jumping on people, restlessness, destructiveness, aggression toward other dogs, territoriality

The largest of terriers, Airedales were originally bred to hunt bears, wolves, and badgers, and are tough and courageous. They are often used in police and guard-dog work, and are very protective of their homes and family—they make good watchdogs. Like most terriers, Airedales can be stubborn, and they benefit from good obedience training. Very independent, they have a distinct sense of humor, often trying to "fool" their owners.

They are excellent companion dogs and are good with children as long as they are introduced to them in early life. Gentle, they are loyal to their families, and are fine in a large apartment as long as they get sufficient outdoor exercise every day.

Their grizzled, short, wiry, black-and-tan coats require minimum care. They should be professionally stripped and clipped every couple of months, and brushed several times a week. If properly groomed, they do not shed.

Possible disorders include hypothyroidism, bleeding disorders, von Willebrand's disease, and hip dysplasia. See Appendix I for more details about these health concerns.

# AKBASH

**Size/Group:** Large/Working
**Breed History:** Agricultural guard dog
**Height:** 26 to 32 inches (males larger)
**Weight:** 75 to 120 pounds
**Life Expectancy:** 10 to 12 years
**Daily Exercise:** 20 minutes
**Behavior Problems:** Strong, consistent training and good fencing requirement; early socialization and constant supervision needed with children

This is not an ideal pet dog. Bred to be an agricultural guard dog over herds of animals, the Akbash is basically a very good watchdog. She is very independent, focused on the job she was bred to do, and is not "into" obedience or cute pet tricks and affectionate behavior. She tends to be single-minded.

If an Akbash puppy is overfed, it may develop joint problems. Care must be taken that a pup does not gain weight too fast, or become overweight gradually.

This is not a good dog to have with other pets. They tend to be very dominant and aggressive with other animals that are less strong, both physically and socially. They may also try to dominate their owners, if allowed. Some are also very curious about the world around them, and require strong, high fencing to prevent escape and becoming a danger to themselves and others.

The Akbash's medium-length coat needs year-round brushing, three times a week during the summer when shedding occurs.

Health concerns may include hip dysplasia, cardiomyopathy, hypothyroidism, bone cancer, bloat, and entropion (eyelids turned inward, causing irritation). For more specifics about these conditions, see Appendix I.

# AKITA

**Size/Group:** Large/Working
**Breed History:** Japan
**Height:** 24 to 28 inches
**Weight:** 75 to 110 pounds
**Life Expectancy:** 10 years
**Daily Exercise:** 1 hour
**Behavior Problems:** Dominance toward owners, stubbornness, territoriality, aggression toward other dogs

A kitas are the official dogs of Japan, where they have lived for hundreds of years. They were originally bred to scent-hunt large prey (bear, boar, and deer) and as protectors of property.

Devoted to their families, Akitas tend to be aloof with people they do not know, and they are wonderful watchdogs. Because of their stubborn natures, these dogs require firm, early training. Akitas should not be "first-time" pets. They need an experienced dog owner to handle them.

They also need a lot of space. They do not do well in apartments unless dwelling is very large. A house with a fenced yard is most suitable for an Akita.

Their short, thick, double coats shed quite a lot, and they should be groomed several times a week. They can be any color, but white, speckled, and brindle are the most common shades.

Possible health problems include hip dysplasia, patellar (kneecap) luxation, progressive retinal atrophy or PRA (leading to blindness), hypothyroidism, von Willebrand's disease, bloat, sebaceous adenitis (degenerating hair follicles and oil glands), pemphigus (an autoimmune skin disease), lupus, and cancer. For more details about these conditions, see Appendix I.

# ALASKAN MALAMUTE

**Size/Group:** Large/Working
**Breed History:** Alaska
**Height:** 23 to 28 inches
**Weight:** 75 to 85 pounds
**Life Expectancy:** 12 years
**Daily Exercise:** 1 hour
**Behavior Problems:** Dominance, food stealing, stubbornness, destructiveness if left alone too long, roaming, howling, aggression toward other dogs, territoriality

Malamutes were bred to haul heavy loads on sleds. Therefore, they are very strong and have great endurance. They require a lot of space, and are not well suited for apartment or city living.

They get bored easily, and thus require a lot of interaction with their families—families with children are ideal for a Malamute. If a Malamute is left alone too long, she can easily destroy a houseful of furniture. Poorly bred Malamutes (from puppy mills) tend to be especially destructive. Professional obedience training is essential for these dogs.

Because they were originally outdoor sled dogs, Malamutes do not tolerate extreme heat well, and they should be provided with shelter during hot, humid weather.

Their heavy, coarse coats shed a great deal in the spring unless they are professionally stripped. They can be light gray to black, or sable with white stomachs, legs, feet, and face.

Health concerns include a condition known as dwarfism (again, most common in poorly bred puppies), hip dysplasia, cataracts, bloat, degeneration of the kidneys, hypothyroidism, heart problems, and bleeding disorders. See Appendix I for more details about these diseases.

# AMERICAN BULLDOG

**Size/Group:** Large/Working
**Breed History:** USA
**Height:** 19 to 28 inches
**Weight:** 65 to130 pounds
**Life Expectancy:** 14 years
**Daily Exercise:** 35 minutes
**Behavior Problems:** Stubbornness and strength, firm handling requirement, aggression toward other dogs, destructiveness, territoriality

These dogs are able to protect ranches from livestock thieves and wild dogs. They were originally bred to handle rough cattle and Brahman bulls.

Because they are so stubborn, willful, and highly protective, American Bulldogs need to be obedience-trained at an early age. They require a strong hand and are not good pets for first-time owners. However, they are good with children as long as they are introduced to them early in puppyhood. American Bulldogs need quite a bit of space and are not happy in a small studio apartment.

Their short, smooth coat can be any solid color, brindle, or white with any other color. They shed little, and require grooming only a few times a week.

They are hardy but have a tendency to develop bloat, sensitive skin, body odor (because of the folds in their skin), and patellar (knee) luxation. To learn more about these health concerns, see Appendix I.

# AMERICAN ESKIMO DOG (Miniature)

**Size/Group:** Tiny-medium/ Non-Sporting
**Breed History:** Germany
**Height:** 12 to 15 inches
**Weight:** 10 to 20 pounds
**Life Expectancy:** 13 years
**Daily Exercise:** 20 minutes
**Behavior Problems:** Independence, difficulty house-training, chewing, barking, destructiveness

This little dog often performs tricks in shows and circuses, and loves to entertain "his" humans with tricks. Highly energetic and playful, the American Eskimo is intolerant of heat, and needs a cool place to go when it is hot and humid.

The American Eskimo needs very little living space but tends to have a high indoor energy level. He is good with well-mannered children, but does not like to roughhouse. He prefers a quiet, well-organized household.

His long white coat sheds a lot, and requires grooming about four times a week. Because of his white fur, tearstains on his face may become a problem.

Health concerns are hip dysplasia, patellar (kneecap) luxation, progressive retinal atrophy (causes blindness), epilepsy, and diabetes. To learn more about these health problems, see Appendix I.

# AMERICAN ESKIMO DOG (Standard and Toy)

**Size/Group:** Medium/ Non-sporting
**Breed History:** Germany
**Height:** 15 to 19 inches for standard and 9 to 12 inches for toy
**Weight:** 20 to 35 pounds for standard and 6 to 10 pounds for toy
**Life Expectancy:** 13 years for both standard and toy
**Daily Exercise:** 35 minutes for standard and 20 minutes for toy
**Behavior Problems:** Possible jealousy of babies and children, independence, chewing, barking, house soiling, aggression

Standard

Both the standard and toy varieties of the American Eskimo like to play and perform tricks and are easy to train in general, but may be difficult to house-train when young. She loves to chew on everything, so plenty of appealing chew toys are a must. The standard's energy level is lower than that of the miniature, but she is still very active indoors and should be walked outdoors for at least thirty-five minutes a day. An interesting trait of all Eskies is that they all cross their front paws when they lie down.

As opposed to her larger relatives who can live outdoors in a fenced yard, the toy Eskie needs to live indoors. This small dog can live in a small apartment or house, but has a high indoor energy level.

Standard Eskies were bred to love cold weather and snow; therefore, in hot, humid weather she needs a cool place to go. Wading pools are greatly appreciated. She is very smart and extremely aware of her surroundings. She may be nervous among strangers. As in all sizes of this breed, her thick white coat sheds continuously and needs brushing frequently. For both breeds, tear stains under the eyes may present a problem.

Bred to be a pet or companion, the toy American Eskimo wants to be around people. She wants to be the center of attention and, therefore, may be jealous of any new arrivals (babies, new spouses, and so forth). She is moderately protective of her property and people, but, if aroused, may make an awful din.

The toy Eskie loves to play and do tricks, often performing in circuses and shows. Boredom may be a problem if this little dog is not given enough to do and enough variety in training. When she becomes bored, a toy American Eskimo may become a problem chewer.

Health problems for both the standard and toy may include: hip dysplasia, patellar (kneecap) dislocation, progressive retinal atrophy leading to blindness, epilepsy, and diabetes. See Appendix I for more specifics about these health concerns.

# AMERICAN PIT BULL TERRIER

**Size/Group:** Large/Terrier
**Breed History:** USA
**Height:** 25 inches
**Weight:** 55 to 80 pounds
**Life Expectancy:** 12 years
**Daily Exercise:** 35 minutes
**Behavior Problems:** possible biting, careful training and socialization requirement, dominance, aggression toward other dogs and people, destructiveness

The American Pit Bull Terrier was bred as a fighting dog, and retains a good deal of his fighting instinct. He also tends to try to dominate his owner. His jaws are very strong and able to lock, so owners should not play tug-of-war with a Pit Bull, because it encourages aggression. However, with strict training and good socialization, this dog can be a good pet. Special care is needed when buying a Pit Bull because careless or unlicensed breeders may produce dogs that are not good physical examples of the breed, or animals with poor temperaments.

Their indoor energy level is high, and they need a lot of living space. A house with a fenced yard is ideal for this dog. They make great watchdogs.

Their short, flat coats come in all colors and can have markings. They hardly shed at all, and need to be groomed only once a week.

Health problems may include hip dysplasia, thickened lower jaw (CMO, craniomandibular osteopathy), cataracts, hypothyroidism, cruciate (overlapping) ligament ruptures, and cancer. See Appendix I for more information about these diseases.

# AMERICAN STAFFORDSHIRE TERRIER

**Size/Group:** Medium/Terrier
**Breed History:** USA
**Height:** 16 to 21 inches
**Weight:** 40 to 75 pounds
**Life Expectancy:** 12 years
**Daily Exercise:** 35 minutes
**Behavior Problems:** Dominance, territoriality, restlessness, house soiling, aggression toward other dogs, destructiveness

Naturally bred for guarding or fighting, this dog nevertheless can be a fine companion dog as long as he is trained firmly, early, and well. According to the U.S. Centers for Disease Control and Prevention, these dogs are known to bite. Like all terriers, they can be stubborn and try to dominate their owners. They tend to be aggressive with strangers and other dogs if an owner is not in control. They are good with children they know, but not to be trusted with strange children. Because of their strong jaws, they can do a lot of damage unless they are trained early not to chew anything except "their" own toys.

"AmStaffs" love to be outside, but extreme care should be taken that the dog cannot escape, either by jumping over or digging underneath a fence. They are very good guard dogs and watchdogs. They love to play and snuggle and enjoy performing agility tests and all types of jobs. They become very restless if bored.

Their short coats come in all colors and shed a little. Grooming with a rubber currycomb once a week is all that is necessary.

Possible health problems include hip dysplasia, thickened lower jaw (CMO, craniomandibular osteopathy), cataracts, hypothyroidism, cruciate (overlapping) ligament ruptures, and cancer. See Appendix I for more information about these health concerns.

# AMERICAN WATER SPANIEL

**Size/Group:** Medium/Sporting
**Breed History:** USA, probably developed from the Curly-Coated Retriever and the Irish Water Spaniel
**Height:** 15 to 18 inches
**Weight:** 25 to 45 pounds
**Life Expectancy:** 12 years
**Daily Exercise:** 1 hour
**Behavior Problems:** Roaming, some sensitivity, excessive barking

American Water Spaniels are not well known, but are greatly prized by their owners for their hunting abilities (duck, quail, pheasant, grouse, and rabbits), ability in the water, love of children, and eagerness to please.

AWS's need a lot of exercise, preferably in the water (fetching a stick, for instance). Their indoor energy levels are high, and they require a lot of outdoor exercise, so are best kept in a large apartment or a house with a yard, but they can adapt to almost any living space as long as their family is nearby.

They should always be kept in an enclosed yard that cannot be dug out of, because they tend to roam. They are good watchdogs, but are not testy with strangers. They are especially good with children and accepting of other pets.

Their medium-length curly coats are light or dark brown and shed a little. Brushing once a week is usually sufficient to keep them in good shape.

Health problems may include hip dysplasia, patellar (knee) luxation; retinal atrophy (which causes blindness), detached retina, cataracts, epilepsy, and hypothyroidism. For more specifics about these diseases, see Appendix I.

# ANATOLIAN SHEPHERD DOG

**Size/Group:** Extra large/ Working
**Breed History:** Turkey, introduced to the U.S. in 1968
**Height:** 28 to 32 inches
**Weight:** 80 to 150 pounds
**Life Expectancy:** 11 years
**Daily Exercise:** 35 minutes
**Behavior Problems:** strict training requirement, territoriality and possessiveness, aggression toward other dogs, destructiveness

The Anatolian Shepherd is a flock-guarding and cart-hauling breed. He requires a lot of space and is very territorial, which makes him an excellent watchdog. He requires early socialization and strict training, or he may try to challenge his owner's authority. His energy level is low, unless he feels that his property or family is threatened—then he springs into action. He is a good jumper and therefore needs a high fence.

These large dogs are very friendly with children and other pets with whom they have been raised, but are apt to be unfriendly with strange dogs and positively nasty toward unneutered males. They may tend to be overprotective of "their" family.

The Anatolian's coat is short and rough, and may be brindle, fawn, white, or irregularly marked. He always has a black mask. He is an average shedder, and requires brushing about once a week, except in the spring, when he sheds heavily.

Physical and health considerations include hip dysplasia, entropion (a hanging lower eyelid), and hypothyroidism. See Appendix I for more details about these disorders.

# AUSTRALIAN CATTLE DOG

**Size/Group:** Medium/Herding
**Breed History:** Australia
**Height:** 17 to 20 inches
**Weight:** 35 to 45 pounds
**Life Expectancy:** 12 years
**Daily Exercise:** 1 hour
**Behavior Problems:** Willfulness, strong-willed; early, consistent socialization and training requirement; aggression toward other dogs; destructiveness

"AuCaDos" are very versatile, tough, courageous dogs, capable of herding steers. They can be fine companions as long as they are socialized early in life. They are very active indoors and need great deal of activity or play in order to stay out of trouble. Quick learners, these dogs like to follow their people around.

Because they are herding dogs, they may try to "herd" their family, especially children at play, by nipping at their heels or pant legs. Toys that can be chased may distract them. Delivery people may find themselves "trapped" in their cars or vans because they are seen as intruders by these very territorial dogs. Because of this trait, AuCaDos naturally make great watchdogs, but they must be socialized early in order to realize that humans are, in fact, "top dogs."

Their short, straight, dense coats are rough to the touch and can be a number of different colors: speckled, red, blue, or blue with tan. They shed little during the year, but a lot during early spring. Ideally, they should be brushed once a week.

Possible health problems are hip dysplasia, OCD (a growth disorder of joints), blindness, glaucoma, lens luxation, and deafness. See Appendix I for more details about these health considerations.

# AUSTRALIAN KELPIE

**Size/Group:** Medium/Working
**Breed History:** Australia
**Height:** 17 to 23 inches
**Weight:** 20 to 45 pounds
**Life Expectancy:** 12 years
**Daily Exercise:** 1 hour
**Behavior Problems:** Independence, tendency toward boredom, not an indoor pet

The Kelpie is a relatively unknown breed. Bred as a working ranch dog, and usually kept as one, she is not at all happy in a small, limited space. She is basically a sheepherder, working mostly in the Australian outback.

If kept as a pet, she requires a large amount of space, exercise, and activity. Without sufficient exercise, she may become destructive. If she has been socialized and obedience-trained early, however, she can develop into a loyal, well-mannered companion dog.

As a herder, she stares at cattle, sheep, or hogs, to force them to obey her; only on occasion does she nip a particularly stubborn animal. Sometimes Kelpies are used to herd turkeys, chickens, emus, and ostriches. She may decide to nip an especially strong-minded child. She will also attempt to "herd" any other household pets.

Her short, dense, straight coat comes in black, black and tan, chocolate, red, red and tan, and fawn. She sheds a little, and requires grooming about once a week.

Possible health problems are hip dysplasia, a growth disorder of the joints (OCD—osteochondritis dissecans), and a heart disorder known as PDA (patent ductus arteriosus). See Appendix I for more details about these health concerns.

# AUSTRALIAN SHEPHERD

**Size/Group:** Medium/Herding
**Breed History:** Spain
**Height:** 18 to 23 inches
**Weight:** 35 to 70 pounds
**Life Expectancy:** 12 years
**Daily Exercise:** 1 hour
**Behavior Problems:** dominance, strong herding instinct, aloofness with strangers

Agile herders, Aussies will indulge in their instinct with adults, children, and all other animals. On a ranch, they not only herd, but also guard both property and livestock, and must have good early training in order not to become dominant over their owners and all other humans. They get along well with children and are devoted to their families. They are not shy, but do tend to treat strangers with reserve.

They require a lot of daily outdoor exercise and chores, and are good learners, easily trained. They especially enjoy flyball, and obedience and tracking exercises. Early training is also strongly recommended to get rid of their heel-nipping instincts.

Aussie coats are medium in length and straight or wavy. They come in a variety of colors, ranging from black with white to red with white, copper, or tan markings. They are average shedders, except during the spring, when they shed heavily. Normally, they require grooming twice a week.

Health concerns include hip dysplasia, progressive retinal atrophy (PRA causes blindness), Collie eye anomaly (a malformation of the optic nerve), cataracts, glaucoma, abnormally small eyes (microphthalmia), and epilepsy. For more particulars about these health problems see Appendix I.

# AUSTRALIAN TERRIER

**Size/Group:** Small/Terrier
**Breed History:** Australia
**Height:** 10 to 11 inches
**Weight:** 12 to 18 pounds
**Life Expectancy:** 14 years
**Daily Exercise:** 35 minutes
**Behavior Problems:** Possible dominance, chasing small animals and getting lost, irritable snapping if teased

This little dog, also referred to as an Aussie, was originally bred to tend sheep and guard mines, and for companionship. A combination of several terrier breeds, he is playful, obedient, and adaptable. He is an ideal apartment pet, although he adapts well to larger homes and also loves to travel—easily carried underneath a human's arm. They are good with children they have been raised with.

Like all terriers, the Australian can be spunky, feisty, and domineering, and requires firm early training and a strong hand. They bark a lot, but are easier to quiet than many terriers. They make excellent watchdogs.

Although they are active by nature, these little dogs do not require a lot of outdoor exercise. They enjoy playing, but are also content to lie quietly at their owner's feet.

Their medium-length coats are straight and rough, and require only moderate grooming, about three times a week. They come in black, silvery black, or reddish, with tan faces, chests, and legs, and shed very little.

Health considerations include Legg-Perthes (disintegration of the hip joint), patellar (knee) luxation, and diabetes. For more details about these health problems, see Appendix I.

# BASENJI

**Size/Group:** Small/Hound
**Breed History:** North Africa
**Height:** 16 to 17 inches
**Weight:** 21 to 24 pounds
**Life Expectancy:** 12 years
**Daily Exercise:** 35 minutes
**Behavior Problems:** Wandering, excessive curiosity and playfulness that may lead to destructiveness, stubbornness

In Africa, Basenjis are used as guides in the forests, warning against dangerous animals. They also hunt small game. In this country they are primarily companion dogs.

These little dogs do not bark, but they make a number of different noises, including one that can only be described as a yodel. They are very curious and cannot leave a hole (or a laundry basket full of clothes) unexplored (or "undumped").

They are very determined and active, and need a lot of daily stimulation and activity. When excited and happy, Basenjis often leap into the air. They require a moderate to high amount of exercise daily, but are quite well suited for apartment or city life. A house with a yard is appreciated.

Basenjis are remarkably catlike in that they lick themselves clean. They also like to climb up on high things. Their short, flat coats require very little grooming—once a week is sufficient. Coat colors include red, black, and black and tan, and they always have white feet, tail tips, and a blaze on their noses.

Possible health problems include progressive retinal atrophy (PRA which causes blindness), other eye problems, malabsorption (an inability to absorb digested food), hemolytic anemia (PKD), and Fanconi syndrome (degeneration of the kidney tubes). For more information about these health concerns, see Appendix I.

# BASSET HOUND

**Size/Group:** Medium/Hound
**Breed History:** France, descended from the Bloodhound
**Height:** 13 to 15 inches
**Weight:** 40 to 60 pounds
**Life Expectancy:** 12 years
**Daily Exercise:** 20 minutes
**Behavior Problems:** House soiling, food stealing, howling, snoring, picky eating

Although Bassets are of medium weight, their extremely short legs make them look more massive than they are. Added to this, their sad, wrinkled faces gives them a mournful appearance. Their long, soft ears are very attractive to children, who have to be reminded not to pull on them.

Like their forebears, Bloodhounds, Bassets have extremely sensitive noses and are excellent field dogs, with a great deal of endurance. They have deep, resonant voices when they bark, but they do not make good watchdogs because they like everybody. Bassets are good-natured dogs, but they do not react well to punishment; rewards work better for training them. They love children and are almost never known to bite. They get along well with their families and love to be included in family activities. Their indoor energy level is low, but they require daily outdoor exercise. A house or large apartment is ideal.

They have naturally oily skin, which gives them a slightly "doggy" smell. Their short coats come in all colors and require little care, although they do shed a lot, so a daily brushing will help cut down on shed hair. Because they are so low to the ground, their stomachs often pick up dirt. Their long, floppy ears require regular cleaning so they do not become infected and develop an odor. Bassets are also very messy drinkers, sloshing water all over the floor.

Health problems include obesity, spinal disease, epilepsy, bleeding disorders, OCD, knee joint problems, elbow dysplasia, blindness, eyelid problems, and glaucoma. See Appendix I for details.

# BEAGLE

**Size/Group:** Small/Hound
**Breed History:** Great Britain
**Height:** 12 to 15 inches
**Weight:** 13 to 30 pounds
**Life Expectancy:** 13 years
**Daily Exercise:** 35 minutes
**Behavior Problems:** Roaming, baying or howling, house soiling, stubbornness, food stealing

Very common pets, Beagles' extreme popularity has led to a number of poorly bred ("puppy mill") specimens, so prospective owners should do their research and know their source before buying a pet.

Beagles are extremely hardy hunting dogs, indifferent to weather conditions, no matter how bad. These dogs normally hunt in packs. This inborn hunting instinct can lead a Beagle to roam far from home, so a high, sturdy fence that cannot be dug under is a must if a Beagle is going to be kept outdoors. Beagles are extremely social and do well with other pets in the home. They do not like to be left alone. They are good with children as long as they have been introduced to them as puppies.

They are calm and gentle, but may be overly shy and submissive, which can make them difficult to train. The best training tool for a Beagle is food, because they really love to eat.

Beagles' short coats shed a little all year round, and require grooming several times a week. Their ears should be cleaned regularly.

Possible health considerations are all kinds of eye problems (glaucoma, cataracts, retinal atrophy), hypothyroidism, epilepsy, and spinal disc problems. For more specifics about these health issues, see Appendix I.

# BEARDED COLLIE

**Size/Group:** Large/Herding
**Breed History:** Great Britain
(known in Scotland since the
15th century)
**Height:** 22 inches
**Weight:** 45 to 60 pounds
**Life Expectancy:** 12 years
**Daily Exercise:** 1 hour
**Behavior Problems:** Possible
herding of other animals and
children, possessiveness, may
knock over toddlers

This joyous, gentle, and affectionate dog is naturally a herder, but she can make a very good pet. A very social dog, she will not be happy if she is left out of things and prefers to be in the middle of all family activities. She loves to play outdoors—Frisbee and flyball are favorite games.

She is very active and needs at least an hour of real daily exercise. She is best suited to country life and loves to run in open space. But Beardies can adapt to urban and apartment living as long as they get long enough daily walks (or runs).

Her ample coat makes her resistant to changes in the temperature, and she likes to sleep outdoors, if possible. She sheds very little, but her coat tends to mat. For the first few years, a Beardie's coat requires a lot of energetic weekly brushing. After about two years, approximately twenty minutes of brushing a week is sufficient.

Possible health problems include hip dysplasia, cataracts, Addison's disease (low adrenaline), hypothyroidism, autoimmune diseases, heart problems, and epilepsy. See Appendix I for more details about these concerns.

# BEAUCERON

**Size/Group:** Large/Miscellaneous
**Breed History:** France (named in 1889)
**Height:** 24 to 28 inches
**Weight:** 66 to 100 pounds
**Life Expectancy:** 13 years
**Daily Exercise:** 45 minutes
**Behavior Problems:** As puppies they tend to be too rough for small children; dominance; strong, thorough training required

Beaucerons were bred in France as agile herders and aggressive big game hunters. They are also known as Bergers de Beauce, Bas Rouges, and French Shorthaired Shepherds. Originally testy sheep-dogs, they have been selectively bred to become good companions to owners who are willing to take the time and have the patience to train and work with them. They are excellent herders, guards (watchdogs), police workers, and rescuers, and are often used as outdoors guard dogs. These dogs need a firm master, and although tolerant of other family members, are often one-man dogs.

Extremely dominant by nature, they are nevertheless eager students, and they really like to carry out jobs and chores. This breed is tolerant of other children and other pets when raised with them, but is not friendly with strange dogs.

Although their indoor energy levels are not particularly high, Beaucerons require a fair amount of space such as a large apartment or a house with a yard. They need at least a forty-five-minute walk daily. Their short, thick, dense coats come in a number of colors: black with rust and white, black with gray, and tricolored. They are moderate shedders and require grooming about once a week.

Their only known health problem is the possibility of hip dysplasia. See Appendix I for more details about this problem.

# BEDLINGTON TERRIER

**Group:** Medium/Terrier
**Breed History:** Great Britain
(developed around 1880)
**Height:** 15 to 17 inches
**Weight:** 17 to 23 pounds
**Life Expectancy:** 14 years
**Daily Exercise:** 45 minutes
**Behavior Problems:** Aggression, incompatibility with other pets, fighting other animals, excessive barking, house soiling, snapping

This dog may look like a lamb, but his personality is anything but lamblike. He positively despises all other animals, of which he is extremely jealous, and will fight them to the death. Care must be taken that he is never off lead outdoors, because he will take off after any animal he sees. He can be good with children if exposed to them early, and is an especially good pet for older people with grown children.

Originally bred as a ratter in mines, these dogs used to be exhibited in fighting pits with other Bedlingtons, badgers, foxes, or rodents. High-spirited, a Bedlington needs long daily walks and enjoys all kinds of play and an occasional run in the country. But he is calm indoors and makes a good apartment pet.

His curly, short coat comes in sand, blue, liver, tan, and combinations of these colors. He needs weekly combing and a professional grooming about every two months. Bedlingtons shed very little.

Health considerations may be liver problems, blindness, cataracts, detached retina, and patellar (knee) luxation. See Appendix I for more particulars about these health problems.

# BELGIAN MALINOIS

**Size/Group:** Large/Herding
**Breed History:** Belgium (developed in 1891)
**Height:** 16 to 22 inches
**Weight:** 55 to 80 pounds
**Life Expectancy:** 12 years
**Daily Exercise:** 1 hour
**Behavior Problems:** Aggression, fear biting, indoor restlessness, destructiveness when left alone

This is one of three breeds (Groenendael, Malinois, and Tervuren) bred in Belgium as shepherds—they protected flocks from wolves as well as from human predators. They make great watchdogs. These dogs are very like German Shepherds and are used extensively by police and for guard work. Needless to say, they are excellent household guard dogs.

Their indoor energy level is high, and they require at least an hour a day of vigorous outdoor exercise. Malinois are fearless dogs that require serious obedience training early in life. Owners must establish control right away by giving strong, clear messages. They are intelligent dogs that will take advantage if allowed to do so. Malinois are not suited for inexperienced owners or busy households—they require a lot of one-on-one attention. They are best housed in a large apartment or house with a yard, and are not really suited for life in urban areas or a modest apartment.

Their short, dense, straight coats come in blackened or reddish fawn, with a black mask and ears. They are average shedders, and require grooming about two times a week.

Possible health considerations include hip dysplasia, progressive retinal atrophy, (which causes blindness), pannus (an eye disorder that can lead to blindness), cataracts, epilepsy, and hypothyroidism. For more information about these issues, see Appendix I.

# BELGIAN SHEEPDOG—GROENENDAEL

**Size/Group:** Large/Herding
**Breed History:** Bred in Belgium for police and rescue work
**Height:** 22 to 26 inches
**Weight:** 55 to 80 pounds
**Life Expectancy:** 12 years
**Daily Exercise:** 1 hour
**Behavior Problems:** Natural protectiveness of owners and aloofness with strangers, early socialization recommended

This intelligent and courageous breed is often used in herding, police work, and search and rescue operations. She makes a very good watchdog, but is not apt to attack unless she sees a good reason to do so. Naturally protective of her family, she remains indifferent to strangers unless they pose a threat. She can be good with children as long as she has had early (puppy) experience with them.

She really needs to be kept busy every day, and requires an experienced owner in order to shape her personality and behavior patterns. She is a very quick learner. An active dog, the Belgian Sheepdog needs good daily exercise—at least an hour a day of outdoor activity.

Her medium-length, straight, dense coat comes in black or black and white, and she sheds a lot. Grooming should be performed at least twice a week, and she may need some occasional professional trimming.

Health problems may include hip dysplasia, progressive retinal atrophy (which may lead to blindness), cataracts, pannus (an eye condition leading to blindness), epilepsy, hypothyroidism. For more information about these disorders see Appendix I.

# BELGIAN SHEPHERD—TERVUREN

**Size/Group:** Large/Herding
**Breed History:** Belgium, 1891
**Height:** 22 to 26 inches
**Weight:** 55 to 80 pounds
**Life Expectancy:** 12 years
**Daily Exercise:** 1 hour
**Behavior Problems:** Posses-
siveness, excitability, fear-biting,
shyness, restlessness indoors,
destructiveness when left alone

Like his cousins, the Groenendael and Malinois, the Tervuren was bred to be a shepherd. He is a devoted pet, very bright and coura-geous, and easily trained. He is not for a first-time pet owner. He is easily bored and enjoys a challenge. He needs an owner with a firm hand. Tervurens are apt to be naughty puppies, and crates are often recommended until the dog matures at eighteen months of age. The Tervuren is very demanding of attention, and if he doesn't get it, he may resort to destructiveness in order to make his owner pay attention to him.

If raised with other pets, he can tolerate them, but he may see a cat as potential prey. He is not particularly good with children but, again, if he is raised with them, he will tolerate them. Their excitability may cause him to become overly excited himself. Good with family, he is wary of strangers and is therefore a good watchdog.

Because he requires a lot of outdoor exercise, he is not recom-mended for apartment living. A house with a yard is much better for him. He can be extremely restless indoors, especially if he doesn't get enough exercise.

His medium-to-long coat is black and tan and sheds some. It needs a moderate amount of care twice a week.

Health problems may include hip and elbow dysplasia, cataracts, epilepsy, and hypothyroidism. For more specifics about these diseases, see Appendix I.

# BERNESE MOUNTAIN DOG

**Size/Group:** Large/Working
**Breed History:** Switzerland
**Height:** 23 to 28 inches
**Weight:** 105 to 120 pounds
**Life Expectancy:** 9 years
**Daily Exercise:** 1 hour
**Behavior Problems:** not good
with strangers, oriented to one
person or family, dominance—
obedience-training requirement,
destructiveness when left alone,
food stealing, timidity

Bernese Mountain dogs are not at all suited for urban or apartment living. Bred to be draft (load-pulling) animals, they are also used for herding and guarding. They are large dogs with heavy coats, and they need a lot of outdoor space and exercise. Very strong, muscular dogs, they prefer to live in unheated kennels all year long, and are not at all happy in hot, humid conditions.

These dogs can have a people phobia, and prefer to stay close to familiar humans unless they have been socialized to other people early in life. They are good watchdogs—they will bark but not bite.

They have thick, soft, silky coats that are usually tricolor (black, tan, and russet), with white markings on the chest and muzzle. They are average shedders, and require grooming about three times a week. Bernese are alert and energetic, stable, and very attentive toward their masters.

Possible health considerations are hip and elbow dysplasia, a growth disorder of the joints (OCD), retinal atrophy (which can cause blindness), thyroid problems, rare malignant and mast cell tumors, bloat, and kidney problems. For more details about these ailments, see Appendix I.

# BICHON FRISE

**Size/Group:** Small/
Non-Sporting
**Breed History:** Southern
Europe/Canary Islands
**Height:** 8 to 12 inches
**Weight:** 10 to 18 pounds
**Life Expectancy:** 14 years
**Daily Exercise:** 20 minutes
**Behavior Problems:** House
soiling, some shyness to the
touch

This little dog, originally bred during the Renaissance to be a lap-dog, is very companionable. He is sociable with just about every-body: children, adults, and strangers alike. He is lively, affectionate, and intelligent, and particularly well-suited for city and apartment life, although his activity level is high indoors. He loves to play, but also knows how to be quiet and calm.

A Bichon's fluffy, medium-length, slightly curly, silky coat comes in all white, or may have cream or apricot markings, or both. His coat re-quires a great deal of professional care and daily grooming, especially during the shedding season, when it can become badly matted instead of shedding onto the rugs.

Health problems may include hip dysplasia, patellar luxation (a slipped kneecap), blindness caused by progressive retinal atrophy (PRA), cataracts, epilepsy, and bleeding disorders. See Appendix I for more information about these health concerns.

# BLACK AND TAN COONHOUND

**Size/Group:** Large/Hound
**Breed History:** USA
**Height:** 23 to 27 inches
**Weight:** 60 to 90 pounds
**Life Expectancy:** 11 years
**Daily Exercise:** 45 minutes
**Behavior Problems:** Food stealing, howling when left alone, patient and firm training requirement

The Coonhound is a very active, strictly outdoor working dog used to hunt almost anything on four legs—from raccoons to bears and large wildcats. Some people do successfully keep Coonhounds in the suburbs, as long as they get a lot of daily exercise. They require a very strong, high fence that cannot be dug under. Once they get a scent, they are relentless in chasing it down. By no means ferocious dogs, they are very gentle with people and will accept other dogs and visitors with a wag of their tails.

Because these dogs are fairly rare, particular care must be taken to find a breeder who specializes in the breed and is careful to preserve good bloodlines.

The Coonhound's short coat is black with tan markings. And it does shed a lot, requiring grooming twice a week.

Health considerations may be hip dysplasia, progressive retinal atrophy (which eventually causes blindness), cataracts, a hanging lower eyelid (ectropion), and bleeding disorders. For more particulars about these health problems, see Appendix I.

# BLACK RUSSIAN TERRIER

**Size/Group:** Large/Terrier
**Breed History:** Russia
**Height:** 26 to 29 inches
**Weight:** 50 to 70 pounds
**Life Expectancy:** 10 to 12 years
**Daily Exercise:** 1 hour
**Behavior Problems:** Dominance, stubbornness

This big dog likes nothing better than to be as close as possible to her family. Since she is devoted to "her" children, care needs to be taken to introduce new children (and adults) to her gradually. She can do almost anything, as long as it seems like fun to her, from performing in a show ring to herding, carting, and sledding. But, because she is a terrier, she will roam if not securely confined.

Despite her size, a Black Russian needs to live indoors, although she loves to play outside.

Her somewhat feathery black coat sheds little as long as it is brushed and combed regularly and trimmed every six to eight weeks.

Health concerns include hip and elbow dysplasia, progressive retinal atrophy (PRA, which can lead to blindness), and allergies. See Appendix I for more information about these problems.

# BLOODHOUND

**Size/Group:** Large/Hound
**Breed History:** Belgium
**Height:** 23 to 27 inches
**Weight:** 80 to 110 pounds
**Life Expectancy:** 10 years
**Daily Exercise:** 45 minutes
**Behavior Problems:** Excessive sniffing in "embarrassing" places, roaming, baying, food stealing, snoring, drooling, stubbornness

Bloodhounds date back over a thousand years, first bred by the monks of Saint Herbert in Belgium. They were developed to scent and track and are used extensively in police and search-and-rescue work. They really love the country and are not suited to urban or apartment living, but can survive in a large house with a big escape-proof yard. Once they are on a scent, it is virtually impossible for an owner to attract a Bloodhound's attention. They will track but never attack—they are very good-natured.

They have loud, deep voices but do not make good watchdogs because they love everybody. In general, Bloodhounds are affectionate and easygoing. Most get along with children, but some breed lines do not. If you have children, it is important to research this carefully.

Their short coats come in red, black and tan, or liver and tan. They shed a little, and should be groomed twice a week.

Health problems may include hip and elbow dysplasia, bloat and torsion (swelling and twisting of the stomach), entropion and/or ectropion (a hanging lower eyelid). For more specifics about these health issues, see Appendix I.

# BLUE TICK COONHOUND

**Size/Group:** Medium/Hound
**Breed History:** USA
**Height:** 21 to 27 inches
**Weight:** 48 to 80 pounds
**Life Expectancy:** 14 years
**Daily Exercise:** 1 hour
**Behavior Problems:** Roaming, chasing small animals

This hound may be a descendant of quick English foxhounds and French hounds, which were used for hunting big game. Blue Ticks are used primarily to hunt raccoons, cougars, and foxes. General Lafayette gave five French hounds to George Washington. Blue Ticks were first registered with the UKC as a separate breed in 1946.

Blue Ticks are fast, muscular dogs that carry their tails up over their backs. They vocalize constantly when on the trail, and bark repeatedly when they have treed prey. Passionate hunters, they are very gentle with children, and make excellent guard dogs.

Their coarse, medium-length coats are smooth and shiny. The preferred color is a mottled dark blue on the body, with irregularly shaped black spots on the back, sides, and ears. There should be more blue than black on the body. Tan spots over the eyes and on the cheeks, and a dark red speckling are also sometimes seen.

Health problems are few, but may include joint diseases (osteochondritis dissecans and osteochondrosis), as well as neurological disorders (lysosomal storage disease and globoid cell leukodystrophy). For more information about these health problems, see Appendix I.

# BOLOGNESE

**Size/Group:** Toy/Rare
**Breed History:** Bologna, Italy,
prior to the 14th century
**Height:** 10 to 12½ inches
**Weight:** 5½ to 9 pounds
**Life Expectancy:** 14 years
**Daily Exercise:** 30 minutes
**Behavior Problems:** Roaming

This rare Old World dog is related to the Bichon, and was referred to as the Italian Bichon of Bologna, thus the "Bolognese." The breed became famous during the Renaissance in the courts of the Medici, Gonzaga, and Este.

The Bolognese is a small, very sturdy dog. Serious, affectionate, and intelligent, she is a bright, quick learner with a pleasing disposition. This dog is devoted to her family, and adores playing with children.

Although she is a family-oriented companion dog, the Bolognese does tend to roam when given the opportunity. A well-fenced yard is recommended if she will be left outdoors alone.

Her white hair is in long locks that cover her entire body and include her tail. Occasionally, a slight tinge of champagne on the ears and back is accepted. The hair stands out, giving her a distinctive fluffy appearance. It is only a bit shorter on her forehead. It is never trimmed, except between her toes and sometimes underneath her belly to keep it clean.

The Bolognese is a particularly hardy breed, but possible health concerns can include luxating patella and eye abnormalities.

# BORDER COLLIE

**Size/Group:** Medium/Herding
**Breed History:** Great Britain
**Height:** 18 to 22 inches
**Weight:** 35 to 50 pounds
**Life Expectancy:** 12 years
**Daily Exercise:** 1 hour
**Behavior Problems:** Restless-ness, destructiveness, and nippiness when bored; not especially good with children; herding every animal and person in sight

Border Collies are descendants of reindeer herders that date back to the Vikings. They often herd sheep simply by using their eyes. They are terrific athletes, have a great deal of energy, and need a lot of outdoor exercise. They also require something active to do, such as Frisbee, agility classes, or a "job" to do. Border Collies are intelligent and trainable; praise works much better with them than punishment.

Very active, and very territorial, they are not friendly toward strangers and therefore make excellent watchdogs. They tend to be wary of most children and are usually not friendly toward other dogs.

Their medium-length straight coats can be red, white, or black with tan markings, blue merle (blue black), or chocolate.

Possible health disorders are hip dysplasia, a growth disorder of the joints (OCD), PRA—progressive retinal atrophy (leads to blindness), cataracts and other eye problems, deafness, epilepsy, and paralysis. For summaries about these health problems, see Appendix I.

# BORDER TERRIER

**Size/Group:** Small/Terrier
**Breed History:** Great Britain
**Height:** 8 to 12 inches
**Weight:** 12 to 16 pounds
**Life Expectancy:** 13 years
**Daily Exercise:** 45 minutes
**Behavior Problems:** Extreme timidity if not socialized as a puppy, possible hyperactivity if not exercised enough, chasing (and possible killing) of any small animal that comes into his sight

These little terriers, not well known in this country, were originally bred to hunt and kill foxes and must be kept behind an escape-proof fence if they are to be prevented from killing a neighborhood cat. They need early, firm obedience training.

Very people-oriented, Border Terriers are loyal and eager to please. They make excellent pets and are very good with children. Active, they love to play but can also be calm and sit on their owners' laps when the occasion warrants it. They are suited for city and apartment life as long as they get sufficient daily exercise.

Their short, rough coats can be blue or gray with tan, and red. They shed very little and should be groomed once a week.

Possible health considerations are hip dysplasia, disintegration of the hip joint (Legg-Perthes), out-of-joint knees, progressive retinal atrophy (PRA leads to blindness), cataracts, autoimmune problems, heart murmurs, seizures, and hypothyroidism. For more information about these conditions, see Appendix I.

# BORZOI (RUSSIAN WOLFHOUND)

**Size/Group:** Extra Large/Hound
**Breed History:** Originally from Arabia, imported to Russia in the 17th century
**Height:** 26 to 31 inches
**Weight:** 55 to 105 pounds
**Life Expectancy:** 11 years
**Daily Exercise:** 30 minutes
**Behavior Problems:** Roaming, picky eating, aversion to touch, snapping, obstinacy

Developed as a coursing sighthound, the Borzoi may be difficult to train and is not appropriate for a first-time dog owner. He requires a lot of exercise and is not well suited for city or apartment dwelling. At the least, he needs a large house with a big yard. If he is going to be allowed to run free, he must be thoroughly trained or he will disappear into the "wild blue yonder."

Borzois have a highly developed chase reaction and should be carefully controlled around other pets (cats, smaller dogs, and wildlife in particular). Usually good-natured, the Borzoi may bite if he is sufficiently annoyed. Extreme care should be taken when buying a Borzoi because there are a good number of poorly bred animals on the market.

Their long, silky coats can be flat or wavy, and come in all colors, sometimes with markings.

Health considerations include progressive retinal atrophy (PRA can lead to blindness), cataracts, retinal problems, bloat, heart problems, and bone cancer. For more details about these diseases, see Appendix I.

# BOSTON TERRIER

**Size/Group:** Small/
Non-Sporting
**Breed History:** USA
**Height:** 10 to 17 inches
**Weight:** 11 to 25 pounds
**Life Expectancy:** 13 years
**Daily Exercise:** 35 minutes
**Behavior Problems:** Excessive
barking, fighting, snoring,
snorting

Bostons were originally bred by crossing an English Bulldog with a white English Terrier. They are smart, outgoing, and very affectionate. They are very social and truly love people, but tend to fight with other dogs, particularly those of the same sex. However, they are tolerant of other pets (such as cats), especially if introduced to them as puppies.

They thrive in any kind of setting, from an apartment to a farm. Small enough to be carried, Bostons are especially well suited for city life and are perfectly satisfied to live in a small apartment. If kept in a yard, they must be kept safe by a sturdy fence. This is a very popular breed, so thorough research of breeders is highly recommended.

Their short, sleek black-and-white coats require minimal grooming once a week. They do not have any odor.

Their short pushed-in (brachycephalic) faces make them prone to breathing problems, especially after prolonged exercise or play. Other health concerns may include Cushings disease, thyroid disease, and heart conditions. See Appendix I for more information about these health concerns.

# BOUVIER DES FLANDRES

**Size/Group:** Large/Herding
**Breed History:** Northern France/Belgium
**Height:** 24 to 28 inches
**Weight:** 65 to 95 pounds
**Life Expectancy:** 11 years
**Daily Exercise:** 45 minutes
**Behavior Problems:** Dominance, unpredictable behavior in puppyhood

This large, cattle-herding dog is not at all suitable for city or apartment life. She is used for police work and as a messenger dog, guide dog for the blind, and guard dog. In World War I Bouviers worked as ambulance dogs. She is an extremely good watchdog, but must be obedience-trained early in life.

Bouviers love to play with children and other animals, with whom they are unusually good. But they can be rough and cannot tolerate small quarters. Basically an outdoor dog, she does not like hot, humid conditions.

Her thick, wiry, rough, medium-length coat comes in black, brindle, gray, and tan. She sheds very little and should be groomed about twice a week. A professional trim is recommended on a regular basis.

Possible health problems include hip dysplasia, cataracts, glaucoma, a hanging lower eyelid (ectropion), twisting of the spleen, hypothyroidism, paralysis of the larynx, and cancerous tumors. See Appendix I for more information about these health issues.

# BOXER

**Size/Group:** Large/Working
**Breed History:** Germany, 1850
**Height:** 21 to 25 inches
**Weight:** 65 to 70 pounds
**Life Expectancy:** 12 years
**Daily Exercise:** 20 minutes
**Behavior Problems:** Puppy-mill-bred individuals may be either very timid or aggressive, restless, and disobedient. Others may be either timid or dominant, and may steal food, drool, and snore. May be flatulent.

This dog has enjoyed a surge in popularity since the 1940s, which continues unabated to this day. The Boxer got his name because he uses his front paws like boxing gloves in a fight. Bred by combining a Bulldog with a Bullenbeisser Mastiff, Boxers used to be used for bull- and bear-baiting, and pit fighting. No longer fighting dogs, they have become calm, loving pets and companions.

Easy to train, boxers are very affectionate with children. They are very active and require a good amount of living space. They are intolerant of cold weather. Their diet must be watched to avoid flatulence, which can be a problem with this and other brachycephalic (pushed-in face) dogs. A breeder will recommend the proper diet.

They are very clean, groom themselves regularly, and their short coats shed only a little. One grooming a week is all that is required. They come in various colors: fawn, sable, or brindle with white markings on their chests, legs, and faces.

Health problems may include hip dysplasia, progressive retinal atrophy (PRA can lead to blindness), heart problems, hypothyroidism, colitis, and cancerous tumors. For more details about these health conditions, see Appendix I.

# BOYKIN

**Size/Group:** Medium/Working
**Breed History:** Southern USA.
Early ancestors may be the
Chesapeake Bay Retriever,
Springer Spaniel, Cocker
Spaniel, and American Water
Spaniel
**Height:** 14 to 18 inches
**Weight:** 25 to 40 pounds
**Life Expectancy:** 13 years
**Daily Exercise:** 1 hour
**Behavior Problems:** Needs a
lot of love, attention, and exercise

Named after W. "Whit" Boykin (1861–1932), a well-known sportsman of Boykin, South Carolina, this little brown spaniel dog is the result of experimental breeding among many breeds to develop a retriever that can easily fit into a small boat and into duck blinds, and at the same time make a good family pet.

Bred by South Carolina hunters in the 1900s to hunt ducks and wild turkeys on the Wateree River, the Boykin is a sturdy spaniel who loves to hunt and retrieve. His size makes him ideal for boat travel through the swamps. He is easy to train because he is smart and has a strong desire to please. He has seemingly boundless endurance, energy, and enthusiasm. He is a good swimmer, so is used for both water and land retrieving. His easygoing disposition makes him an excellent pet and companion. He is a relative newcomer in the recognized dog world, but can now be found throughout the United States.

His coat is either short and straight or medium-length, flat or slightly curly. There may be some feathering on his legs. He is either solid color liver or dark brown; sometimes he has a small white spot on his chest. He has a docked tail.

Potential health problems can include cataracts, hip dysplasia, and skin allergies.

# BRIARD

**Size/Group:** Large/Herding
**Breed History:** France
**Height:** 22 to 27 inches
**Weight:** 75 to 90 pounds
**Life Expectancy:** 11 years
**Daily Exercise:** 30 minutes
**Behavior Problems:** Restlessness indoors, disobedience, and challenging to owners

This ancient breed (Charlemagne is supposed to have owned Briards) was developed as a herding dog, but these dogs do not require a great deal of exercise. So, some say they are able to adapt to city life as long as they live in a large house with a yard, but in general, they like to live outside. They carried supplies and acted as sentries in World War I.

A very independent breed, Briards need early, strong training if they are going to grow up to be obedient. They are very protective of their families, and must be carefully controlled before they meet a strange person or animal.

Their long, wavy coats come in all colors, often with markings on the muzzle and chin.

Possible health problems include hip dysplasia, progressive retinal atrophy (PRA) and retinal degeneration, other eye problems, bloat, and hypothyroidism. To learn more about these ailments, see Appendix I.

# BRITTANY (Spaniel)

**Size/Group:** Medium/Sporting
**Breed History:** France, first shown in 1896
**Height:** 18 to 21 inches
**Weight:** 28 to 35 pounds
**Life Expectancy:** 13 years
**Daily Exercise:** 1 hour
**Behavior Problems:** Restlessness, destructiveness, excessive barking if left alone, phobias, roaming, stealing food, fearfulness of cities

The Brittany is very long-legged to be called a spaniel, but she is referred to in this manner by many. She is a descendant of the bird dog and enjoys pointing, retrieving, swimming, and hunting. She is the only spaniel that points. She requires a lot of daily exercise and loves to play and interact with her owner(s). If she is not provided with enough exercise, she resorts to all kinds of restless behavior. She is not well suited for city or apartment life—a house with a large yard is a better home.

She is easy to train, and really wants to please her owner(s). This dog is often fearful of strangers unless she is socialized to people outside the family as a puppy. She may also become timid if she is treated roughly.

Her medium-length, dense, and wavy coat comes in several different color combinations: tricolored, orange, liver, or black—with white markings on the nose, chest, belly, and legs. She sheds a little and should be groomed twice a week.

Possible health problems include cleft palate, hip dysplasia, glaucoma, spinal paralysis, heart and liver problems, and seizures. For more information about these health issues, see Appendix I.

# BRUSSELS GRIFFON (Rough and Smooth)

**Size/Group:** Tiny/Toy
**Breed History:** Belgium, since at least the 15th century
**Height:** 7 to 8 inches
**Weight:** 6 to 12 pounds
**Life Expectancy:** 12 years
**Daily Exercise:** 20 minutes
**Behavior Problems:** Excessive barking, house soiling, stubbornness, picky eating, wheezing and snoring

Rough

Smooth

These tiny dogs were originally bred to be ratters and companions. They make very good watchdogs, setting up a terrible din if a stranger comes to the door. But they require firm early training because they can be very stubborn and challenge their owners at every step of the way. They dislike walking on a leash, as a rule—again, early training can overcome that hurdle. Griffons do make excellent students, as long as a trainer is not harsh with them.

Saucy and perky, they are excellent, loving, companion pets. Because of their small size and minimal exercise requirements, these little dogs are excellent city and apartment dwellers.

Their coats come in two types—rough and smooth—and can be many different colors: black, red, black and red, black and tan. They often have dark whiskers and masks. White is not permitted in either coat type for show dogs.

Their health problems are few: patellar (knee) luxation and progressive retinal atrophy leading to blindness are the two most common. See Appendix I for more information about these conditions.

# BULLDOG (English Bulldog)

**Size/Group:** Medium/Non-Sporting
**Breed History:** Great Britain
**Height:** 14 to 16 inches
**Weight:** 40 to 50 pounds
**Life Expectancy:** 9 years
**Daily Exercise:** 20 minutes
**Behavior Problems:** snoring, wheezing, stubbornness, and food possessiveness

The national dog of England, this dog was bred to fight bulls and possibly other animals such as bears. He was trained to bite the nose or leg of a staked bull, driving the poor animal into paroxysms of anger. When the bull reacted by kicking out, the bulldog simply held on even more tightly. This practice was outlawed in England in 1835. Nowadays bulldogs have very low aggressive tendencies and almost never bite. If they are sufficiently aroused, however, they revert to type.

Today, the bulldog is a gentle companion pet. Affectionate and slightly sluggish, he needs to feel dominant in a household. A bulldog really likes his food and tends to be extremely possessive about it—best to keep your distance when he is eating. He is extremely intolerant of heat due to his brachycephalic face—it is hard for him to breathe when it is hot and humid.

Bulldogs and cats get along well together, as long as the cat doesn't threaten the food bowl. They love to walk, but become less active with age. They do well in any living space, from a farm to a city apartment. They are very poor watchdogs.

Their short coats come in brindle, fawn, white, and red, and in combinations of these colors. They shed little and require grooming about twice a week.

Health considerations include intolerance of heat and breathing problems. For more details about these health issues, see Appendix I.

# BULLMASTIFF

**Size/Group:** Extra Large/Working
**Breed History:** Great Britain; cross between mastiffs (60%), and bulldogs (40%)
**Height:** 25 to 27 inches
**Weight:** 90 to 130 pounds
**Life Expectancy:** 10 years
**Daily Exercise:** 20 minutes
**Behavior Problems:** dominance toward people, aggression, leash pulling, stubbornness

These dogs were bred to be guard dogs, watchdogs, and bodyguards, and are used extensively by police, security organizations, and the army. Even so, they are extremely loving with their families and good with children.

Very lively, powerful, and energetic outdoors, they were bred for short spurts of speed, but are otherwise content to spend downtime with their owners. They need a lot of space and are not suited to city or apartment life. They dislike exercising in hot weather, and tend to become overweight, so they need daily exercise to stay in shape. They are very territorial and protective of their family and property, although not aggressive with strangers.

Bullmastiffs are very serious animals and make good obedience students, but they need to be kept under strict owner control. They may take children's raucous, active, physical play too seriously, and the Bullmastiff Organization recommends that families with children choose the least dominant puppy in a litter.

Their short, stiff coats shed little, and need brushing about once a week. They come in brindle, fawn, and red, always with a black mask.

Health considerations include hip and elbow dysplasia, progressive retinal atrophy (PRA leads to blindness), ectropion and entropion (eyelid problems), bloat, and swelling and twisting of the stomach (torsion). See Appendix I for more specifics about these health problems.

# BULL TERRIER (Colored and White)

**Size/Group:** Medium/Terrier
**Breed History:** Great Britain; cross between Bulldog and Old English terrier, 1830
**Height:** 21 to 22 inches
**Weight:** 52 to 62 pounds (There is also a miniature bull terrier, 10 to 14 inches high; 25 to 35 pounds.)
**Life Expectancy:** 11 years
**Daily Exercise:** 20 minutes
**Behavior Problems:** chewing, hostility toward other animals, stubbornness, willful disobedience, snoring

Colored

White

Bull Terriers were originally bred to be pit fighters and have well-developed jawbones and strong teeth. They have long heads, and their eyes are very close together. Although they are always prepared to fight, they have become loyal, obedient, companion pets. They are also used as watchdogs and to guard flocks.

"Bullies" are very affectionate, but they are also stubborn and need firm, calm, good obedience training and not recommended for inexperienced dog owners. They have a great deal of energy and often tear through the house. They love to play and "clown" around.

Their short, shiny coats shed little, and need grooming only once a week. They are most often white with black markings, but can be brindle or sable with white chest and markings, or any color with white markings.

Health problems can be patellar (knee) luxation, lens luxation, deafness, kidney degeneration, and heart problems. See Appendix I for more information about these health considerations.

# CAIRN TERRIER

**Size/Group:** Small/Terrier
**Breed History:** Isle of Skye, Scotland
**Height:** 10 to 12 inches
**Weight:** 13 to 16 pounds
**Life Expectancy:** 14 years
**Daily Exercise:** 20 minutes
**Behavior Problems:** Dominance, guarding, stubbornness

The Cairn was originally bred as a working terrier to hunt small prey such as otters, foxes, and other vermin. (The word *cairn* refers to a small pile of stones often used to mark graves or property lines—small prey often took up residence in these cairns.) Though stubborn and hardheaded, at the same time she is cheerful and lively and a loving family member, although she is not especially gentle with children or even adults (although she likes kids). She loves to do tricks and can be easily trained to do them. Terrier-like, she is smart, independent, inquisitive, and stubborn. Cairns are independent and able to burrow beneath most fences in order to get closer to an intruding squirrel or other animal.

She is territorial and makes an extremely good watchdog, barking furiously at anything or anybody. Because of her small size and moderate exercise requirements, a Cairn is a good city or apartment dweller and an excellent companion dog. Unlike many other terriers, a Cairn walks on leash very well.

Her medium-length rough coat comes in all colors except all white, doesn't shed, and needs moderate grooming about three times a week.

Possible health problems include Legg-Calvé-Perthes disease (disintegration of the hip joint); knee luxation; a painful, thickened lower jaw (CMO); progressive retinal atrophy (PRA), leading to blindness; cataracts and glaucoma; kidney and blood problems. For more details about these health considerations, see Appendix I.

# CANAAN DOG

**Size/Group:** Medium/Herding
**Breed History:** Israel
**Height:** 19 to 24 inches
**Weight:** 35 to 55 pounds
**Life Expectancy:** 13 years
**Daily Exercise:** 45 minutes
**Behavior Problems:** Roaming, independence, wariness of strangers, territoriality, firm obedience training requirement

These dogs originally appeared in Israeli deserts as nomads. Now that they are somewhat domesticated, they act as property and livestock guards. They have also served in the Israeli army as messengers and guard dogs, and are also used to guide the blind, in therapy, and to locate missing people. They do not require a tremendous amount of exercise and are suitable for apartment living.

Due to their originally solitary life, in which they were responsible for their own safety, they have a highly developed sense of self-protection, and are therefore very territorial and will bark at the slightest intrusion. Canaan dogs are so observant of their surroundings that they do poorly in obedience classes. (They do not pay enough attention to the instructor, but more to all the other dogs and people.) However, they do require firm training by a self-assured owner who is able to provide it. They are not good pets for inexperienced owners.

They are affectionate to their own people, loyal and protective of them. They communicate mostly by using body language and making small sounds.

Their medium-length rough coats come in white with black, brown, or red markings; or black or brown, sometimes with white markings. They shed continuously (more during the spring) and need to be brushed at least once a week.

Their only possible health problems are hip dysplasia and progressive retinal atrophy (PRA), which can lead to blindness. For more particulars about these conditions, see Appendix I.

# CANE CORSA

**Size/Group:** Large/Rare/ Working
**Breed History:** Italy
**Height:** 23 to 27 inches
**Weight:** 84 to 110 pounds
**Life Expectancy:** 10 years
**Daily Exercise:** 1 hour
**Behavior Problems:** Aggression, stubbornness, dominance, serious training required

The breed dates back to the Roman Empire, where they fought lions and bears in the Coliseum. The Cane Corsa is very intelligent, self-confident, and alert. Possessing great strength and courage, he is a natural guard dog. It is vital to train and socialize this dog early to ensure good temperament and control. He should have ample outdoor space to move around in.

The Cane Corsa's coat is thick, short, and rough to the touch, requiring minimal care. In winter he grows a denser coat. Color ranges from black and blue to chestnut, fawn, and red, and any or all of these colors brindled.

Health concerns include hip dysplasia, elbow dysplasia, bloat, and hypothyroidism. For more details about these problems, see Appendix I.

# CAVALIER KING CHARLES SPANIEL

**Size/Group:** Small/Toy
**Breed History:** Great Britain, 15th and 16th centuries
**Height:** 12 to 13 inches
**Weight:** 12 to 18 pounds
**Life Expectancy:** 12 years
**Daily Exercise:** 15 minutes
**Behavior Problems:** Barking with joy

These lively, spunky little dogs get along with any age group—they love everybody! They are especially well-suited for moderately active apartment-dwelling seniors, but also enjoy children and all people in between. "Cavs" are outgoing and rugged enough to delight in strenuous activities outside. They possess unusually good olfactory and vision senses and enjoy short hunts in the country.

They are easy to housetrain, unlike most toy dogs, and are very good-natured and eager to please their owners. They are not perfect in formal obedience training because they do have minds of their own. However, they respond well to their owners' wishes and instructions.

Their medium-length silky coats come in black and tan, tricolored, red, and white with chestnut markings. They shed moderately and should be brushed and combed once a week.

Possible health considerations are patellar (knee) luxation, cataracts, retinal disease, and heart valve abnormalities (MVD). See Appendix I for more details about these health problems.

# CESKY TERRIER (Bohemian or Czech Terrier)

**Size/Group:** Small/Terrier
**Breed History:** Czechoslovakia, early 1900s
**Height:** 10 to 12 inches
**Weight:** 13 to 22 pounds
**Life Expectancy:** 14 years
**Daily Exercise:** 20 minutes
**Behavior Problems:** Stubbornness, threat to small pets (e.g., gerbils and hamsters), digging, house soiling

This is a relatively new, rare breed of dog worldwide, coming to the United States in the late 1980s. There are now approximately over two hundred Cesky Terriers in the U.S. Frantisek Horak, of Czechoslovakia, set out to breed a dog small enough to go into burrows and not become stuck, and hunt small vermin. He crossed a Scottish and Sealyham terrier to develop the Cesky.

The Cesky is not only an excellent small animal hunter, especially useful against mice and rats, she is also a charming, loyal, adaptable, and obedient pet, although she can be stubborn at times. She is good with children and other pets, unless they are small enough for her to view as prey. An excellent house guard, she is very aware of what is going on both inside and outside the home.

She requires little outdoor exercise and is perfectly content to live in a city apartment or house with no yard. Like all terriers, she likes to dig, so if she is kept in a yard the fence needs to be "dig-proof."

The Cesky has a bushy beard and eyebrows. Her thick, long, wavy, soft coat can be tan or gray blue, sheds very little, and requires grooming about twice a week. A professional electric clipping is recommended on a regular basis. Hair is left long over the eyes, under the chin, and on the dog's sides and legs.

This is a robust, healthy dog.

# CHESAPEAKE BAY RETRIEVER

**Size/Group:** Large/Sporting
**Breed History:** USA
**Height:** 21 to 26 inches
**Weight:** 55 to 80 pounds
**Life Expectancy:** 12 years
**Daily Exercise:** 1 hour
**Behavior Problems:** Willfulness, stubbornness, dominance, excessive barking

In 1807, a British boat with two Newfoundlands on board was wrecked off Maryland. The dogs were bred with local retrievers to produce the Chesapeake Bay Retriever. This dog retrieves enthusiastically and loves the water, whatever the weather or temperature. No matter where he lives, he should be given frequent opportunities to exercise in the water—retrieving thrown sticks or other objects as well as ducks. The "Chessie" needs a lot of exercise, and is not suitable for city or apartment living. He needs a house with a lot of space and a large yard or country grounds.

He is a better watchdog than most sporting breeds, often being overly aggressive toward strangers and barking excessively. Owners need to show that they are pack leaders from the very beginning and give firm, early obedience training to these dogs, who work best with people they love and respect. He is good with gentle children.

His short, thick brownish coat sheds water almost immediately. He sheds little and needs to be brushed about once a week. (Use a bristle brush.)

Chessies' possible health problems include hip and elbow dysplasia, a growth disorder of the joints (OCD—osteochondritis dissecans), progressive retinal atrophy (PRA can lead to blindness), and cataracts. For more information about these health concerns, see Appendix I.

# CHIHUAHUA (Smooth and Long Coat)

**Size/Group:** Tiny/Toy
**Breed History:** Mexico; thought to be originally from China
**Height:** 5 to 9 inches
**Weight:** 2 to 6 pounds
**Life Expectancy:** 12 years
**Daily Exercise:** 10 minutes
**Behavior Problems:** Stubbornness, snappishness, fearfulness

Smooth Coat

Long Coat

The oldest breed in North America, this very popular little dog is the smallest of breeds, but she is not "small" in personality. The Chihuahua is lively, intelligent, very affectionate, bold, and clever. She is also quite fragile physically and should be protected from extremes of temperature as well as rough handling by children or other people. Toddlers should not handle them, or should only do so under strict supervision.

Although she requires little exercise, and some owners never even take a Chihuahua outdoors (they litter-box train them), these dogs really require stimulation, and a daily outing will make for a much happier pet.

Their coats can be either smooth or longhaired and come in all colors. The smooth-coated dogs require very little grooming and shed all the time. The longhaired variety needs a bit more grooming and sheds only in the spring. Brushing is recommended, and the long coats sometimes need a little trimming.

# CHIHUAHUA

Health problems may include patellar (knee) luxation, progressive retinal atrophy (PRA can lead to blindness), glaucoma, lens luxation, eyelids turned inward (causing irritation), heart problems, tracheal collapse, hypoglycemia (low blood sugar level), and open fontanel (which is a bone in the skull not covered by skin). For more details about these concerns, see Appendix I.

# CHINESE CRESTED (Hairless and Powderpuff)

Hairless

Powderpuff

**Size/Group:** Small/Toy
**Breed History:** China (some think the breed originated in Turkey or Ethiopia)
**Height:** 11 to 13 inches
**Weight:** 5 to 12 pounds
**Life Expectancy:** 15 years
**Daily Exercise:** 30 minutes
**Behavior Problems:** Tendency toward boredom

This tiny dog comes in two varieties. (Surprisingly, both types can be in the same litter.) Very intelligent and sensitive, these dogs bond intensely with their owners and want constant companionship; otherwise, they become bored. They are quick learners and benefit from training. They get along well with other animals and do especially well in a small pack of the same breed.

They require very little living space and are perfectly happy in a small apartment as long as they get a half-hour walk once a day. She is very sensitive to temperature extremes and must be protected from them (both the sun and the cold). She is prone to dry eyes: drops can help—ask your veterinarian or breeder what type of drops to use.

Both types may be any color. The Powderpuff has a medium-length silky coat and sheds a little; she should be groomed about five times a week. The hairless has little tufts of hair on her head and ears, feet, and the tip of her tail. Her skin requires extensive care. It must be wiped with a wet cloth every day, and then rubbed with hand lotion. She also needs a weekly bath in order to avoid skin problems. The tufts need regular brushing.

The hairless Cresteds have poor dentition and require regular dental care. Other health considerations include Legg-Calvé-Perthes (disintegration of the hip joint), detached retinas, skin problems, and lens luxation (in which the lens may slip, leading to glaucoma). See Appendix I for more details about these health problems.

# CHOW CHOW

**Size/Group:** Medium/Non-Sporting
**Breed History:** China, 2,000 years ago
**Height:** 18 to 20 inches
**Weight:** 45 to 70 pounds
**Life Expectancy:** 11 years
**Daily Exercise:** 45 minutes
**Behavior Problems:** Possible aggression, stubbornness, dominance, guarding possessions and food, irritable snapping, touch shyness possible

Chows once were used for hunting, guarding, and pulling carts and sleds, but now they are primarily companion dogs. Stubborn and independent, these dogs need early socialization and training and are not good choices for inexperienced dog owners. Good watchdogs, they are very loyal toward their owners. Most do not like to walk on a leash.

They often seem to be indifferent or fearful, but this is due in part to the fact that their peripheral vision is poor. Their eyes are small, slanted, and dark. It is best to approach a Chow from the front in order not to startle him.

Chows need a lot of living space and should not be kept in a small apartment. They require quite a bit of daily exercise, as well. They are not especially good with children, unless they have been raised with them. They should be carefully supervised around children from outside the household. They are generally not playful, although some may play ball if exposed to the activity early in life.

Chows are the only dogs with black tongues, and they have beautiful, heavy coats that shed a lot, especially in the spring. They should be groomed at least three times a week. Coat color can be red, blue, black, cream, or cinnamon.

Health considerations are hip dysplasia, a growth disorder of the joints (OCD—osteochondritis dissecans), patellar (knee) luxation, glaucoma, eyelids that turn inward and cause irritation (entropion), stenotic nares (pinched nostrils), degeneration of the kidneys, and hypothyroidism—see Appendix I for more specifics.

# CLUMBER SPANIEL

**Size/Group:** Medium/Sporting
**Breed History:** First developed in France; perfected in England
**Height:** 18 to 20 inches
**Weight:** 55 to 80 pounds
**Life Expectancy:** 12 years
**Daily Exercise:** 30 minutes
**Behavior Problems:** Minimal—some snore and drool, may be stubborn and strong-willed

Bred to be hunters, they used to hunt in small packs, but today they usually hunt alone. Favorite prey is partridge and pheasant, but they will also retrieve any thrown object, either on land or in the water. They need a fenced yard if they are going to be let out alone.

These childlike dogs are loving, sweet, charming, appealing, and naughty all at the same time. Not very energetic, they do, however, have stamina and can be taken on long walks. They get along well with all children. Clumbers are not very well known, and there are few of them on the market, so it may be difficult to find a reputable breeder.

Their medium-length, slightly wavy, silky coats can be several colors: tan or sable with white markings, or white with lemon or apricot markings on the head and face. They shed a little and should be brushed every day. Once in a while they need their ears cleaned and the bottoms of their feet trimmed of excess fur. The "feathers" on their ears and feet may be trimmed occasionally.

Health problems may include hip dysplasia, cataracts, spinal disc problems, hanging lower eyelids (ectropion), and eyelids that turn inward and irritate the eyes (entropion). For more details about these health issues, see Appendix I.

# COCKER SPANIEL (American)

**Size/Group:** Small/Sporting
**Breed History:** Bred from the English Cocker
**Height:** 14 to 16 inches
**Weight:** 20 to 32 pounds
**Life Expectancy:** 13 years
**Daily Exercise:** 30 minutes
**Behavior Problems:** Poorly bred dogs can be yappy and snappish (may even be vicious); fearful; dominant. All may be stubborn

Cockers are among the most popular dogs in this country, so care must be taken to find a reliable breeder before buying one. Although they were originally bred to hunt small prey, they are rarely used to hunt nowadays, but are kept as companions.

Well-bred Cockers are affectionate, friendly, happy, playful, curious, full of energy, and able to be trained. They are sociable with other animals and are often kept with other pets. Cockers are good with children. They love to play and "fetch." Their small size makes them ideal city or apartment dwellers as long as they get enough daily exercise. Because they are so sociable they do not make particularly good watchdogs.

Their long, wavy, silky coats need frequent care. Daily brushing is recommended, and bathing and trimming every few months. If left unbrushed, the long hair on their ears and legs especially becomes matted and snarled.

Health considerations include hip dysplasia, progressive retinal atrophy (PRA) that eventually leads to blindness, cataracts, epilepsy, skin diseases, and autoimmune diseases. For more information about these health problems, see Appendix I.

# COCKER SPANIEL (English)

**Size/Group:** Medium/Sporting
**Breed History:** Great Britain
**Height:** 15 to 17 inches
**Weight:** 26 to 34 pounds
**Life Expectancy:** 13 years
**Daily Exercise:** 30 minutes
**Behavior Problems:** House soiling, food stealing, occasionally excessive submissiveness, urination when afraid or excited

In 1800, spaniels were divided into seven breeds: Clumber, Sussex, Welsh Springer, English Springer, Field, Irish Water, and Cocker. Originally bred as hunting dogs, English Cockers can flush and retrieve game, but today they are mostly kept as companion pets. They play games enthusiastically.

The English Cocker is less popular than his American cousin and has therefore avoided puppy-mill breeding and its subsequent health problems. He is taller and heavier than the American Cocker. He is obedient, sweet-tempered, and affectionate. He gets along very well with children and is friendly toward strangers. He barks a moderate amount and is altogether usually a very social dog. However, he needs to be socialized and trained early in life, or he can be willful and indulge in guarding behavior with "his" toys.

His long, wavy coat sheds all year long, and requires a good weekly brushing and occasional clipping and trimming. He comes in all solid colors, and in combinations of colors.

Health considerations include a tendency to become overweight, hip dysplasia, progressive retinal atrophy (PRA can lead to blindness), cataracts, deafness, and kidney disease. For more specifics about these health problems, see Appendix I.

# COLLIE (Rough and Smooth)

**Size/Group:** Large/Herding
**Breed History:** The Rough was introduced in the 1860s in Scotland. The Smooth is a cross of black and white Rough Collies with Greyhounds.
**Height:** 22 to 26 inches
**Weight:** 50 to 75 pounds
**Life Expectancy:** 12 years
**Daily Exercise:** 45 minutes
**Behavior Problems:** Possible timidity, irritable snapping, roaming, restlessness

Rough

Smooth

This breed, known particularly because of the movie and TV dog Lassie, is very popular. Potential owners must be sure to find a reliable breeder—poor, puppy-mill bred examples may exhibit the behavior problems above. Both varieties are very family oriented and, if left alone too long, may vocalize excessively. Bred to be herders, they may try to "herd" children and other pets. They are not especially good watchdogs and more often greet a stranger with a wagging tail and friendly bark. The rough variety may be more suspicious of strangers because of its intense family loyalty. They really want to please and are excellent obedience pupils. But inexperienced owners should not expect Lassie-like behavior. These dogs are bred to be companion pets, not to perform heroic rescues and complicated tricks, although these attributes can be developed with a great deal of time, patience, and training ability. Collies can adapt to almost any environment, but are best suited to a large house or apartment with a yard if they live in the city.

Both varieties have coats of white, blue merle, sable, and tricolors.

# COLLIE

The rough, or longhaired, dogs require frequent brushing and occasional bathing in warm weather; they shed a lot. Smooth collies require little coat care—perhaps once a week—and shed little.

Health considerations for both types include arthritis, progressive retinal atrophy (PRA can lead to blindness), collie eye anomaly (this needs to be checked at eight weeks of age), epilepsy, heart problems, hypothyroidism, and dermatomyositis (a skin disease). See Appendix I for more information about these problems.

# COTON DE TULEAR

**Size/Group:** Small/Rare/ Companion
**Breed History:** Madagascar, port of Tulear, brought on trade ships in the late 16th century and became the pet of royalty
**Height:** 10 to 11 inches
**Weight:** 12 to 15 pounds
**Life Expectancy:** 16 years
**Daily Exercise:** 30 minutes
**Behavior Problems:** Aversion to strangers and harsh training, clinginess to owners

This small, rare longhaired dog was bred to be a companion pet with a sweet, adoring nature. She is very playful and a bit shy of strangers. Neither overly active nor aggressive, a Coton wants to be near her owners all the time and will happily sleep all day in an office or shop. Once home, a good run in a fenced yard will be enough exercise for this little dog.

She will always try to please, needs very little discipline, and is so happy and laid back that she will not defend herself, but she is always alert and will let her owner know about any unusual happenings.

Cotons often jump and walk on their hind legs, an unusual and charming habit. They also love water and will often play in their drinking bowls (making a mess!). Swimming pool owners must keep a careful eye out for their safety.

Cotons require brushing three times a week between baths, which they should have every three to six weeks.

They are generally sturdy and have no known genetic health problems.

# CURLY-COATED RETRIEVER

**Size/Group:** Large/Sporting
**Breed History:** Great Britain,
1800; mix of Irish Water Spaniel,
Poodle, and Labrador Retriever
**Height:** 22 to 27 inches
**Weight:** 60 to 80 pounds
**Life Expectancy:** 12 years
**Daily Exercise:** 1 hour
**Behavior Problems:** Timidity, if
not socialized early may be-
come a fear biter, dominance,
territoriality, aggression

Not well known in the United States, this large, agile, hardy, and affectionate dog is easy to train, but must never be harshly treated. Intensely loyal toward his family, a Curly-Coated Retriever is very smart, easily bored, and requires daily exercise, playtime, and stimulation such as hide-and-seek, hidden toys or food, and water exercise whenever possible. If he doesn't get enough exercise and stimulation, he will literally drive his owners crazy with his frenetic antics.

This breed is not suited for city or apartment dwelling. He needs a lot of space, at the least a large house with a yard, and he is better off in the country with access to swimming water. A Curly-Coated Retriever can get along well with other dogs and with people. He can easily live in a pack, made up either of people or other dogs. He is particularly loyal to his owners and bonds strongly with them.

His curly, short coat comes in black or brown and sheds a little. Grooming is recommended at least twice a week.

Health problems may include hip and elbow dysplasia, progressive retinal atrophy (PRA can lead to blindness), cataracts, hypothyroidism, bloat, inturned eyelids (leading to irritation), and epilepsy. For more information about these concerns, see Appendix I.

# DACHSHUND

**Size/Group:** Small/Hound
**Breed History:** Germany
**Height:** 6 to 9 inches (Mini: 5 to 6 inches)
**Weight:** 15 to 25 pounds (Mini: 8 to 11 pounds)
**Life Expectancy:** 14 years
**Daily Exercise:** 10 minutes
**Behavior Problems:** Digging, excessive barking, irritable snapping, house soiling, food stealing

Smooth

This little dog is very popular, so it is important to go to a reliable breeder to purchase one. Lively, intelligent, and eager to please, the "Dachsie" is a perfect city or apartment dog. One, because she takes up so little space, and two, because her short legs result in minimal exercise requirements.

She loves to play, has a lot of energy indoors, and is a good obedience student. Longhairs and wirehairs are very sturdy, and will play outdoors in any kind of weather. Shorthairs are pickier, and many owners paper-train them in case of foul weather.

Standard longhairs are the best with children, and you have to be careful around children with Minis, because they can easily be stepped on or hurt in rough play.

All varieties come in many colors: shorthaired in black, gray, chocolate, red or tan, yellow, brindle, gray, and blue and white; wirehaireds' coats come in all colors; longhaireds' coats come in the same varieties as the short.

Health considerations include excess weight, elbow dysplasia, cataracts, diabetes, epilepsy, all sorts of spinal and disc problems, patellar (knee) luxation, and progressive retinal atrophy (PRA). For more details about these health problems, see Appendix I.

# DACHSHUND

Wirehaired

Longhaired mini

Longhaired

Wirehaired mini

Smooth mini

# DALMATIAN

**Size/Group:** Large/Non-Sporting
**Breed History:** Some say they originated in ancient Egypt and Yugoslavia; others, that they came from England in the 1700s
**Height:** 19 to 24 inches
**Weight:** 50 to 65 pounds
**Life Expectancy:** 12 years
**Daily Exercise:** 1 hour ·
**Behavior Problems:** Restlessness, destructiveness, shyness and viciousness in fearful puppy-mill animals, dominance, jumping up on people, excitable barking

The up-and-down popularity of this breed has been due, in part, to the Walt Disney movie and the subsequent proliferation of poorly bred specimens. Dalmatians are also known, of course, as firehouse mascots. They are the only spotted breed that the AKC recognizes.

They are full of energy and spirit and learn quickly. When socialized and well trained early in life, a Dalmatian can be a good household pet as long as he gets enough daily exercise. Without it, he is not well suited for city or apartment living. A large apartment or house with a yard is minimal space for a Dalmatian. They love to run with horses and really need a lot of activity in their lives.

Their short black and white, or brown and white, coats require little grooming, but they do shed a great deal. A rubber curry brush is recommended (available in most pet-supply stores).

Health problems may include deafness (a common inherited tendency), hip dysplasia, progressive retinal atrophy (PRA leads to blindness), glaucoma, bladder stones, diabetes, and pannus (another eye condition that can lead to blindness). For more specifics about these health concerns, see Appendix I.

# DANDIE DINMONT TERRIER

**Size/Group:** Small/Terrier
**Breed History:** Scotland; bred by combining Scottish, Skye, and Bedlington Terriers
**Height:** 8 to 12 inches
**Weight:** 18 to 24 pounds
**Life Expectancy:** 13 years
**Daily Exercise:** 20 minutes
**Behavior Problems:** Digging, dominance, willful disobedience, object guarding, house soiling, snoring, territoriality

Raised originally by gypsies, the breed's popularity dates from an 1800 Sir Walter Scott novel, in which the hero is named Dandie Dinmont. She is very bright, playful, affectionate, and a great companion who is devoted to her owner. A determined digger, if she is kept, or let, outdoors she must be protected with a dig-proof fence. She is a fairly good watchdog and likes tracking and terrier trials.

Originally bred to hunt small prey, this little dog is now a fine companion dog that can live in any situation. A small apartment is fine as long as she gets enough daily exercise and attention. She is good with children and other pets with whom she has been raised or if introduced to them early in life.

The Dinmont is stubborn and strong-willed and may be difficult to train. Training should begin early and continued regularly.

Her medium-length rough coat comes in black, mustard, pepper, or apricot. Her head may be white. She sheds only a little, but must be brushed and combed regularly and professionally hand-stripped on a regular basis. Without proper care, her coat may become matted and have to be stripped.

Health problems may include elbow deformities, spinal disc disease, glaucoma, hypothyroidism, and knee or shoulder luxation. For more details about these diseases, see Appendix I.

# DOBERMAN PINSCHER

**Size/Group:** Large/Working
**Breed History:** Germany; developed by a tax collector in 1860 to be a guard dog, probably a cross between German shepherds, Rottweilers, terriers, and Great Danes
**Height:** 22 to 27 inches
**Weight:** 65 to 90 pounds
**Life Expectancy:** 12 years
**Daily Exercise:** 45 minutes
**Behavior Problems:** Snapping, biting, challenging toward owner for dominance, timidity, indoor restlessness, touch shyness, territoriality, quick-temperedness in some puppy-mill individuals

Fierce and fearless police dogs during World War I, now they are bred to be calmer and mellower. Even so, they should never be trained to attack. They need a strong hand throughout their lives. "Dobes" are definitely not suitable for inexperienced owners; they are far "too much dog." These very bright dogs are happiest when they have a job to do, but whatever the job, their independent natures will usually result in their doing it their way. They require a lot of daily exercise.

Males may also be aggressive toward strangers and require strong, early training and a firm owner. Females tend to be calmer and less aggressive, but are still suspicious of unknown people. Both sexes are highly territorial. They can be either one-person or one-family animals. If they are raised with children, they tolerate them; otherwise, children and Dobermans are not a good combination.

Their short coats can be black, blue, red, or fawn with rust markings and shed a little for most of the year (but with heavier seasonal shed). They should be groomed about once a week and have an occasional bath, after which they can be allowed to drip-dry.

Possible health problems include hip dysplasia, cancer, bloat, hemorrhaging (von Willebrand's disease), liver disease, spinal problems in old age, and hypothyroid disease. For more health information, see Appendix I.

# DOGO ARGENTINO (Argentinean Mastiff)

**Size/Group:** Large/Working
**Breed History:** Argentina; developed from at least 10 different breeds
**Height:** 24 to 27 inches
**Weight:** 80 to 100 pounds
**Life Expectancy:** 12 years
**Daily Exercise:** 1 hour
**Behavior Problems:** Aggression, dominance, territoriality, destructiveness

This big dog was originally developed to track and hold large game such as wild boars and mountain lions. He now is also used to guide the blind, for police work, and as a companion pet. He is a very good watchdog. He is fearless, has great endurance, and is very strong. Early obedience training and an owner who is very sure of himself are both requirements with this dog. The Dogo Argentino is basically an aggressive dog and is not suitable for an inexperienced or timid owner. (He has been banned in the United Kingdom.)

Once the Dogo Argentino is well trained, he is an affectionate member of the family. Nevertheless, he really needs to hunt and be given a lot of daily exercise and challenges. He requires a lot of space; a large apartment or house with a yard is suitable, but the country is the best home for this breed. He is not particularly energetic indoors.

His short, thick, smooth coat is always white and sheds some. He should be groomed about three times a week.

Health problems may include hip dysplasia, bloat, and skin problems (allergies, and so on). For more particulars about these health problems, see Appendix I.

# DOGUE DE BORDEAUX (French Mastiff)

**Size/Group:** Extra Large/ Working
**Breed History:** France; bred to fight other dogs, bulls, and bears
**Height:** 23 to 27 inches
**Weight:** 90 to 145 pounds
**Life Expectancy:** 10 years
**Daily Exercise:** 45 minutes
**Behavior Problems:** Excessive drooling, extreme aggression, territoriality, destructiveness indoors

Equipped with both an extra-large bark and body, the Dogue de Bordeaux does not need to be aggressive to warn strangers off his property. She is often used as a guard dog. Still, she is extremely gentle and affectionate with her family as long as she is exercised enough and has had early obedience training and socialization. Some say she longs to be a lapdog!

The Dogue de Bordeaux has a mind of her own and needs a firm owner who is sure of himself. She gets along well with children, but not with strange dogs.

She is a very strong, athletic dog, but can even be kept in an apartment as long as she has sufficient daily exercise. Because of her brachycephalic (pushed-in) face, she hates heat and humidity, and really needs to be kept in an air-conditioned environment when it's hot. During hot weather, she should be exercised outdoors only in the early morning or after sunset.

Her soft, short coat can be fawn, speckled, or brown, with white markings. She sheds little (except for heavy seasonal shedding) and should be brushed about twice a week. She has a very "doggy" odor.

The Dogue de Bordeaux is a healthy animal. Hip dysplasia, skin problems, and cancer are her only health problems. For more specifics about these conditions, see Appendix I.

# ENGLISH SETTER

**Size/Group:** Large/Sporting
**Breed History:** France, 1500;
brought to England in the 1800s
**Height:** 24 to 25 inches
**Weight:** 50 to 70 pounds
**Life Expectancy:** 14 years
**Daily Exercise:** 1 hour
**Behavior Problems:** House
soiling, roaming, possible
stubbornness and destructive-
ness

B red to gracefully traverse a large amount of territory in a hunt, the English Setter is a good-looking, sweet dog with an excellent field reputation. She points birds and other small game and enjoys runs with her owner(s). The English Setter has a very strong sense of smell and is indefatigable, active, and vigorous, with excellent reflexes.

She can be kept in a kennel, but is happiest in a home with lots of family interaction. Though best with a fenced-in yard, she is all right in an urban/apartment environment and is well behaved, mild, and friendly indoors as long as she gets enough daily outdoor exercise. She is less vigorous than many other setters and is very playful with other dogs.

She wants to please her owners, but does not like strict obedience training, although she is very receptive to general training. Patience and persuasiveness are best. She likes gentle, playful interaction. She is an affectionate family dog, but she may be a bit too rough and exuberant for toddlers.

The English Setter's long, flat coat can be sable or brown with white, blue, apricot, tricolor, black, brown, or white. Her legs and tail have beautiful "feathers," and her eyes are brilliant with a sweet expression. She is an average shedder, and requires brushing every couple of days.

Health problems may include hip dysplasia, cancer, deafness, hypothyroidism. See Appendix I for more details about these considerations.

# ENGLISH SPRINGER SPANIEL

**Size/Group:** Medium/Sporting
**Breed History:** First of all English hunting spaniels during the Renaissance; American popularity began in the 1700s
**Height:** 19 to 20 inches
**Weight:** 44 to 55 pounds
**Life Expectancy:** 12 years
**Daily Exercise:** 1 hour
**Behavior Problems:** Some fearfulness or aggression in badly bred pups, destructiveness, excessive barking, jumping on people, phobias, food stealing

Millie Bush made English Springers famous. Strong and friendly dogs, they really look like large Cockers with heavier coats, longer legs, and bigger bodies. They are good hunters, and are used in the field for upland game, finding birds and flushing them out.

They are cheerful, courageous, loving, good-natured family dogs. They are extremely devoted to their owners, friendly, affectionate and loyal, and are good with children. English Springers may be a bit cautious, standoffish, and aggressive with strangers.

Although bred to be field dogs, they adapt well to urban or apartment life as long as they get enough daily exercise. They have a tendency to become overweight, which should be monitored with care. They love the country, and should be given the opportunity to run and have long walks as often as possible.

Their long, smooth coats come in several colors (tricolored and black or brown with white), and they shed moderately, requiring brushing once or twice a week, and need moderate professional trimming.

Health considerations include hip and retinal dysplasia, progressive retinal atrophy (PRA may lead to blindness), hanging lower eyelids (ectropion), glaucoma, epilepsy, hemorrhagic disorder (von Willebrand's disease), and a heart anomaly (SAS). See Appendix I for more information about these health problems.

# ENGLISH TOY SPANIEL
## (Blenheim and Prince Charles)

**Size/Group:** Tiny/Toy
**Breed History:** England; popular with English nobility
**Height:** 9 to 10 inches
**Weight:** 8 to 13 pounds
**Life Expectancy:** 12 years
**Daily Exercise:** 10 minutes
**Behavior Problems:** Picky eating, wheezing, snoring

There are several color varieties of the English Toy Spaniel. The Blenheim is red and white with a spot on the center of the head. The Prince Charles is tricolor, white with markings under the tail and on the face. The King Charles is black with tan markings. The Ruby is pure red. Ancestry of the breed can be traced back to the Italian Maltese, the British Pug, and the Korean Japanese Spaniel. He is solely a companion dog.

This is a hardy toy dog that gets along well with everyone, including children. He was a favorite of all the English nobility, and adjusts to any lifestyle. Small children (toddlers) are apt to drop this small, fragile dog, and he is therefore not recommended in this situation. Older children and adults are preferable owners. He requires a lot of attention and is not at all happy if he doesn't get it.

He is sociable with humans who approach with care, and timid with those who don't. He requires little exercise. He likes other dogs, with which he is sociable and somewhat submissive. They often lie upside down in their owners' arms or laps.

His long, soft, wavy coat sheds little and needs brushing about twice a week, with occasional trimming of whiskers and the hair on the feet.

Health considerations include patellar (knee) luxation, cataracts, heart murmurs, abnormally small eyes (microphthalmia), hernias, and sensitivity to anesthesia. For more details see Appendix I.

# FIELD SPANIEL

**Size/Group:** Medium/Sporting
**Breed History:** Great Britain
**Height:** 18 to 20 inches
**Weight:** 35 to 50 pounds
**Life Expectancy:** 12 years
**Daily Exercise:** 1 hour
**Behavior Problems:** Roaming, food stealing, snoring, excessive barking

This is the least-known spaniel in the United States, and it may be difficult to find a reputable breeder. The Field Spaniel has a wonderful personality; she is sweet, calm, even-tempered, intelligent, and tranquil as long as she gets enough daily exercise. She can live contentedly in a city apartment, again, with plenty of exercise, but is happiest in a large house with a yard or in the suburbs or the country. She loves to be outdoors, but if she lives outside all the time, she must have a lot of interaction with people because of her social nature. Wherever she lives, she needs obedience training.

Bred to hunt in open country and underbrush, she has a keen sense of smell, a lot of endurance, a sense of humor, and good problem-solving instincts. She loves people and gets along well with other animals that she lives with. In her enthusiasm, the Field Spaniel tends to be a bit sloppy, gulping water and spilling food. This dog is a fairly good watchdog and a very companionable house pet.

She has shorter legs than her cousin, the Cocker, and a longer body. She has a flat, wavy, longish coat and is always one-colored: either black, brown, liver, or mahogany red, with possible tapering off to a lighter shade. She sheds a little and needs brushing at least three times a week and regular professional trimming of her ears, tail, neck, and head.

Health considerations include cataracts, progressive retinal atrophy (PRA can lead to blindness), hip dysplasia, and hypothyroidism. For more specifics about these health issues, see Appendix I.

# FILA BRASILEIRO

**Size/Group:** Giant/Rare/ Working
**Breed History:** Plantation guard dogs, dating back to 16th century Brazil
**Height:** 24 to 30 inches
**Weight:** 90 to 100 pounds
**Life Expectancy:** 10 years
**Daily Exercise:** 1 hour
**Behavior Problems:** Dominance, aggression, extreme territoriality, serious training requirement

Agile and hardy, these ancient fighting dogs were admired for their courage and strength in protecting their masters' homes and properties. Today, the breed can be found in many environments as good watchdogs but their stubborn and dominant temperament requires serious professional training. The Fila Brasileiro is not recommended for the first-time dog owner.

The Fila's coat is short and dense, allowing easy monthly grooming.

Hip dysplasia and bloat can be common health problems to the breed. Consult Appendix I for more details about these conditions.

# FINNISH SPITZ

**Size/Group:** Medium/Non-Sporting
**Breed History:** National dog of Finland for hundreds of years
**Height:** 15 to 20 inches
**Weight:** 31 to 35 pounds
**Life Expectancy:** 13 years
**Daily Exercise:** 30 minutes
**Behavior Problems:** Independence, dominance, excessive barking, aggression

Once used to hunt large prey such as polar bears and elk, the Spitz is now used to hunt birds and small animals. He barks to flush out and tree his prey, at which time he barks (or yodels) to alert his owner. (His rapid barks, 160 times per minute, sound like yodeling.) He communicates with his master with small barks and purring throat noises.

He is independent and willful, yet friendly and outgoing and thrives on encouragement and praise. Harsh discipline may cause him to retreat. The Spitz is basically a one-person dog, performing best for his master in obedience, showing, and hunting. Although he gets along well with other animals with which he has been raised and also relates well to children, he does not care for roughhousing. He is a moderately good watchdog. He needs obedience training and consistent, positive reinforcement.

One of the cleanest of dogs, the Spitz regularly grooms himself like a cat, and has little, if any, odor. His medium-length, thick coat comes in various shades of red and honey and sheds some (more during the spring shedding season). He normally requires brushing about once a week.

The Spitz is a healthy dog. The only health problems he may suffer from are cataracts and hip dysplasia. To find out more information about these disorders, see Appendix I.

# FLAT-COATED RETRIEVER

**Size/Group:** Large/Sporting
**Breed History:** Developed in Great Britain in the early 19th century by combining Labradors, Irish Setters, Curly-Coated Retrievers, and possibly Newfoundlands
**Height:** 22 to 25 inches
**Weight:** 60 to 80 pounds
**Life Expectancy:** 12 years
**Daily Exercise:** 1 hour
**Behavior Problems:** Stealing food and garbage, overfriendliness consisting of jumping up on people, timidity in some poorly bred dogs, excessive barking

Because the Flat-Coat is not well known in the United States, it may be difficult to find a breeder. This is too bad, because she is one of the most obedient, affectionate, intelligent, and easily trained retrievers. She is also extremely good with children, other animals, and people in general. Her tail almost never stops wagging except when she's asleep.

Devoted to her family, she requires a lot of human interaction. She needs a good deal of daily exercise and should be given a chance to swim as often as possible. Weather is not a consideration—she will swim in any water and any climate. She will even roll in mud puddles! She loves to play and fetch objects. She can live in a large house with a yard, but must be given plenty of opportunities to work off her energy. She is a moderately good watchdog. Although she may be somewhat stubborn, she makes a good obedience student and should be provided with training early in life. She becomes bored easily and needs a trainer with a good imagination.

Her medium-length dense coat comes in shades of black or brown, sheds some, and requires brushing once or twice a week.

Possible health considerations are hip dysplasia, cataracts, progressive retinal atrophy (PRA may lead to blindness), inturned eyelids leading to eye irritation (entropion), cancer, patellar (knee) luxation, and hypothyroidism. For more details about these problems, see Appendix I.

# FOXHOUND (American)

**Size/Group:** Large/Hound
**Breed History:** May date back to de Soto's Florida landing in 1539; once known as Virginia Hound
**Height:** 21 to 25 inches
**Weight:** 65 to 75 pounds
**Life Expectancy:** 11 years
**Daily Exercise:** 1 hour
**Behavior Problems:** Destructiveness, jealousy, unfriendliness toward strangers, tendency to go "stir crazy" if kept locked up, baying, roaming, house soiling

The American Foxhound has extremely good staying power, a very well-developed sense of smell, and the ability to run fast for distances that would leave many other breeds exhausted. He is faster than the English Foxhound, but less sturdy. He is very determined, has a keen nose, and can work in any weather. This dog is very loyal and protective of his family and unsure of strangers. He is not aggressive or snappy toward strangers, just very careful around them. Because he was originally bred as a pack hound, he gets along well with other dogs of all breeds. He is usually submissive with humans.

A hunting dog used to long runs in open country, he is not at all suited for city or apartment life, unless he lives with extremely active owners. He is active both indoors and out. Ideally, he needs to live in a large suburban house with unlimited space or in the country, where he can run at will. Without enough exercise he may become destructive indoors.

His short coat comes in all colors, and he sheds little. Brushing once a week is more than sufficient coat care. No trimming is needed.

The American Foxhound is a sturdy dog with few, if any, health problems.

# FOXHOUND (English)

**Size/Group:** Large/Hound
**Breed History:** 18th century; a cross between Greyhounds and other hounds, Bulldogs, and Fox Terriers
**Height:** 23 to 27 inches
**Weight:** 55 to 75 pounds
**Life Expectancy:** 11 years
**Daily Exercise:** 1 hour
**Behavior Problems:** Roaming, house soiling, baying, barking, destructiveness indoors

George Washington is said to have imported packs of English Foxhounds into this country as hunting dogs. These dogs are not generally kept as pets, although they can be kept in a house as long as they are provided with enough exercise. At the least, they require a large house and yard, and are not suited for city or apartment life.

Essentially pack-oriented hunting dogs (in packs of fifteen to twenty), they do tend to roam, but are usually devoted to their owners or handlers. Larger and somewhat stouter than their American cousins, English Foxhounds have almost the same temperament. They are loyal and protective of family, wary of strangers, somewhat submissive with owners and handlers, and friendly with other dogs.

Their short, tricolored coats shed a little and require grooming about once a week.

They are generally healthy and vigorous, but because of the enormous amount of energy they expend, they are ready for retirement from field work at about seven or eight years of age.

# FOX TERRIER (Smooth, Wire, Toy)

**Size/Group:** Small/Terrier (tiny, Toy)
**Breed History:** Great Britain
**Height:** 12 to 16 inches (Toy, 9 to 11 inches)
**Weight:** 14 to 19 pounds (Toy, 6 to 12 pounds)
**Life Expectancy:** 13 years
**Daily Exercise:** 45 minutes (Toys need less)
**Behavior Problems:** Excessive barking, guarding of food and objects, dominance, may be destructive, territoriality

Wire

There is little difference between the various Fox Terriers except their coats and size. The smooth-haired and toy are white with markings on the head and sometimes the body; wirehaireds may be red, brindle, liver, or blue with white markings. They shed little, and should be groomed about once a week. Wirehaireds need regular professional grooming.

They were originally developed to find foxes and tease them out of their lairs so that Foxhounds could then chase them. They are very energetic and extroverted and are often trained to be trick dogs. They make excellent obedience students, except they may forget their manners if they become overexcited. They require a lot of exercise and may become destructive if bored and restless.

Fox Terriers are loyal and devoted to their owners. They are sociable with other animals except that males will fight with other males of the same breed. Many people own more than one toy. All three varieties are good city and apartment dwellers as long as they get enough daily exercise. Wirehaireds are good watchdogs, but the smooth and toy terriers are only moderately protective.

Health considerations may include thyroid problems, patellar (knee) luxation, and hemorrhaging (von Willebrand's disease). See Appendix I for more specifics about these health concerns.

Smooth

Toy

# FRENCH BULLDOG

**Size/Group:** Small/
Non-Sporting
**Breed History:** A native French
breed; possibly mixed with
English Bulldogs.
**Height:** 10 to 12 inches
**Weight:** 22 to 28 pounds
**Life Expectancy:** 11 years
**Daily Exercise:** 35 minutes
**Behavior Problems:** Possible
snoring and wheezing, sensitiv-
ity to temperature extremes,
snappishness when overheated

Bred as a companion dog, and very popular in the late 1980s, this is a perfect apartment dog. She is small, clean, neat, affectionate, smart, dependable, alert (she makes a good watchdog), brave and bright, sensitive, and she requires little daily exercise.

She is friendly, sturdy, quiet, and affable, but she must first become dominant with the other animals and children in her home before she is entirely comfortable in any environment. Because of her brachy-cephalic (pushed-in) face, she does not tolerate extreme heat. She does best with one or two adult owners who give her their undivided atten-tion, and is not especially fond of children.

Although generally well mannered, she does not do well in formal obedience training, due to her playful and independent nature. "Frenchies" have heart, humor, and friendliness all packed into a small package.

Her short coat comes in brindle, brindle with white, tan and white and sheds only a little, requiring grooming once a week.

Health considerations include hip and elbow dysplasia, cataracts, patellar (knee) luxation, allergies, spinal problems, elongated soft pal-ate, and an extra row of eyelashes that cause tearing (distichiasis). For more particulars about these problems, see Appendix I.

# GERMAN SHEPHERD DOG

**Size/Group:** Large/Herding
**Breed History:** Bred from farm dogs in Germany, longhaireds were introduced in Hanover, in 1882; shorthaireds in Berlin in 1880
**Height:** 22 to 26 inches
**Weight:** 70 to 95 pounds
**Life Expectancy:** 12 years
**Daily Exercise:** 45 minutes
**Behavior Problems:** Possible destructiveness, restlessness, nervousness, fear-biting (especially puppy-mill–bred pups), challenging owners for dominance

Thought to be the result of accidental mating between a shepherd dog and a wolf, German shepherds are a very popular breed. They love to work with people, and are best known as herders or guardians of flocks, for their work as police dogs, guard dogs, messengers during wartime, search-and-rescue dogs, and guides for blind people. Unfortunately, they are also often trained to be attack dogs and then turn into lethal weapons. They love to work, and should never be left to idle in inactivity. If left alone outdoors, a high, strong fence is a necessity. Shepherds should never be tied up.

Highly intelligent, German shepherds require firm, early obedience training. When well trained, they are affectionate and loyal toward their masters and good with children. But fiercely one-person, one-family individuals may be so wary of strangers that they may fear-bite. There is little difference in personality between the longhaired and shorthaired varieties.

Both types shed a great deal and must be brushed often (brushed and combed during shedding season). Their coats can be black, gray, white, or black and tan.

Health considerations include degenerative myelopathy, hip and elbow dysplasia, a growth disorder of the joints (osteochondritis dissecans, OCD), torsion and bloat, diabetes, pancreatitis, epilepsy, draining open tracts around the anus (perianal fistulas), spinal diseases, and eye problems. For more details about these health concerns, see Appendix I.

# GERMAN SHORTHAIRED POINTER

**Size/Group:** Large/Sporting
**Breed History:** A descendant of the Spanish Pointer, crossed with English and Italian Pointers
**Height:** 21 to 26 inches
**Weight:** 45 to 75 pounds
**Life Expectancy:** 12 years
**Daily Exercise:** 1 hour
**Behavior Problems:** Restlessness indoors, barking and destructiveness when left alone, house soiling, food stealing, roaming, possible behavior problems if raised in a kennel or pet shop

The German Shorthaired Pointer is exuberant, easily trained, cheerful, obedient, and good with children, except that in her very enthusiasm she may knock over a small child. This is an active breed, and should not be kept in the city or an apartment. She needs a lot of daily exercise, and is best suited to a situation in which she has access to a large yard or a chance to run in the country. Long, daily runs or walks, fetching games, and interactions with people are all musts for this breed. If she is left outdoors alone at all, she must have a secure fence.

Bred to be excellent pointers and hunters and for guarding, they can work well in almost any terrain or situation, as long as they get enough daily exercise. They can be stubborn, and are not especially territorial, and therefore are not particularly good guard dogs. They are not a good choice for inexperienced owners. Given the opportunity to exercise enough, they can become good family dogs, but basically they thrive on hunting and running.

Their short coats are spotted liver or black with white; solid liver or black. They shed little and need brushing with a currycomb about twice a week—more during shedding season.

Health concerns include hip and elbow dysplasia, cataracts, eyelids that turn inward and cause irritation to the eyes (entropion), von Willebrand's disease (a hemorrhaging disorder), and epilepsy. For more particulars about these health problems, see Appendix I.

# GERMAN WIREHAIRED POINTER

**Size/Group:** Large/Sporting
**Breed History:** Cross between the German Pointer, Wirehaired Griffon, Bloodhound, and Airedale
**Height:** 22 to 26 inches
**Weight:** 50 to 75 pounds
**Life Expectancy:** 12 years
**Daily Exercise:** 1 hour
**Behavior Problems:** Distractibility, possible clownishness, jumping up on people, dominance, guarding, roaming, food stealing, indoor restlessness

This dog is very friendly toward family and friends, but may be wary of strangers and other animals. He is a good family pet, but only when he gets enough daily exercise. Like his shorthaired cousin, he is not well suited to city or apartment life and really needs to live in a large house with a lot of indoor and outdoor space, or in the country. His thick, dense coat provides protection in all kinds of weather, and is essentially water repellent. He is perfectly happy to go into icy cold water.

Basically a hunting dog, he has a keen sense of smell, and needs to run in the field often. He is a wonderful retriever, determined and friendly, and a good companion dog and not particularly active indoors. He is not an especially protective watchdog.

Wirehaired pointers have a sense of humor and are great with children. These qualities may make them hard to train, but if they are given early, firm, gentle persuasion, they can become model citizens.

Their short, wiry coats come in all brown or brown with white, shed little, and require brushing about twice a week.

Health problems may include hip and elbow dysplasia, bloat, and cataracts. For more information about these diseases, see Appendix I.

# GLEN OF IMAAL TERRIER

**Size/Group:** Small/Miscellaneous
**Breed History:** Glen of Imaal in County Wicklaw; first seen at an Irish dog show in 1933; introduced to the U.S. in 1968
**Height:** 12 to 14 inches
**Weight:** 31 to 35 pounds
**Life Expectancy:** 13 years
**Daily Exercise:** 20 minutes
**Behavior Problems:** overexuberance for tots and seniors, stubbornness, possessiveness of belongings and people

Very curious and cocky, with a fighting spirit, these little dogs are hunters of small prey (especially mice). They need a good fence or strong leash to keep them safe. Very courageous and strong, they can be stubborn and independent and can also be trained to hunt foxes and badgers. They are "food-hounds," and will do anything for a tasty treat.

Glens love to play Frisbee and other games, and enjoy rough-and-tumble activities. Therefore, they may be a bit too much for small children and older people to handle comfortably. Terrier-like, they are tenacious and slightly quarrelsome with other animals, but are devoted to their families and are basically companion dogs. They are not demanding, but love attention and can coexist with other dogs and even cats, with supervision.

Their medium-length, somewhat dense coats come in blue-gray brindle and wheaten. They are average shedders, and should be combed about twice a week, professionally stripped once a year.

Health considerations may include hip dysplasia and progressive retinal atrophy (PRA), which can lead to blindness. For more details about these health problems, see Appendix I.

# GOLDEN RETRIEVER

**Size/Group:** Large/Sporting
**Breed History:** Thought to have been a cross between a Bloodhound and a golden-coated dog in a Russian circus in the mid 1800s; brought to England in the early 1900s
**Height:** 22 to 24 inches
**Weight:** 55 to 80 pounds
**Life Expectancy:** 13 years
**Daily Exercise:** 45 minutes
**Behavior Problems:** Few, with socialization—excessive exuberance, jealousy of humans' relationship with each other, possible timidity

A very popular and gifted hunting dog, the Golden is smart, easily trained, and affectionate.

Bred to be a retriever, she has a wonderful sense of smell, a soft mouth, and is used both in the field and in thickly wooded areas. She is also a very good swimmer, and can retrieve in marshes and open water. A hardy dog, she is able to tolerate all extremes of weather. If she is going to spend time alone outdoors, she needs a strong, high fence.

As a pet she is devoted to her owners and very good with children. She tolerates all kinds of high jinks, which include kids climbing all over her body and riding on her back. Loyal and very affectionate, she loves everyone and every animal, including kittens and cats. She is therefore an extremely popular family pet and companion. There are virtually no negative comments to be made about the breed. Because she is large and active, she should not live in small quarters. Her best home is a house with a yard, at least.

Her dense, straight or wavy medium-length coat is always gold in color. She sheds moderately or profusely, and requires brushing at least twice a week.

Possible health problems include hip dysplasia (common in all large breeds), a growth disorder of the joints (OCD), cataracts, inturned eyelids leading to irritation (entropion), allergies, heart problems (SAS), epilepsy, cancer, and hypothyroidism. For more details about these health concerns, see Appendix I.

# GORDON SETTER

**Size/Group:** Large/Sporting
**Breed History:** Scotland; developed in the late 1600s by a Duke of Gordon
**Height:** 23 to 27 inches
**Weight:** 40 to 80 pounds
**Life Expectancy:** 13 years
**Daily Exercise:** 1 hour
**Behavior Problems:** house soiling, roaming, picky eating, occasional aggression, protectiveness of family, stubbornness

Daniel Webster originally brought this big dog to the United States in the 1800s. Bred to be primarily a hunting dog, he has an excellent sense of smell and is a very good retriever. He especially likes to hunt woodcocks and other birds, and is a good swimmer. The Gordon setter is slower and not so agile as his Irish and English cousins, but is considered to be outstandingly intelligent and conscientious.

He is an excellent companion pet for families with children. A Gordon does, however, need firm training. Because he requires a great deal of daily exercise, he is not a good city or apartment dweller. As long as he gets enough exercise, he is calm indoors. If he is left outdoors at all, he must be kept in a yard with a secure fence.

His medium-length coat is silky and wavy and comes in all black or black with tan or reddish-brown (mahogany) markings. He sheds a lot, and his coat should be groomed every day to avoid snarls and mats. Health problems may include hip dysplasia, progressive retinal atrophy (PRA may lead to blindness), hypothyroidism, ear problems, and bloat. For more particulars about these health issues, see Appendix I.

# GREAT DANE (Brindle, Harlequin, Tawny)

**Size/Group:** Extra Large/ Working
**Breed History:** Germany
**Height:** 30 to 32 inches
**Weight:** 120 to 160 pounds
**Life Expectancy:** 8 years
**Daily Exercise:** 35 minutes
**Behavior Problems:** Possible dominance and aggressiveness in poorly bred dogs—very dangerous, given their size! Be careful to find a reputable breeder.

This breed dates way back, and may originally have been developed to hunt bears and wild boar. These dogs were also used as bodyguards, and are still often employed as watchdogs.

Despite their size, Danes cannot tolerate extremes of temperature and should not be kept outdoors. They are really happiest when close to their families. They get along well with other pets and children with whom they have been raised, but can easily knock over small toddlers accidentally. Their long, waggy tails very often knock objects off tabletops. Harlequins in particular often injure the tips of their tails, which need to be surgically repaired. Very gentle, companionable, and playful, these dogs need a lot of daily exercise to remain calm indoors. Early training is a must. A grown Dane that jumps up on people is not especially amusing. Although people do sometimes keep them in city apartments, their size alone makes this difficult. Also, lack of sufficient exercise can cause these big dogs to become stiff and sore.

Their short coats may be gray/blue, brindle, black, tan, or harlequin (white with black marking), and shed little. A weekly brushing is enough to keep a Dane's coat in shape.

Many Danes overeat, which can cause bone disease. They are prone to bloat if exercised immediately after eating. Other concerns may be hip dysplasia, painful and swollen joints (HOD), bone cancer, deafness, enlarged heart, cataracts, and difficulty walking. For more specifics about these diseases, see Appendix I.

# GREAT PYRENEES

**Size/Group:** Extra Large/
Working
**Breed History:** Mastiff group;
descended from the Hungarian
Kuvasz and the Maremmano-
Abruzzese; related to Saint
Bernards and Newfoundlands
**Height:** 26 to 32 inches
**Weight:** 90 to 125 pounds
**Life Expectancy:** 11 years
**Daily Exercise:** 35 minutes
**Behavior Problems:** Domi-
nance, guarding, protective-
ness, aggression

These large, good-natured, obedient, hardworking, and affectionate dogs were originally bred to herd sheep, and they are just as gentle and caring with children. They are devoted to owners they respect, and will do anything those owners want.

Originally born to mountain living, they also serve as guides in the snow, rescue dogs for lost victims of avalanches, and guard dogs for people and property. They can also be used to guard sheep, and as guide dogs through heavy snow. They are willing and able to take on large prey, but have been currently bred to serve as family dogs. Nevertheless, they are still aggressive with perceived intruders—perhaps including the UPS deliveryman. Early socialization and training are musts if a "Pyr" is going to turn into a socially acceptable pet.

Their long, thick coats come in solid white, or white with markings, and they shed a lot. They should be groomed at least three times a week, combed and brushed weekly, and their eyebrows need to be trimmed regularly to keep the hair out of their eyes.

Health concerns include hip and elbow dysplasia, patellar (knee) luxation, entropion (inward-turned eyelids leading to eye irritation), cataracts, spinal problems, and bleeding disorders. See Appendix I for more details about these health problems.

# GREATER SWISS MOUNTAIN DOG

**Size/Group:** Extra Large/ Working
**Breed History:** Oldest and largest of the Swiss breeds
**Height:** 23 to 28 inches
**Weight:** 85 to 140 pounds
**Life Expectancy:** 10 years
**Daily Exercise:** 45 minutes
**Behavior Problems:** Guarding behavior, dominance, aggression

Not well known in the United States, the breed originated in Switzerland during Roman times, when they were used as fighting dogs. At the end of the Middle Ages, these dogs were used as bodyguards and attack dogs. They also assisted farmers by pulling carts to market and working as farm dogs.

Then they became herding guards in Switzerland, and are still used to guard stables or homes. Today they are often used by police.

Loyal and courageous, bright and wise, they are closely related to the Bernese Mountain Dog and work calmly with other animals. After work, they play happily with children and get along well with all family members and other pets. Naturally quiet, they will alert the approach of strangers with a deep, loud bark. They are very tolerant of bad, or cold, weather.

Their smooth coats come in black or rust and white. They shed seasonally and require little grooming at other times of the year. A good brushing once a week to release dead hair and keep the coat shiny is all that is needed.

Health considerations may include hip dysplasia, a growth disorder of the joints (OCD), torsion and bloat, splenic torsion (twisting of the spleen), hypothyroidism, and dilated esophagus. For more information about these health problems, see Appendix I.

# GREYHOUND

**Size/Group:** Large/Hound
**Breed History:** A very ancient breed, the Greyhound was probably brought to Europe by the ancient Phoenicians
**Height:** 27 to 30 inches
**Weight:** 60 to 70 pounds
**Life Expectancy:** 10 years
**Daily Exercise:** 45 minutes
**Behavior Problems:** timidity, house soiling, fear-biting and irritable snapping, phobias, touch shyness, and stubbornness

These are racing dogs, able to run almost forty miles per hour, and they must have plenty of space to run. Although primarily outdoor dogs, they do like soft bedding, which also helps to prevent elbow calluses and bursitis. They are also very sensitive to the cold. Young dogs especially are not well suited to city or apartment life unless they get a lot of daily exercise. However, many pet Greyhounds are retired runners, and they do adapt well to small quarters. The breed has an unusually good ability to escape and must be securely fenced in if left outdoors alone.

Greyhounds tend to be nervous dogs and are usually reserved with strangers. Many are also reserved with their owners. Although they are usually friendly with children and other animals, they don't play for long, losing interest quickly. Some strains are bred primarily for racing, and may be unreliable around children. When choosing a pet, look for a breeder who raises his dogs to be companion pets.

Their short, firm coats come in all colors and shed little. They should be groomed about once a week. Unlike other dogs, they groom themselves all over, catlike.

Health concerns include progressive retinal atrophy (PRA can lead to blindness), hypothyroidism, throat problems, bloat, and bleeding disorders. They are also very sensitive to anesthesia. For more specifics about these health issues, see Appendix I.

# HARRIER

**Size/Group:** Medium/Hound
**Breed History:** Great Britain; developed by crossing Fox Terriers, Greyhounds, and Bulldogs.
**Height:** 18 to 22 inches
**Weight:** 45 to 60 pounds
**Life Expectancy:** 11 years
**Daily Exercise:** 1 hour
**Behavior Problems:** House soiling, indoor restlessness, destructiveness, excessive barking, digging, stubbornness

Dating back to the mid-1200s, the Harrier is a hardy, active dog with a very keen nose, used mostly in packs to hunt fox and hares. His prey has been reported to simply collapse from the effort of trying to evade this very persistent hunter.

He requires a lot of daily exercise, is very restless indoors, and is not well suited to city or apartment life unless he has long daily walks and frequent opportunities to run in the country. He is a good fence jumper and can dig well, so care must be taken to keep him secure if he is left outdoors.

He is a lively dog and is easy to train, although he may display a stubborn streak. (He should be obedience trained early in life.) Gentle and cheerful, he is good with children and gets along well with other pets.

The Harrier's coat is short and glossy and requires very little care. He sheds little, and brushing once a week will keep his coat gleaming. He is tricolored with white underside, legs, chest, and possibly face and tail tip. The rest of his body is tan with a black saddle.

Health concerns include hip dysplasia, epilepsy, lens luxation, and progressive retinal atrophy (PRA can lead to blindness). For more particulars about these health problems, see Appendix I.

# HAVANESE

**Size/Group:** Small/Toy
**Breed History:** Cuba
**Height:** 8 to 11 inches
**Weight:** 7 to 13 pounds
**Life Expectancy:** 12 years
**Daily Exercise:** 15 minutes
**Behavior Problems:** Excessive barking, house soiling, stubbornness

Related to the Bichon Frise, the Havanese is a gleeful, charming, sturdy, playful dog, excellent for families with children, and friendly toward other animals. She will play for long periods of time with her children without tiring, and is also often used as a therapy dog. She was bred to be a companion pet, and these qualities remain her primary attributes.

She is a quick learner and does not often challenge her owners' dominance. If she is taught as a puppy, she can become an excellent swimmer. Very alert and aware of her surroundings, curious, and very active, this little dog is an excellent watchdog. Wary of strangers, she is not especially protective, but will warn her owners of anyone approaching.

The Havanese has a very impressive, long, soft, curly or wavy coat that sheds little. It comes in solid cream, black, blue black, and gold. Brushing every other day keeps her coat in good condition and prevents mats from forming. Occasional clipping may be desired, especially around the eyes to prevent stains.

Health considerations may include patellar (knee) luxation, which is very common; hypothyroidism; and cataracts. For more information about these health concerns, see Appendix I.

# IBIZAN HOUND (Shorthair and Wirehair)

Shorthaired

**Size/Group:** Large/Hound
**Breed History:** An ancient breed, found in the time of King Tut, possibly brought to Egypt long before then
**Height:** 23 to 28 inches
**Weight:** 45 to 55 pounds
**Life Expectancy:** 12 years
**Daily Exercise:** 1 hour
**Behavior Problems:** Sensitivity to change and to strangers, with whom he may be aloof, irritable snapping, touch shyness

Wirehaired

The Ibizan is not well known in this country, although the breed has lived around the Mediterranean for at least four thousand years. It has only recently been recognized by the AKC.

This Sighthound is good at hunting, agility trials, lure coursing, tracking, and is also an excellent obedience student. He requires a lot of daily exercise and is not well suited for city or apartment life unless he gets it. He likes to jog and play ball with his owners, and a run in the open country is needed now and then. Ibizans do not fare well in cold weather. Their ears in particular must be protected if they are going to be out in freezing temperatures for any length of time.

The Ibizan is gentle, easy to house-train, friendly with other pets, and a loyal friend to his family. Unusually clean and quiet, he is an excellent athlete, able to jump extremely high. Therefore, if he is going to be left outdoors alone, he must have a jump-proof fence for his own protection.

His short and smooth, or medium-length and wiry, coat comes in solid red or white, or red with white. He hardly sheds at all and needs only a weekly brushing (Wirehairs require brushing two times a week) to be kept in good shape.

Health problems are few, and they include cardiomyopathy (a non-inflammatory disease of the heart muscle), a rare brain disorder (axonal dystrophy), and copper-associated liver damage. For more specifics about these health considerations, see Appendix I.

# IRISH RED AND WHITE SETTER

**Size/Group:** Medium/Rare/ Sporting
**Breed History:** Originated in Ireland in the 1700s for retrieving game
**Height:** 22 to 25 inches
**Weight:** 60 to 70 pounds
**Life Expectancy:** 13 years
**Exercise:** 1 hour
**Behavior Problems:** Destructiveness, hyperactivity, excessive barking, training requirement

These athletic dogs have boundless enthusiasm, energy, and zest for life. Red and Whites are extremely people-oriented, and can develop separation anxiety. As puppies, they can be timid, so early socialization and training are recommended. They require a lot of daily exercise (an hour a day, minimum), and a yard to run in.

Regular brushing will reduce minimal shedding.

Health issues include bloat, ear infections, hip dysplasia, and eye problems. Check Appendix I for more information about these diseases.

# IRISH SETTER

**Size/Group:** Large/Sporting
**Breed History:** Originally descended from the Spanish Pointer mixed in with Spaniel, Pointer, English Setter and Gordon Setter
**Height:** 25 to 27 inches
**Weight:** 60 to 70 pounds
**Life Expectancy:** 13 years
**Daily Exercise:** 1 hour
**Behavior Problems:** Flightiness and overexuberance (primarily seen in puppy-mill individuals), house soiling, roaming, playful destruction, jumping on people, barking, pulling on leash

Generally speaking, this breed remains puppylike, both mentally and physically, for longer than normal. The Irish needs early, gentle, consistent obedience training, because an untrained dog can be very stubborn and naughty. All Irish Setters tend to be excitable and energetic, but they really want to please their owners.

They are good with children, but their sheer exuberance may cause them to accidentally knock over toddlers. They love to play and are always ready for a game. They are great "kissers," and love a lot of attention. Some are very independent and are not always friendly toward strangers.

Irish setters require a good deal of daily exercise and are not suitable for city or apartment life. A walk will not take the place of a good run for these dogs, and they act very strangely if they are overconfined, jumping around in elevators and hallways. They tend to roam and must be securely fenced if they are let outdoors alone.

The Irish Setter's long hair needs to be brushed twice a week and they need an occasional bath. Health concerns may include hip dysplasia, epilepsy, bloat, progressive retinal atrophy (PRA may lead to blindness), and hypothyroidism. For more details about these problems, see Appendix I.

# IRISH TERRIER

**Size/Group:** Medium/Terrier
**Breed History:** This breed is 2000 years old
**Height:** 17 to 19 inches
**Weight:** 25 to 30 pounds
**Life Expectancy:** 13 years
**Daily Exercise:** 45 minutes
**Behavior Problems:** Guarding behavior, house soiling, dominance challenges toward owner, aggression toward other dogs

This dog can adapt to any environment and climate, and does well in the city or an apartment as long as she gets sufficient daily exercise. She is an excellent watchdog, a good hunter and retriever both on land and in the water, where she catches rats and otters. She is also an excellent companion pet.

A good escape artist, the Irish Terrier needs a sturdy fence if she is going to be left outdoors alone. She is fearless and courageous, and must be leashed securely in order to avoid a fight.

Terrier-like, she learns quickly and also becomes bored fast. She loves to play games and to be included in all types of activities with children and adults alike. She should be trained early by someone who is able to pique her interest and gain her respect.

Her short wiry coat comes in reddish brown, and she sheds very little when she is well groomed, about twice a week. She needs professional hand-stripping twice a year.

Health considerations include abnormally small eyes and urinary stones. For more information about these, see Appendix I.

# IRISH WATER SPANIEL

**Size/Group:** Large/Sporting
**Breed History:** Probably a cross between an Irish Setter and a Poodle in the early 19th century or perhaps much earlier
**Height:** 20 to 24 inches
**Weight:** 45 to 65 pounds
**Life Expectancy:** 12 years
**Daily Exercise:** 1 hour
**Behavior Problems:** Timidity, fear, fear-biting or -snapping, barking at little noises, drooling, shyness

This is the largest of the spaniels, with a long, thin, ratlike tail. His tail tip often bleeds as a result of hitting things. Primarily used to hunt wild ducks in lakes and marshes, he has a really good combination of traits: he is very obedient and bright; he is a real sporting dog, loves water, and has a wonderful fetching instinct. He is very affectionate with his family and gets along very well with children, whom he is apt to guard. He is wary of strangers and therefore makes a good watchdog.

A true outdoor dog that needs a lot of exercise, the Irish Water Spaniel is not suited for city or apartment life. He loves to play games, retrieve, and swim (he has webbed feet), and when he has enough of these activities he can be a very satisfactory house pet. He is generally friendly toward other animals, but two unaltered males are apt to fight. Curious, this dog does not like to be left out of anything and is apt to want to join you in any activity, including taking a bath!

His medium-length curly coat is thick, oily, waterproof, and sheds little. He is always solid brown (liver, to some). He should be brushed regularly to remove loose hair and mats, and professionally trimmed when necessary.

Health concerns may include hip dysplasia, epilepsy, hypothyroidism, and autoimmune diseases. For more details about these health problems, see Appendix I.

# IRISH WOLFHOUND

**Size/Group:** Extra Large/Hound
**Breed History:** As long ago as the 3rd century
**Height:** 28 to 35 inches
**Weight:** 105 to 160 pounds
**Life Expectancy:** 6 years
**Daily Exercise:** 35 minutes
**Behavior Problems:** Dominance, stubbornness, clumsiness

This huge dog was used to hunt wolves and elks by the ancient Celts. Romans later introduced the breed to Ireland, where it became the national dog. In the late 1800s it was crossbred with Deerhounds and Great Danes. He is the most powerful and tallest of all breeds. Despite his huge size, this is a gentle dog. But he needs firm handling and training and is not a good pet for an inexperienced owner. He is good with children, but may knock small ones over because of his size and clumsiness. The Wolfhound is apt to be a one-person dog, attaching strongly to one owner.

He is a good companion dog, but must have a lot of space and the opportunity for long, unrestrained runs. He tends to be quiet indoors, but still needs a lot of space just to lie down! He is still used to hunt wild boars, wolves, coyotes, and stags, but is now primarily a pet and gets along well with other animals, even much smaller ones as long as he hasn't been trained to course, or chase. The Wolfhound is an excellent guard dog.

His medium-length, rough coat comes in solid gray, red, white, brindle, black, and tan and sheds a little. He should be brushed about twice a week and requires some hand-stripping on a regular basis.

Health considerations include bloat, cataracts, progressive retinal atrophy (PRA may lead to blindness), hip dysplasia, cardiomyopathy (a disease of the heart muscle), and bone cancer. For more specifics about these health problems, see Appendix I.

# ITALIAN GREYHOUND

**Size/Group:** Small/Toy
**Breed History:** Very old breed, brought to Europe by the Phoenicians, further developed in Italy
**Height:** 13 to 15 inches
**Weight:** 5 to 15 pounds
**Life Expectancy:** 13 years
**Daily Exercise:** 30 minutes
**Behavior Problems:** Wariness of strangers and larger dogs, aggression with dogs their own size or smaller, barking, possible house soiling

This gentle, timid, submissive companion dog is very attached to her master and always wants to be physically close. As a matter of fact, Italian Greyhounds have been known to break a limb while jumping off a high place to follow "their" people. She can be friendly to other people, and likes children, but she is not suited for a family with rough or boisterous youngsters. She is very obedient and well mannered, never snappish or mean. Elegant and graceful, these dogs are a pleasure to look at and have around.

She is highly suitable for city or apartment life. She needs little daily exercise, and she doesn't take up much space. Because of her small size and short coat, she is very sensitive to the cold and needs a warm bed and an outer coat in cold weather.

Her short coat comes in all colors, hardly sheds at all, and only requires gentle brushing about once a week, at most.

Health considerations include progressive retinal atrophy (PRA may lead to blindness), epilepsy, autoimmune diseases, and patellar (knee) luxation. For more details about these health concerns, see Appendix I.

# JACK RUSSELL TERRIER

**Size/Group:** Small/Terrier
**Breed History:** Developed in the 1800s by Parson Jack Russell in England
**Height:** 11 to 15 inches
**Weight:** 10 to 18 pounds
**Life Expectancy:** 13 years
**Daily Exercise:** 45 minutes
**Behavior Problems:** Possessiveness of toys or food, barking, chasing cats or any other small pets, destructiveness when bored, aggression toward other dogs

This small terrier, like all of his cousins, is especially capable of burrowing into small holes to reach small game. In addition, he can face down raccoons, woodchucks, and foxes. He is full of courage, very obedient, and devoted to his owners. A happy little dog, the Jack Russell is a favorite of children, but he will not sit (or stand) still if poked or prodded. He is often extremely possessive of toys and food. He is a moderately good watchdog.

Extremely agile and energetic, these small dogs can climb almost anything, and it is very difficult to successfully confine them if they are left alone outdoors. Because of his relatively high exercise requirements, the Jack Russell is not particularly well suited to city or small apartment life. A house with a yard or the country is best for this active little dog, which needs early, strict training.

His coat comes in several forms—smooth, short, rough and broken—and all shed a lot. It may be tricolored, plain white, or white with black or tan markings. They require frequent brushing; the broken coat needs to be professionally hand-stripped.

Health concerns may include eye problems; deafness; wobbliness (ataxia), affecting the animal's ability to stand or walk well; patellar (knee) luxation; and disintegration of the hip joint (Legg-Calvé-Perthes). For more about these health issues, see Appendix I.

# JAPANESE CHIN (Spaniel)

**Size/Group:** Tiny/Toy
**Breed History:** Japan; Commodore Perry presented a pair to Queen Victoria
**Height:** 8 to 9 inches
**Weight:** 4 to 7 pounds
**Life Expectancy:** 12 years
**Daily Exercise:** 10 minutes
**Behavior Problems:** Wheezing and snoring, house soiling, stubbornness

Often compared to cats, these tiny dogs grab naps whenever possible. Otherwise very lively, they will play with any other dogs, and they love to learn and perform tricks. Intelligent and responsive, they like to be with people and will follow their owner(s) anywhere. They love to be spoiled, and their owners usually are happy to comply.

Great climbers, they often scale bookshelves and manage to get themselves up onto mantelpieces, where they stretch out decoratively. Although they are not the most responsive obedience pupils, their cheerful nature and appealing ways make this a small problem. The Chin does not bark as much as most other toy dogs and is not an especially good watchdog. Because of their small size and low exercise requirements, they are ideal city or apartment dwellers, and are often kept as companions by seniors and invalids.

Their thick, long, silky coats shed a lot, especially during the spring. They should be combed about twice a week and have an occasional bath. They come in white with tan, reddish-brown, or black markings.

Health problems may include progressive retinal atrophy (PRA may lead to blindness), cataracts, seizures, breathing problems because of their pushed-in faces, patellar (knee) luxation, sensitivity to anesthesia, and a lack of brain enzymes that can cause blindness and retardation (gangliosidosis). For more descriptions of these health complications, see Appendix I.

# JAPANESE SPITZ

**Size/Group:** Small/ Non-Sporting
**Breed History:** Directly descended from the Nordic Spitz, brought into Japan hundreds of years ago
**Height:** 12 to 14 inches
**Weight:** 11 to 13 pounds
**Life Expectancy:** 12 years
**Daily Exercise:** 45 minutes
**Behavior Problems:** Wariness of strangers, stubbornness, aggression, barking

A relatively new breed, this small dog is a very good watchdog. She will growl and put up a loud fuss at the approach of strangers. She is loyal and affectionate with her family, friendly toward all children, and an excellent companion pet. She may be somewhat stubborn at times.

If she has sufficient daily outdoor exercise, she is content to live in a small city house or apartment, and her small stature makes her an excellent urban pet.

Her thick, soft, long white coat needs a lot of care and should be brushed at least twice a week. She also should be bathed when necessary. As long as she is groomed regularly, she sheds moderately. She has a large head and slanted, dark eyes. Her tail is long and fluffy and is usually carried rolled up over her back.

Health problems may include cataracts, entropion (eyelids turned inward, irritating the eyes), and knee and elbow luxation. For more details about these health concerns, see Appendix I.

# KEESHOND

**Size/Group:** Medium/Non-Sporting
**Breed History:** A mixture of the Chow Chow, Elkhound, Pomeranian, and Samoyed
**Height:** 17 to 19 inches
**Weight:** 40 to 45 pounds
**Life Expectancy:** 12 years
**Daily Exercise:** 45 minutes
**Behavior Problems:** Attention-demanding, barking if left outdoors or indoors alone, house soiling, stubbornness, aggression

This bright, lively, and patient dog loves to be with people of all ages and gets along well with other pets. She is an excellent house pet; her only drawback is that she is sometimes too demanding of attention, constantly nudging her owner for a pat. She can live happily almost anywhere, from a city apartment to a farm. She is a good swimmer and was used to perform many different tasks when she lived on Dutch barges. Nowadays she is primarily a companion pet. She is an excellent obedience student, except when she becomes bored or overexcited and acts up. Keeshonden are often used as therapy dogs. They are also very good watchdogs.

Poor breeding can be a problem with this popular dog, so it is important to do plenty of research and find a reputable breeder.

Her thick, rough, long coat is gray and black, sometimes with white markings on the neck, chest, and legs. She sheds normally through most of the year, more heavily during the spring. She should be brushed once or twice a week, more during shedding season.

Possible health problems include hip dysplasia, patellar (knee) luxation, diabetes, progressive retinal atrophy (PRA can lead to blindness), cataracts, heart problems, degeneration of the kidneys, incomplete development of an organ, hypothyroidism, and autoimmune disorders. See Appendix I for more information about these health issues.

# KERRY BLUE TERRIER

**Size/Group:** Medium/Terrier
**Breed History:** Developed by shepherds in Ireland, a cross between the Irish Terrier, the Dandie Dinmont, and the Bedlington
**Height:** 17 to 20 inches
**Weight:** 33 to 40 pounds
**Life Expectancy:** 14 years
**Daily Exercise:** 45 minutes
**Behavior Problems:** Aggression; stubbornness; guarding of food, places, objects, and family members; possible food stealing and excessive barking

Although he is stubborn and assertive, the Kerry Blue is trainable and very loving toward his family and is good with children. With early training and socialization and a firm (alpha) owner, he can be a good companion pet. Sturdy and always ready to play outdoors, he still can be an excellent indoor dog as long as he gets enough daily exercise. He is moderately well suited for city life, but an apartment may be too small for him.

He is an excellent hunter and retriever. A guard of house, flocks, and herds, he is beloved by farmers. He is also often used in police work.

His short, silky coat comes in blue (or blue-black to most people), slate blue, and light blue gray and sheds very little. He should be brushed and combed one or two times a week, and professionally trimmed once a month.

Health problems are few. The Kerry Blue may suffer from hip dysplasia, cataracts, and blood disorders. See Appendix I for more specifics about these health problems.

# KOMONDOR

**Size/Group:** Extra Large/ Working
**Breed History:** Originally descended from Tibetan dogs and brought to Hungary by nomads in the late 1800s
**Height:** 25 to 27 inches
**Weight:** 80 to 100 pounds
**Life Expectancy:** 12 years
**Daily Exercise:** 1 hour
**Behavior Problems:** House soiling, aggression, willful disobedience, possible dominance challenges toward owner and family

These large dogs were originally bred to guard livestock, and their unusually thick, dense, corded white coats help to protect them from extremes of weather, and also afford some protection from other animals, such as wolves and bears, that might attack them.

Because of their heritage as guard dogs, they are extremely loving and protective of their homes and families. They are all right with children they have been raised with. Very wary of strangers, they make excellent watchdogs. Early socialization is a must, or the Komondor may attack anyone who approaches the house. Obedience training and a firm hand are also necessities, or these willful dogs will take over the household. They require a lot of daily exercise and, with it, are calm indoors. They are not suited for city or apartment living.

An adult's coat can grow to reach the ground. They do not shed at all, but they do mat easily. They should be groomed regularly, which takes a lot of care. (The Komondor Club of America has complete care instructions.) Bathing a Komondor is a time-consuming chore, and owners often try to protect the dog's coat from soiling with bibs, T-shirts, or by tying the cords to avoid urine staining, especially with males.

Health problems may include bloat, hip dysplasia, eyelids that are turned inward and cause irritation (entropion), and cataracts. For more explanation of these health concerns, see Appendix I.

# KUVASZ

**Size/Group:** Extra Large/ Working
**Breed History:** Probably came to Hungary from Tibet in the 13th century
**Height:** 22 to 30 inches
**Weight:** 70 to 115 pounds
**Life Expectancy:** 12 years
**Daily Exercise:** 35 minutes
**Behavior Problems:** Overprotectiveness, one-person or one-family dogs, dominance challenges, restlessness, territoriality, aggression

These sturdy dogs are able to live outdoors, but prefer to be with their people wherever they are. Like their closely related cousins, the Komondors, they were used to guard flocks, and their protection level is high. They were also used in packs for hunting, and eventually became companion pets. They are very good watchdogs. They have strong parental instincts and may decide to adopt other animals.

They are not well suited to city or apartment life, and because of their very intelligent and willful nature, they must be obedience trained early in life and kept under supervision by all family members. They are good and gentle with children with whom they have been raised, but may be overprotective of them; therefore, other children may seem to pose a threat. They are not good pets for inexperienced owners.

Their medium-length wavy white coats shed a great deal, especially in the spring, and they need to be brushed several times a week.

Health concerns may include hypothyroidism, torsion, hip and elbow dysplasia, and a growth disorder of the joints (osteochondritis dissecans, OCD). See Appendix I for more details about these problems.

# LABRADOR RETRIEVER

**Size/Group:** Large/Sporting
**Breed History:** Originally from Newfoundland, brought to England via Labrador in the early 19th century
**Height:** 22 to 25 inches
**Weight:** 55 to 75 pounds
**Life Expectancy:** 12 years
**Daily Exercise:** 1 hour
**Behavior Problems:** Chewing and destructiveness when puppies, incessant barking, roaming, house soiling, poor temperaments in puppy-mill individuals

Labs are among the most popular dogs in the United States. This is why it is well worthwhile to do careful research to find a reputable breeder, and wait for a pup if necessary. There are a lot of poorly bred, unhealthy examples around.

Bred to be hunting retrievers, they are unexcelled in the field, but they are also excellent companion pets and are often used as seeing-eye dogs. Steady and adaptable, Labs can live in almost any environment as long as they get enough daily exercise. They need a sturdy, high fence if they are going to be left outdoors alone. Lively and affectionate, these dogs are lovable pets. They swim well and should be given the opportunity to get in the water as often as possible. Their oily coats shed water easily, but their ears should be cleaned after swimming. They are able to withstand rough handling and get along wonderfully with children and other animals. As a matter of fact, they get along with just about everyone, and do not, therefore, make very good watchdogs. Because they are so active and willful, obedience training is a must.

Their short, dense coats can be chocolate, yellow, or black, and they do shed a lot. They should be groomed with a slicker brush at least once a week.

Health concerns may include cataracts and other eye problems, including progressive retinal atrophy (PRA), which can lead to blindness; hip and elbow dysplasia; diabetes; epilepsy; a joint growth disorder (OCD); swollen, painful joints (HOD); patellar (knee) luxation; bloat; strokes; heart problems; cardiomyopathy; spinal arthritis; and hypothyroidism. See Appendix I for more explanation of these diseases.

# LAKELAND TERRIER

**Size/Group:** Small/Terrier
**Breed History:** Thought to be a cross between an Old English wirehaired terrier and a Bedlington; developed in the 1800s
**Height:** 14 to 16 inches
**Weight:** 15 to 17 pounds
**Life Expectancy:** 13 years
**Daily Exercise:** 45 minutes
**Behavior Problems:** Dominance, wariness of strangers, excessive barking, picky eating, aggression toward other dogs, stubbornness

Not well known in the United States, this hardy little dog was once used in England to follow foxes and badgers that preyed on livestock, going into their underground lairs and killing them. She is competent both on land and in water. The hunting instinct remains, and she is still a curious and active dog. Originally from the English Lake District, she was once called a Patterdale Terrier, and is one of the oldest of English terriers. As opposed to most other terriers, she does not dig. She is calmer, more stable, and less excitable and aggressive than many other terriers, although if a male is left alone with another male dog, he may fight. She is the strongest of all terriers of the same weight. Cheerful and affectionate, she gets along well with children and other dogs, but is easily distracted and may be difficult to train in a formal setting. She needs a firm, patient owner and tends to be a "one-man" dog, wary of strangers. She loves to hike on leash and explore in the country.

The Lakeland is often bored and emotional, like all terriers, and is easily distracted. Obedience classes have to be peppered with imagination and novelty. She is able to live in almost any environment, urban, suburban, or country, as long as she gets enough daily exercise.

Health concerns may include lens luxation, von Willebrand's disease (a hemorrhagic disorder), elbow dysplasia, cataracts, and disintegration of the hip joint (Legg-Calvé-Perthes). For more details about these health problems, see Appendix I.

# LEONBERGER

**Size/Group:** Large/Rare/ Working
**Breed History:** German water rescue dog in existence since 1846
**Height:** 25 to 32 inches
**Weight:** 80 to 150 pounds
**Life Expectancy:** 11 years
**Daily Exercise:** 45 minutes
**Behavior Problems:** Protectiveness, territoriality, some aggression, dominance, stubbornness, strong will

Bred by the mayor of Leonberger to resemble the town's crest, this breed was developed from Landseer Newfoundlands, Saint Bernards, and Great Pyrenees. Leonbergers are high-energy dogs with amazing intelligence. They can become an ideal family dog, but they need a lot of training and socialization. It takes constant work and participation from all members of the family.

"Leos" need a lot of exercise. They love to swim, dig, and are inherently playful throughout their lives. Because of their size and daily need for exercise, these dogs are not suited for cities and apartment life.

Medium-soft to rough in texture, the Leo's coat is water repellent and comes in two colors: yellow gold and red brown, resembling a lion's mane. The look is distinguished, but they shed heavily twice a year.

Health considerations include hip dysplasia, bloat, hypothyroidism, and a growth disorder of the joints. For more specifics about these health concerns, see Appendix I.

# LHASA APSO

**Size/Group:** Small/ Non-Sporting
**Breed History:** From the sacred city of Lhasa, Tibet
**Height:** 9 to 11 inches
**Weight:** 14 to 16 pounds
**Life Expectancy:** 14 years
**Daily Exercise:** 20 minutes
**Behavior Problems:** Stubbornness, bossiness, wariness of strangers, aversion to rough play, irritable snapping, touch shyness, fighting when kept in pairs, aggression, territoriality

One of four breeds from the Tibetan mountains, this dog appears to be a large Shih Tzu. She is a friendly, childlike dog that loves to show off, and will often drop a toy into an unsuspecting stranger's lap. She is stubborn, but can be trained with patience. Devoted to her owner and family, the Lhasa tends to be wary of strangers, harking back to her earlier role as a watchdog.

She likes to be her own boss, but is trainable if coached inventively. Intervals of play can be good diversions.

The Lhasa does not require a lot of exercise, but she does demand a great deal of attention. She may not be the best choice for a family with children—she wants to be an only child!

Her thick, long coat protected the dog from the harsh Tibetan weather. She may be gold, brown, black, tan, white, or multicolored, sheds little, but needs regular daily brushing and a bath a week. She doesn't shed a lot when groomed and bathed regularly.

Health considerations include patellar (knee) luxation, cataracts, progressive retinal atrophy (PRA can lead to blindness), intervertebral disc disease, hip dysplasia, eyelids turned inward and causing irritation (entropion), and von Willebrand's disease—a hemorrhagic disorder. For more information about these health problems, see Appendix I.

# LÖWCHEN

**Size/Group:** Small/Non-Sporting
**Breed History:** Dates back to ancient France; painted by Goya in 1795
**Height:** 10 to 14 inches
**Weight:** 10 to 18 pounds
**Life Expectancy:** 14 years
**Daily Exercise:** 20 minutes
**Behavior Problem:** Attention demanding

This affectionate, lively, intelligent breed is not well known in this country. High-spirited, the Löwchen is happy to sit on his owner's lap as long as he's had a good walk. This is a dog that really wants to be near his people all of the time.

The Löwchen is an excellent obedience student and often passes the Canine Good Citizen Test. He likes all people and other animals, and is good with well-mannered children. He is a perfect apartment dweller because of his moderate indoor energy level.

His thick, long, wavy coat comes in all colors and demands frequent grooming to prevent mats from forming, unless he is kept in a "puppy cut," which many owners opt for. A good brushing at least four times a week will keep his coat in shape, and once in a while he needs a professional trim. (He needs to be clipped for showing.) He sheds very little.

Health concerns may include progressive retinal atrophy (PRA can lead to blindness), cataracts, and knee luxation. See Appendix I for more specifics about these health problems.

# MALTESE

**Size/Group:** Tiny/Toy
**Breed History:** An ancient breed, probably a cross between a Poodle and a miniature Spaniel
**Height:** 7 to 10 inches
**Weight:** 4 to 6 pounds
**Life Expectancy:** 14 years
**Daily Exercise:** 10 minutes
**Behavior Problems:** Fussy eating, house soiling, fear of loud or unusual noises, wariness of strangers, irritable snapping, attention-demanding, excessive barking

This little dog always wants to be close to her family and demands playtime and attention. She is gentle and well mannered and makes a very good obedience student as long as she is taught with imagination. Because of her devotion to her family, she is a very good watchdog.

She is an excellent city or apartment pet and easy to take along in a carrying case. Although she is quite hardy for her size, she does not like to roughhouse and should not be kept with very young children. She needs to be protected from the cold, and some owners opt to paper-train these little dogs to avoid walking them in bad weather.

Her minimal exercise requirements are well made up for by the amount of time that must be spent grooming her. Her long silky coat comes in white or cream and must be brushed every day to prevent matting. If left to grow long, it needs to be tied up to prevent sweeping the floor or becoming stained with urine. To avoid these problems, some owners have their pets' coats trimmed.

Health problems include poor teeth—brushing by owners and regular cleaning by a veterinarian are recommended; progressive retinal atrophy (PRA), which can lead to blindness; glaucoma; inturned eyelids that irritate the eyes (entropion); knee luxation; hypothyroidism; hypoglycemia (low blood sugar); and deafness. For more particulars about these health issues, see Appendix I.

# MANCHESTER TERRIER (Toy and Standard)

Toy

**Size/Group:** Tiny/Toy; Small/Terrier
**Breed History:** Originated in Manchester, England
**Height:** 7 to 12 inches; 12 to 16 inches
**Weight:** 6 to 12 pounds; 12 to 22 pounds
**Life Expectancy:** 12 to 14 years or more
**Daily Exercise:** 10 minutes; 35 minutes
**Behavior Problems:** House soiling, irritable snapping, excessive barking, attention-demanding, dominance, food guarding or stealing

Standard

Once considered two different breeds, the Toy and Standard Manchester Terriers are actually identical in personality and temperament. The toy requires slightly less daily exercise than his larger cousin. Clean, responsive, gentle, and odorless, both sizes are perfectly well suited to city or apartment life and make excellent companion pets and good watchdogs. They are good with older children and may be overprotective of their family. Therefore, if there are visiting children, the dog must be watched carefully or confined.

Very affectionate with their owners, these little dogs are wary of strangers. Excellent hunters of small animals such as rodents, rabbits, and even birds that have landed upon the ground, Manchester Terriers will not give up while "on the hunt."

Their short black and tan coats shed little and require brushing about once a week.

Health concerns include seizures, progressive retinal atrophy (PRA can lead to blindness), hypothyroidism, a hemorrhagic disorder known as von Willebrand's disease, and disintegration of the hip joint (Legg-Calvé-Perthes). See Appendix I for more details.

# MASTIFF

**Size/Group:** Extra Large/ Working
**Breed History:** An ancient breed, descended from the Tibetan Mastiff and brought to England before 55 B.C.
**Height:** 28 to 30 inches
**Weight:** 170 to 200 pounds
**Life Expectancy:** 8 years
**Daily Exercise:** 20 minutes
**Behavior Problems:** Snoring, drooling or wheezing, possible food stealing, possible fear-biting, wariness of strangers, tendency to track in dirt

This enormous breed is one of the heaviest of all dogs—they take up a lot of space and are not at all suited for city or apartment life. Used by the Romans to fight bulls, bears, lions, and tigers, they were also used as pit-fighting dogs in England up to a hundred years ago.

These powerful and courageous dogs must be socialized and trained early, with patience and consistency, or they may become dangerous. They are generally very good obedience students, and should never be hit or threatened. When properly trained and socialized, they are good with children, but can easily knock small ones over and should be supervised with toddlers.

Usually easygoing and good-natured, some are quite agile, while others are not. It depends on the individual and his lineage. They love to swim and explore with children and adults alike, and often get very dirty during their explorations. Their large feet also regularly track in dirt, so they are not particularly suitable for fastidious housekeepers.

Their short coats come in brindle, fawn, and apricot and shed a little. A shedding blade should be used about once a week to remove loose, dead hair.

They have a number of possible health problems, including hip and elbow dysplasia, knee luxation, hypothyroidism, a growth disorder of the joints (OCD, osteochondritis dissecans), painful and swollen joints (hypertrophic osteodystrophy, HOD), eye defects, strokes, epilepsy, cardiomyopathy, bloat, and arthritis of the spine (spondylosis). For more details about these health concerns, see Appendix I.

# NEAPOLITAN MASTIFF

**Size/Group:** Extra Large/ Miscellaneous
**Breed History:** Not recognized officially until 1946, a direct descendant of the Tibetan Mastiff
**Height:** 24 to 30 inches
**Weight:** 110 to 155 pounds
**Life Expectancy:** 10 years
**Daily Exercise:** 30 minutes
**Behavior Problems:** Drooling, snoring, dribbling food and water and scattering it around when they shake their heads, knocking things over, aggressiveness, roaming, wariness of strangers, very demanding of attention

Although these dogs have several contradictory histories, they are certainly from the Neapolitan area of Italy. These massive dogs were bred to be first and foremost outdoor watchdogs, fighting dogs, and keepers of flocks; they were used by both police and criminals and as bodyguards. Because of their huge size and protective nature, they must have early socialization and obedience training. They are not at all suitable for inexperienced, frail, or elderly owners, and are not good with children unless they have been raised with them. They are friendly toward other household pets, and to all livestock, which they want to guard. They are not meant to live in apartments unless they get enough daily exercise. They are very sensitive to heat and humidity.

Gentle by nature, mastiffs want to be physically close to their owners and often follow them around. They are stoical and courageous and able to bear pain with no complaint.

Their short, smooth coats come in gray, blue, black, mahogany, and tawny. They may be brindled. Shedding is minimal, and grooming consists of an occasional brushing.

Health considerations include hip and elbow dysplasia, hypothyroidism, heart problems, bloat, turned-in eyelids that irritate the eyeballs (entropion), and a growth disorder of the joints (osteochondritis dissecans, OCD). For more details about these health considerations see Appendix I.

# NEWFOUNDLAND

**Size/Group:** Extra Large/ Working
**Breed History:** The most common theory is that they are a cross between Tibetan Mastiffs and Labradors
**Height:** 26 to 28 inches
**Weight:** 100 to 150 pounds
**Life Expectancy:** 8 years
**Daily Exercise:** 45 minutes
**Behavior Problems:** Few— drooling; they love any water and may even try to climb into their water bowls!

This huge, patient, intelligent, courageous breed has almost no faults. She is friendly with everyone, including children of all ages, for whom she often acts as a "nanny." She is also very friendly toward other pets, and especially likes to live with another dog or two.

"Newfs" need a lot of exercise. They love to swim and are very good at it because of their webbed feet. They are excellent rescue dogs, both in and out of the water, and are often used to track down lost campers and hikers. Not only because of their size, but also because of their daily exercise requirements, these big dogs are not suited to city or apartment life.

Their dense, medium-length coats come in all sorts of colors and color combinations and shed a lot. They should be brushed with a slicker brush and combed at least once a week, more often in the summer.

Health considerations include bloat, eyelids that turn inward and irritate the eye (entropion), lower eyelids that hang down (ectropion), hip dysplasia, hypothyroidism, a growth disorder of the joints (osteochondritis dissecans, OCD), and a heart abnormality (subaortic stenosis, SAS). For more specifics about these health problems, see Appendix I.

# NORFOLK AND NORWICH TERRIERS

**Size/Group:** Tiny/Terrier
**Breed History:** England; the Norwich disappeared during WWI but was redeveloped by breeding Bedlingtons, Irish Terriers, and Bull Terriers
**Height:** 9 to 11 inches
**Weight:** 10 to 12 pounds
**Life Expectancy:** 14 years
**Daily Exercise:** 35 minutes
**Behavior Problems:** Excessive barking, stubbornness

Norfolk Terrier

Norwich Terrier

These dogs make up for their small size by their large personalities. They think that they are big dogs, and are not at all content to be lapdogs. As a matter of fact, they greatly dislike being held tightly on a lap or in a person's arms. Like most terriers, they can be very stubborn and willful—far be it from a Norfolk or Norwich to slavishly obey his master's every whim.

They were originally bred to hunt small game such as rodents and foxes and drive them out of their hiding places so that the hounds and hunters could chase them. Now they are primarily companion pets and excellent watchdogs.

They love attention and affection (as long as it doesn't involve being restrained), and are able to live in any environment, from a small apartment to a large farm. They need a moderate amount of daily exercise, but their short legs make a walk around the block a sufficient outing.

Their rough, wiry, medium-length coats are either wheat-colored, red, or black and tan, and shed very little. They need very little daily grooming, but should be professionally hand-stripped on a regular basis.

Possible health concerns include cardiomyopathy (enlarged heart), collapsed trachea, epilepsy, and knee luxation. For more details about these disorders, see Appendix I.

# NORWEGIAN ELKHOUND

**Size/Group:** Medium/Hound
**Breed History:** An ancient
breed from Norway
**Height:** 19 to 21 inches
**Weight:** 44 to 55 pounds
**Life Expectancy:** 12 years
**Daily Exercise:** 35 minutes
**Behavior Problems:** Excessive
barking, roaming, digging,
stealing and guarding food,
dominance, protectiveness,
stubbornness, assertiveness

This breed was developed to hunt, track (Norwegians relied on her scenting ability to find elk), herd, and to pull sleds. She was a companion of the Vikings and has changed little since then. She is a medium-size, powerfully built dog with a lot of stamina.

She is moderately suited for urban or apartment life, but prefers a house with a large yard and unlimited space or the country. She should never be allowed to roam freely alone throughout a neighborhood, because she is a powerful and assertive animal. She needs an owner with a firm hand and should be firmly discouraged from any tendency to attack.

She is more closely related to the northern breeds (Siberians, and the like) rather than to hounds, and is classified as a hound only because of her hunting ability. She is alert and makes a fine watchdog, She really likes cold weather and snow, and must have sufficient daily exercise in order not to escape, roam, or be excessively noisy.

Her thick silver-gray coat tipped with black is designed to protect her from the icy cold of the Scandinavian winters. Her medium-length coat sheds a little and should be brushed three times a week with pin and slicker brushes, and combed with a Greyhound comb.

Health considerations include a tendency toward cysts, hip dysplasia, cataracts, hypothyroidism, progressive retinal atrophy (PRA can lead to blindness), and degeneration of the kidney tubes (Fanconi syndrome). See Appendix I for more specifics about these health problems.

# NOVA SCOTIA DUCK TOLLING RETRIEVER

**Size/Group:** Medium/Miscellaneous/Sporting
**Breed History:** Originally called the Little River Duck Dog, the breed was developed in early 18th century Canada to retrieve waterfowl
**Height:** 18 to 20 inches
**Weight:** 37 to 51 pounds
**Life Expectancy:** 13 years
**Daily Exercise:** 1 hour
**Behavior Problems:** Territoriality, excessive barking, stubbornness, aggressiveness at times, training requirement

The Toller, a frolicsome, busy dog, gets his name from the seventeenth-century Middle English word *tolling*, which means to "lure or decoy game." Rather than simply retrieving game, the Toller first has to capture the curiosity of the waterfowl by pacing and using playful action to lure them to shore.

Energetic and playful, they need exercise, structure, and discipline. Early training is a must. One must be very patient and persistent with the Toller, because he is easily distracted. Channeling their energy and training into performance events such as field and agility will make your Toller a happy and contented family dog.

The Toller has a water-repellent outer coat and a soft, dense undercoat, which sheds seasonally.

Health issues may include Addison's disease, pulmonic stenosis, and thyroid and heart disease. See Appendix I for further health information.

# OLD ENGLISH SHEEPDOG

**Size/Group:** Large/Herding
**Breed History:** Uncertain; possibly related to the Briard and Bergamasco
**Height:** 24 to 25 inches
**Weight:** 60 to 65 pounds
**Life Expectancy:** 12 years
**Daily Exercise:** 1 hour
**Behavior Problems:** Puppy-mill individuals may steal or guard food, objects, and places; fear-bite; be restless; willfully disobey; bark excessively; be destructive; challenge owner dominance; be timid; develop phobias; and snap when irritated

This large breed is familiar to almost everyone. Her wonderful long fur was once used in England to make coats. She is basically a hardworking breed, still used to guard and herd sheep, but she is now primarily a companion pet. Unfortunately, the breed's popularity, engendered by a Disney movie, has led to puppy-mill production and the proliferation of badly bred animals. (See "Behavior Problems," above.) Be very careful to find a reputable breeder who has the best interests of this wonderful dog as a priority.

The ideal Old English is first and foremost a herding, guard, and sled dog. She is also a retriever and companion dog that is especially good with children, often "guarding" them against all comers. She tends to "herd" her owners, pushing and directing them toward their families. Affectionate and gentle, she is not a fighter and shuffles around, as some say, "like a bear."

Her thick, long coat comes in gray or black with white markings and should be properly groomed. Brushing should be frequent, about four times a week, in order to prevent snarls and mats. With proper grooming, the sheepdog sheds little and requires professional trimming only occasionally.

Health concerns include hip dysplasia, glaucoma, cataracts, progressive retinal atrophy (PRA can lead to blindness), entropion (eyelids turned inward that can lead to irritation), diabetes, hypothyroidism, deafness, and a disease affecting a dog's ability to walk (wobblers). See Appendix I for more details about these health issues.

# OTTERHOUND

**Size/Group:** Large/Hound
**Breed History:** An old breed, developed from Bloodhounds, Harriers, Griffons Nivernais, and Rough-Haired Terriers
**Height:** 23 to 27 inches
**Weight:** 65 to 120 pounds
**Life Expectancy:** 12 years
**Daily Exercise:** 45 minutes
**Behavior Problems:** Roaming, food stealing, house soiling, clumsiness, and embarrassing sniffing of people

There are not very many of this charming breed of dog around. As her name suggests, she was originally bred to hunt otters. Her webbed feet make it easy for her to traverse rough terrain and, of course, to swim well. She is often used for search and rescue, agility and tracking trials, and as a therapy dog. She is still used to track big game or raccoons, but is now primarily a companion pet. Her strong chase instinct makes it important to protect smaller pets. Although she is able to live outdoors, she really prefers to be close to her human family.

She has a loyal, cheerful, affectionate, and playful personality and is also a moderately good watchdog. She loves to play and wrestle with children, although her strong, waggy tail may knock little ones over. Basically a pack dog, she loves to work and play with others—people as well as other dogs.

Because of her strength and persistence, the Otterhound should have strict obedience training early in life. She needs a lot of space and exercise and is not suited for city or apartment living. If kept outdoors, she needs a strong, high fence to prevent her from roaming, but she prefers to be inside with her family.

Her rough, medium-length coat comes in all colors and has a strong odor. She is an average shedder and should be groomed once a week with a slicker brush and comb, her ears and beard cleaned often.

Health considerations include bloat, seizures, bleeding disorders, and hip dysplasia. See Appendix I for more information about these health issues.

# PAPILLON

**Size/Group:** Tiny/Toy
**Breed History:** Popular in Italy during the Renaissance, the Papillon was bred to perfection by French breeders
**Height:** 8 to 11 inches
**Weight:** 6 to 10 pounds
**Life Expectancy:** 13 years
**Daily Exercise:** 10 minutes
**Behavior Problems:** Fear-snapping, house soiling, attention-demanding, jealousy, barking

This little dog was bred to be a companion pet and is good with gentle children; many breeders will not sell these small dogs to families with young children or large dogs. She can be badly hurt if dropped or stepped on. However, despite her small size, she is robust and very able to adjust to different living conditions and climates. She is an ideal city or apartment pet and requires very little daily exercise. She is an excellent watchdog.

She loves to be petted, cuddled, and played with—in fact, she demands it. She has a wonderful attention span and really enjoys hearing her master's voice. As an adult she will watch her owner's face for long periods of time as long as she is being spoken to. She may be jealous and possessive of her family and does need positive obedience training.

Her thick, long coat comes in white with any other color markings, or in a mixture of several colors. She sheds and should be groomed about twice a week. Sometimes she should be professionally trimmed.

Health concerns include knee luxation, progressive retinal atrophy (PRA may lead to blindness), other eye problems, epilepsy, heart defects, an opening in the skull bones, congenital liver malformation, and hemolytic anemia (an autoimmune disease that destroys red blood cells). For more specifics about these health issues, see Appendix I.

# PEKINGESE

**Size/Group:** Tiny/Toy
**Breed History:** A favorite of the imperial family in Peking for many centuries, brought to Europe in the mid-19th century by French and British soldiers who found them in the palace ruins
**Height:** 6 to 9 inches
**Weight:** 7 to 14 pounds
**Life Expectancy:** 12 years
**Daily Exercise:** 10 minutes
**Behavior Problems:** Possible aloofness and independence, stubbornness, demanding of attention, irritable snapping, excessive barking, guarding behavior, wheezing and snoring

These little pug-faced dogs are second only to the Toy Poodle in popularity among Toys. They are willful and independent and need patient training and gentle handling. They want to be at the center of everyone's attention. "Pekes" are often rather aloof and do not readily join in with family activities; they prefer to watch and supervise. A perfect apartment dweller and lapdog, the Peke can also be a very good watchdog. He can tolerate very well behaved children, but is happiest with an adult couple and can live perfectly well in a small apartment, with a minimum of daily exercise. Owners often carry these little dogs around underneath their arms. As a matter of fact, the smallest Pekes are called "sleeves," because their Chinese masters used to carry them there.

The Pekingese is highly intolerant of heat and must be protected with air-conditioning and restricted outdoor exercise during hot summer months. His large, very prominent eyes are very susceptible to injury and should be checked every day.

His thick, long coat can be many colors and sheds a little, except in the spring, when it sheds a lot. Frequent brushing with a bristle brush and regular combing, will keep his coat in good condition.

Health concerns include foot or knee luxation, eye injuries, dry eyes, and spinal problems. For more particulars about these health issues, see Appendix I.

# PERRO DE PRESA CANARIO

**Size/Group:** Large/Rare/ Working
**Breed History:** Brought to the Canary Islands by the Spanish conquistadors to guard cattle
**Height:** 25 inches
**Weight:** 85 to 110 pounds
**Life Expectancy:** 9 years
**Daily Exercise:** 1 hour
**Behavior Problems:** Dominance, aggression, territoriality, training requirement

Powerful and intelligent, these dogs have an intuitive instinct for guarding. These dogs should be trained as early as possible, and socialized to establish proper control. This breed is not recommended for the first-time dog owner. The Presa Canario requires a knowledgeable and experienced owner for responsible care and handling.

Space is needed for exercise: a large yard or countryside. Grooming needs include monthly bathing and coat care. Coat is short and smooth and somewhat oily.

Health issues may include hip dysplasia, elbow dysplasia, bloat, and heart disease. Check Appendix I for summaries of these health problems.

# PETIT BASSET GRIFFON VENDÉEN

**Size/Group:** Medium/Hound
**Breed History:** Originally from the west coast of France, in Vendéen
**Height:** 13 to 15 inches
**Weight:** 30 to 45 pounds
**Life Expectancy:** 12 years
**Daily Exercise:** 45 minutes
**Behavior Problems:** Barking, bossiness, roaming

A persistent Scenthound, this dog may not pay attention to you once she's on the scent. Energetic, bright, friendly, and lively, with a high energy level, her greatest drawback is her persistent barking. Sturdy and bold, she has a very strong urge to chase every rabbit or other small animal she sees. A very good escape artist, she can jump most fences and dig under those she can't quite manage to get over, so good security or confinement is a must. She can live in a large apartment or house with a yard, but is happiest with lots of outdoor exercise.

Although highly social with everyone, including children and other dogs, her highly developed hunting instincts make her an unsuitable housemate with cats or other smaller pets.

Her medium-length thick and wiry coat comes in white with lemon, black, or apricot markings or may be tricolored. This harsh coat helps to protect the Griffon from underbrush and should always look slightly mussed, and should not be clipped or trimmed. She sheds and should be combed and brushed a couple of times a week. Hair should be plucked out of her ear canal from time to time.

Health concerns include progressive retinal atrophy (PRA can lead to blindness), knee luxation, hip dysplasia, epilepsy, juvenile cataracts, hypothyroidism, and spinal meningitis when young. See Appendix I for more details about these problems.

# PHARAOH HOUND

**Size/Group:** Medium/Hound
**Breed History:** Thought to be an ancient Egyptian breed brought to Spain during pre-Islamic nomadic invasions
**Height:** 21 to 25 inches
**Weight:** 45 to 60 pounds
**Life Expectancy:** 12 years
**Daily Exercise:** 45 minutes
**Behavior Problems:** High energy level; roaming

O ne of the most important things an owner of one of these dogs must do is to keep him secure. His extremely keen eyesight, curiosity, and passionate hunting instinct can get him into a lot of trouble unless he is securely leashed or well fenced in. He can spot a small animal miles away, long before a person's eyes can make it out.

He really needs a lot of daily exercise and is not suited for city or apartment life. He has a unique quality among dogs—he blushes when he is excited. He also sometimes actually smiles with pleasure.

Very calm, playful, and affectionate, the Pharaoh Hound is wonderful with children and really loves to work and run with his owners. He tends to be cautious with unknown people or animals and should be allowed to get to know them gradually.

His rough, short, soft coat is tan, sometimes with white markings on the face, chest, legs, and tail. He sheds and should be brushed or "gloved" at least once a week.

The only health problem that the Pharaoh hound may suffer from is optic nerve hypoplasia (an underdeveloped optic nerve). For more information about this disorder, see Appendix I.

# PINSCHER, GERMAN

**Size/Group:** Medium/Rare/
Working
**Breed History:** Germany
**Height:** 17 to 20 inches
**Weight:** 25 to 35 pounds
**Life Expectancy:** 13 years
**Daily Exercise:** 1 hour
**Behavior Problems:** Domi-
nance, aggression, stubborn-
ness, excessive barking, training
requirement

Originally bred to control rodents, the German Pinscher is strong-willed, sturdy, alert, active, and tenacious. This is a good breed for those who admire the looks of the Miniature and Doberman Pinscher, but want a more moderate size. Yet don't be fooled by his size. This medium-size Pinscher is fearless and capable of stopping an intruder. His strength and energy demand a great deal of exercise.

It's recommended to start early training and socialization with the German Pinscher, as they can be very stubborn and manipulative. With commitment to training, this dog can excel in obedience and other sports.

Shedding and grooming are minimal.

Possible health issues are hip dysplasia and eye problems. Read more about these disorders in Appendix I.

# PINSCHER, MINIATURE

**Size/Group:** Tiny/Toy
**Breed History:** Many feel that this little dog has been around longer than his larger cousin, the Doberman; he has become popular in the U.S. since the late 1920s
**Height:** 10 to 12 inches
**Weight:** 8 to 11 pounds
**Life Expectancy:** 13 years
**Daily Exercise:** 10 minutes
**Behavior Problems:** Barking, stubbornness, dominance, nippiness

Because of his tiny frame, this is not a breed suited for households with young, raucous children who might get bitten. He does not like to be handled too much and then only very gently. He is definitely not suited to outdoor living.

Terrier-like, he is courageous and lively. Small toys and game pieces must be kept out of the very intelligent and curious Minpin's reach. Owners often use pressure gates, screens, or crates to keep this little dog safe and out of trouble, especially if they are not around to keep a watchful eye out, or are busy carrying things in or out of open doors. If he is to be left outside, fences should be carefully checked for small spaces that this little dog could squeak through.

His short coat comes in black with tan, red, or brown markings. He sheds only a little, and needs to be brushed once a week, at most.

Health concerns include progressive retinal atrophy (PRA may lead to blindness), cataracts, pannus (an eye condition that may lead to blindness), knee luxation, and disintegration of the hip joint (Legg-Calvé-Perthes). For more details about these health issues, see Appendix I.

# PLOTT HOUND

**Size/Group:** Medium/Miscellaneous
**Breed History:** Germany
**Height:** 20 to 25 inches
**Weight:** 45 to 60 pounds
**Life Expectancy:** 14 years
**Daily Exercise:** 1 hour
**Behavior Problems:** Baying

This is a little-known breed in this country, though Jonathan Plott brought them to the United States in the mid-1700s. They are strong and tenacious dogs, bred to hunt wild boar, coyotes, wolves, stags, and wildcats in packs. These dogs are very good at their jobs. They can work around the clock without showing fatigue. Although sweet-tempered and loving to their families, they are not especially good obedience students and should be socialized early in life. They often greet their owners with a happy howl and many wags and licks, and are great with children, other dogs, and household pets.

They require a lot of daily exercise and room to explore, and are not well suited to city or apartment life. Besides, they would drive any nearby owners crazy with their constant howling and baying. They are really best with owners who seriously want to hunt.

Their thick, short coats come in black, white, gray, blue, and brindle and shed little. A short brushing twice a week is all that is needed to keep a Plott Hound's coat in good shape.

These dogs are very sturdy and virtually without health problems.

# POINTER

**Size/Group:** Large/Sporting
**Breed History:** Thought to have originally been a mix of the Bull Terrier, Bulldog, Greyhound, Newfoundland, and Italian Pointer
**Height:** 23 to 28 inches
**Weight:** 35 to 90 pounds
**Life Expectancy:** 13 years
**Daily Exercise:** 1 hour
**Behavior Problems:** independence, roaming, attention-demanding, compulsive "working," stubbornness

The Pointer as we know it today was developed about eighty years ago. This breed of dog is highly energetic and needs a lot of exercise and attention. She is happiest and at her best when she has a job to do, and the jobs can be quite varied. They can range from fetching something for you in the house, playing flyball, doing field work, or performing obedience tasks. She is an untiring hunter with a very good sense of smell, and makes an excellent bird dog. Although she may bark at unusual noises, she is not a good watchdog.

She is playful, loving, and protective with children and makes a good choice for junior handling. Once grown, the Pointer can live outdoors as long as she has a dry, draft-free shelter, but she really would rather be indoors with her family. She is not at all suited for city or apartment life.

Her short coat sheds and should be brushed with a bristle brush on a daily basis to minimize shedding. It comes in many colors: liver, liver and white, lemon and white, orange with white, and solid orange, black, liver, and lemon.

Health concerns include progressive retinal atrophy (PRA may lead to blindness), cataracts, turned-in eyelids that may irritate the eyeball (entropion), epilepsy, and hip dysplasia. For more specifics about these health problems, see Appendix I.

# POLISH LOWLAND SHEEPDOG

**Size/Group:** Medium/Herding
**Breed History:** From the central plains of Poland, he can be traced back to the Puli in ancient times
**Height:** 16 to 20 inches
**Weight:** 30 to 66 pounds
**Life Expectancy:** 13 years
**Daily Exercise:** 45 minutes
**Behavior Problems:** Suspiciousness of strangers, stubbornness, strong will

Ancestor of many herding dogs, including the Bearded Collie, the Polish Lowland Sheepdog, or PONS, needs a great deal of affection, attention, and exercise and requires a firm hand and early, consistent training and socialization. His curiosity and intelligence make it imperative that he be kept out of trouble if he is left alone, outdoors or inside. He is dependable once he is sure what his owner wants.

A really intelligent working dog, this breed is happiest when he is doing a job. Even though he is able to withstand cold when he is working outdoors, he really wants to be included in family activities indoors. But he is in no way a cuddly lapdog. He has a charming personality and a sharp memory and is usually friendly with other animals unless his leadership is threatened. He is very good with children he has been raised with.

His thick, long coat needs brushing several times a week in order to avoid mats, because he sheds into his coat (not onto the carpet). He does not require clipping.

He has few health concerns, but owners should watch for signs of a heart disorder known as patent ductus arteriosus (PDA), and also hip dysplasia. See Appendix I for more particulars about these health problems.

# POMERANIAN

**Size/Group:** Tiny/Toy
**Breed History:** Developed in the Russian region of Pomerania many centuries ago; a much scaled-down descendant of the Spitz
**Height:** 5 to 7 inches
**Weight:** 3 to 8 pounds
**Life Expectancy:** 15 years
**Daily Exercise:** 10 minutes
**Behavior Problems:** Willful disobedience, irritable snapping, dominant guarding behavior, barking

This very small dog makes up for his size with a large personality. He loves to be pampered and will in fact demand it. He wants to be in on everything that is going on in the house, and does like outdoor play or exercise, although he really hates snow and rain. He loves to go along on errands with his owner (he is often carried in a tote bag or backpack) and must always be kept on a leash or in a secure yard because his curiosity and bravado with larger dogs can get him into trouble. Very quick to learn, he often performs tricks and is even seen in circuses.

He will bark at strangers and so, despite his small frame, does make a good watchdog. He is good with well-behaved children who are at least six or seven, but bears watching if he has not grown up with them, because he may snap if annoyed.

His thick, straight, long coat sheds and should be brushed several times a week. He may need some professional trimming.

Health concerns may include progressive retinal atrophy (PRA), which may lead to blindness; cataracts; inturned eyelids, which can irritate the eyeballs (entropion); knee luxation; hypoglycemia; tracheal collapse; skull bones not fully closed; and a heart disorder known as patent ductus arteriosus (PDA). For more about these conditions, see Appendix I.

# POODLE (Miniature and Standard)

**Size/Group:** Miniature: Small/ Non-Sporting; Standard: Large/ Non-Sporting
**Breed History:** A descendant of an almost extinct dog called a Barbet, a French water dog
**Height:** Miniature: 10 to 15 inches; Standard: 15 to 26 inches
**Weight:** Miniature: 15 to 18 pounds; Standard: 45 to 70 pounds
**Life Expectancy:** 13 years
**Daily Exercise:** Miniature: 20 minutes
Standard: 45 minutes
**Behavior Problems:** Dominance; owners assume leadership role early on

Minature Poodle—show clip

Minature Poodle—pet clip

These extremely intelligent dogs are always very attached to their owners and want to be with them at all times. They should never be ignored or kept in a kennel. Because of their high intelligence level, they may try to outsmart their owners to get their own way.

Both sizes enjoy a lot of exercise, swim well, and will retrieve objects from the water. They are courageous, adaptable, and able, and are excellent at obedience training. They get along well with other pets and with children, although the standard may be too much for a small toddler.

Whether an owner prefers to keep her dog in a "kennel cut" (same length all over) or in a show cut (with pom-poms on the legs and a topknot on the head), a Poodle's coat needs daily grooming with a slicker brush, ear hairs plucked, and clipping and scissoring, which is

# POODLE

Standard Poodle—show clip

Standard Poodle—pet clip

often done professionally. They do not shed at all as long as they are properly groomed.

Health problems in both sizes may include cataracts, progressive retinal atrophy (PRA can lead to blindness), epilepsy, and hip dysplasia. Minis may develop patellar (knee) luxation; glaucoma; deafness; epilepsy; disintegration of the hip joint (Legg-Calvé-Perthes); a heart problem (PDA); deafness, and a lack of brain enzymes (gangliosidosis), which causes retardation and blindness. Standards may suffer from bloat, entropion (turned-in eyelids that irritate the eyeball), degenerating hair follicles and oil glands (sebaceous adenitis, or SA), low adrenal function (Addison's disease), and degeneration of the kidneys (renal cortical hypoplasia). For more information about these health issues, see Appendix I.

Toy Poodle—pet clip

**Size/Group:** Tiny/Toy
**Breed History:** A descendant of an almost extinct French water dog called a Barbet
**Height:** 7 to 11 inches
**Weight:** 5 to 8 pounds
**Life Expectancy:** 14 years
**Daily Exercise:** 15 minutes
**Behavior Problems:** Excessive barking, irritable snapping, dominance, myriad problems in puppy-mill individuals

Toy Poodle—show clip

Like his larger relatives, the Toy Poodle is a people dog: playful, active, and affectionate. He bonds closely with his owner(s), but because of his tiny, delicate frame, he should not be handled by toddlers or rough children. He should always be kept indoors—no outdoor kennel for this little dog.

Toy Poodles are one of the most popular breeds of dog. That's why you must select a breeder carefully; there are a large number of "puppy-mill" individuals on the market. Their owners too often spoil them into brats. These little dogs are excellent city or apartment dwellers, and their owners often carry them around in tote bags or backpacks. However, they do require some daily running-around-outdoors time.

Because they were bred to be water retrievers, what we call the "show cut" was originally designed to protect their joints and vital organs from the cold. Many owners now prefer to keep their pet's coats in a kennel cut—the same length all over. They need a lot of grooming and must be professionally clipped on a regular basis. They shed little, and what loose hair they do shed becomes matted into their coats without proper grooming.

Health problems may include cataracts, progressive retinal atrophy (PRA may lead to blindness), knee (patellar) luxation, hypoglycemia, and epilepsy. For more details about these ailments, see Appendix I.

# PORTUGUESE WATER DOG

**Size/Group:** Large/Working
**Breed History:** Unknown; have lived on boats with Portuguese fishermen for hundreds of years
**Height:** 17 to 23 inches
**Weight:** 35 to 60 pounds
**Life Expectancy:** 12 years
**Daily Exercise:** 1 hour
**Behavior Problems:** Chewing, jealousy, territoriality, barking, attention-demanding

These dogs are real water lovers who can be very useful in retrieving objects dropped from boats. They were once used to help fishermen catch fish that had escaped from the nets. They may become deaf when young because they spend so much time in the water.

"Porties" demand a lot of attention from their owners. With enough attention, they can be calm house pets. They are very playful and curious and investigate the world around them with their mouths. All dropped objects are fair game for these dogs. They love children and often indulge in guarding and herding behavior with them. They get along well with other dogs, although intact males, in particular, may be territorial. They can live happily in any quarters, but do need sufficient daily exercise wherever they live.

Their thick, long, wavy coats can be many colors—solid black, white, brown, and dark brown, and black or brown with white. They shed very little, but need a lot of brushing, combing, and professional clipping or scissoring.

Possible health concerns include progressive retinal atrophy (PRA can lead to blindness), hip dysplasia; and a glycogen storage disease. For more details about these health considerations, see Appendix I.

# PUG

**Size/Group:** Small/Toy
**Breed History:** Originally from China, brought to Holland in the 1500s; further developed in England
**Height:** 10 to 11 inches
**Weight:** 14 to 18 pounds
**Life Expectancy:** 13 years
**Daily Exercise:** 10 minutes
**Behavior Problems:** snoring and wheezing, stubbornness, house soiling

These very popular pets are childlike dogs that are fun-loving, clever, and not at all aggressive. They are excellent companions for all humans, from children to the elderly, although young toddlers may seem to be a threat to them. They are usually calm with other animals. Sturdy enough to play with children, they are also light enough to be carried around in a tote bag or in someone's arms. Because they love all people, they are terrible watchdogs.

They require very little exercise or living space and are very suitable for city or apartment life. They are easy to train using positive reinforcement. (They do not respond well to harsh training.) Because of their brachycephalic (pushed-in) faces, Pugs swallow a lot of air and therefore have stomach and intestinal gas with the predictable results.

Their short coats are all black, fawn, silver, or tan with black markings on the face and ears. They shed a lot and need to be groomed every day with a hound's glove. Their facial wrinkles must also be cleaned out daily. They do not drool.

Health considerations include excessive weight gain, easily injured eyes (because of their prominence), and dry eyes (eye drops help). For more particulars about these health problems, see Appendix I.

# PULI

**Size/Group:** Medium/Herding
**Breed History:** Similar to the
Tibetan terrier; brought to
Hungary by nomads from the
Orient around A.D. 1000
**Height:** 14 to 19 inches
**Weight:** 20 to 40 pounds
**Life Expectancy:** 12 years
**Daily Exercise:** 1 hour
**Behavior Problems:** Barking,
demanding, stubbornness,
assertiveness, guarding, indoor
restlessness, willful disobedi-
ence

This water-loving breed was probably used to hunt in the marshes in the past. In Hungary she is still used to guard flocks. Because she is hardworking and needs a lot of outdoor exercise, she is not particularly well suited for city or apartment life.

She is wary of strangers and other dogs, but is good with her family and with children with whom she has been raised. Because she is so headstrong and needs firm training and handling, the Puli is not a good pet for a first-time dog owner. She is a very good watchdog.

Her long, corded coat comes in white, black, or gray, and hardly ever sheds. However, it mats very easily and requires daily specialized grooming. Some owners clip the coat to cut back on grooming time. Both her rear end and her face need constant cleaning to remove waste and food that may become stuck in her abundant fur.

Health concerns may include von Willebrand's disease (a hemorrhagic disorder), cataracts, progressive retinal atrophy (PRA may lead to blindness), and hip dysplasia. For more information about these diseases, see Appendix I.

# REDBONE COONHOUND

**Size/Group:** Medium/Rare/Hound
**Breed History:** USA
**Height:** 23 to 27 inches
**Weight:** 55 to 75 pounds
**Life Expectancy:** 13 years
**Daily Exercise:** 1 hour
**Behavior Problems:** Destructiveness, excessive howling, stubbornness, dominance, some aggressiveness

With an ancestry dating back to the 1700s, this American-born breed was prized for his ability to tree raccoons and possums. With a highly developed sense of smell, the Redbone Coonhound is able to detect scents even underwater, whether he is in the water, on a boat, or on the shore. They have tremendous staying power and concentration, and can remain focused for hours.

Redbones are sweet and laidback, but bore easily and need to work, otherwise they can be very destructive. Redbones respond well to structured playtime or training. A combination of exercise and work, such as hiding objects and toys for him to seek out, does the trick.

They should be bathed on a regular basis, paying special attention to the ears, to avoid hound odor and inner-ear infections. Their coats are smooth, short, and reddish-brown.

This breed is prone to allergies, thyroid conditions, and ear infections. See Appendix I for more information on these health problems.

# RHODESIAN RIDGEBACK

**Size/Group:** Large/Hound
**Breed History:** Developed by the Boers in the late 1800s, standardized in 1922
**Height:** 24 to 27 inches
**Weight:** 65 to 85 pounds
**Life Expectancy:** 12 years
**Daily Exercise:** 1 hour
**Behavior Problems:** house soiling, aggression, dominance, challenging people in family

This powerful dog was developed as a hunting and guard dog for herds and homes, and is a mix of many European breeds. She has a lot of energy and stamina. Her name stems from the backward-growing ridge of hair on her spine. Known for tracking African lions and holding them at bay for hunters, these dogs are intelligent, sturdy, and confident enough to control large game. They are excellent watch-dogs, but tend to roam and chase mindlessly and require strong fencing to remain safe. They can be dangerous with small animals unless they have been raised with them.

Ridgebacks are generally one-person dogs, but once an owner has gained her respect and remains in control, the dog will adapt quickly. However, these dogs still have an independent streak that may cause them to challenge an owner from time to time. They are not especially good obedience students and become bored easily. They are good with children and are always ready to play. Because they are so large, adult supervision is a must with small children.

Their short, thick coats are either red or apricot, and they shed some. Brushing once a week with a stiff brush or currycomb is enough to keep their coats in good shape.

Health considerations include cataracts, deafness, hypothyroidism, cancer, hip and elbow dysplasia, and a tubelike cyst in the spinal cord (dermoid sinus). For more specifics about these health concerns, see Appendix I.

# ROTTWEILER

**Size/Group:** Large/Working
**Breed History:** Bred in Rottweil, Germany, thought to be descended from the Italian Mastiff
**Height:** 26 inches
**Weight:** 85 to 100 pounds
**Life Expectancy:** 9 years
**Daily Exercise:** 35 minutes
**Behavior Problems:** Biting; wariness of strangers; food stealing; guarding food, places, and objects; willful disobedience; aggression; snoring; excessive barking

An ancient breed, used as a herd dog in the Middle Ages, they were almost extinct in the 1800s before becoming popular again in the early 1900s. Very powerful and strong, the "Rottie" needs early socialization and early strict obedience training. This is not an appropriate breed for a first-time dog owner. Nor is it suitable for city or apartment living. It is very important to choose a breeder wisely in order to get a dog with an even temper, because the recent popularity of this breed has led to some pretty poor specimens on the market.

Originally bred to haul loads and to guard livestock and drive them to market, this is a calm, courageous dog that is very sure of himself. His droving instinct is so strong that he may try to herd people and other animals. Very small children may be knocked over by the dog's nudging, and although most Rotties are good with children, they should be supervised. Games that involve dominance, such as tug-of-war, should be avoided because they might not understand that it's a game. They make excellent watchdogs. Although they can live outdoors, they really do not tolerate heat well, so are really better off in the house.

Their short coats are all black or black with tan markings. They shed a lot, but require brushing only once a week to get rid of dead hair.

Health concerns include a growth disorder of the joints (osteochondritis dissecans, OCD), hip and elbow dysplasia, progressive retinal atrophy (PRA can lead to blindness), other retinal problems, heart defects, bloat, cancer, and hypothyroidism. For more details about these problems, see Appendix I.

# SAINT BERNARD (Rough and Smooth)

**Size/Group:** Giant/Working
**Breed History:** Brought to a monastery in Saint Bernard Pass in the Swiss Alps in the mid-16th century; eventually, used to find lost travelers
**Height:** 25 to 30 inches
**Weight:** 110 to 118 pounds
**Life Expectancy:** 7 years
**Daily Exercise:** 35 minutes
**Behavior Problems:** Food stealing, barking, willful disobedience, dominance (especially true of puppy-mill individuals)

Rough

Smooth

These strong, massive dogs are calm and make fine pets as long as they have enough room and daily exercise. They are definitely unsuited for city or apartment life. They have very loud barks, and their protection level is very high. They will bark at the slightest noise or intrusion and need to be discouraged from barking excessively. If they are raised with children, most are good with them. You must research the bloodlines of any animal you are interested in to be sure she is from a "child-friendly" family, and also that she has been bred from healthy stock. Because of their popularity, there are a number of poorly bred individuals out there. Some puppy-mill dogs are aggressive. Others are overtimid and fearful and develop phobias and fear-biting.

The Saint Bernard's big, hanging jowls result in copious drooling. Some lines have drier mouths and tighter lips than others. They prefer cold weather, and suffer in the heat without a wading pool or air-conditioning.

They do not automatically perform rescue operations; they learn this skill as puppies if they socialize with packs of experienced adult dogs. They get along well with other animals they have been raised with.

Both rough (longhaired) and smooth-haired dogs have coats that are either red with white or black with white. The longhairs shed a lot and need to be brushed about three times a week. Smooth, or short-hairs, shed some and need brushing less often.

Hip dysplasia is a major concern in these dogs so, again, it is important to choose an individual with care. See Appendix I for more information.

# SALUKI

**Size/Group:** Large/Hound
**Breed History:** An ancient breed from Iran, thought to be a cross between Egyptian and Asian Greyhounds. Named for an ancient Arab city, Salug
**Height:** 22 to 28 inches
**Weight:** 45 to 65 pounds
**Life Expectancy:** 13 years
**Daily Exercise:** 45 minutes
**Behavior Problems:** House soiling, roaming, irritable snapping, phobias, stubbornness, undemonstrativeness

The royal dog of Egypt, the Saluki hunts gazelle in her native land. This breed needs a lot of space, and is not well suited to city or apartment life unless she gets several daily walks, and is sometimes taken to the country to run. She is an excellent watchdog and has a keen sense of hearing. She thrives in hot weather and does not require much drinking water.

She is very clean and is a calm companion pet. Friendly with older children who have been taught to respect her, she may snap at anyone (child or adult) who teases or annoys her. She gets along well with other dogs, but she may consider smaller pets as prey. Although she is headstrong, she is affectionate and sensitive to her owner's wishes and responds well to patient training.

Her silky, short coat comes in all colors except solid black, and it sheds little. Her tail and ears should be brushed, and the rest of her body should be groomed with a hound glove about twice a week.

Health concerns may include heart defects, tumors, and hypothyroidism. For more about these health issues, see Appendix I.

# SAMOYED

**Size/Group:** Large/Working
**Breed History:** An ancient breed, has lived in Siberia for centuries; brought to England in 1889 by explorer, Robert Scott
**Height:** 19 to 24 inches
**Weight:** 40 to 75 pounds
**Life Expectancy:** 12 years
**Daily Exercise:** 45 minutes
**Behavior Problems:** Roaming, house soiling, barking, restlessness and mischievous destructiveness if not exercised and left alone too long, digging

Originally developed to pull sleds, this is a loyal, obedient, gentle, good-natured, sociable, and calm dog. When her mouth is closed, she appears to be smiling—right in tune with her loving personality. Because she is used to working in a team, a single dog kept as a pet may become extremely attached to her owner. She takes well to patient training and will guard, hunt, herd, be a watchdog (she is very vocal), or simply a loving companion pet.

Because of her thick coat she can withstand cold weather, and she is also very active. However, she seems to be able to live happily in a city apartment as long as she receives enough loving attention and plenty of daily exercise, especially when the weather is very cold. She especially loves snow and dislikes hot weather.

She is very beautiful, with a long, straight all-white coat. She sheds some and should be brushed at least twice a week and have an occasional bath.

Health concerns include arthritis, progressive retinal atrophy (PRA may lead to blindness), cataracts, diabetes, hypothyroidism, and hip dysplasia. For more information about these illnesses, see Appendix I.

# SCHIPPERKE

**Size/Group:** Small/Non-Sporting
**Breed History:** Originally bred by a canal boat captain in Flanders; was first shown in the late 19th century
**Height:** 10 to 13 inches
**Weight:** 12 to 18 pounds
**Life Expectancy:** Up to 15 years
**Daily Exercise:** 45 minutes
**Behavior Problems:** House soiling, stealing and guarding objects and food

This sturdy, short-legged little dog was originally bred to be a shoemaker's and bargeman's dog and was used to guard and hunt. He was used extensively as a ratter on the barges in Belgium. He is an excellent swimmer, and is still a tenacious watchdog.

The Schipperke is virtually fearless and very inquisitive, so an owner needs to take care to keep him from harm because of his own devil-may-care attitude toward cars, heights, and unsafe places. He is very responsive to his family and is excellent with friendly children to whom he has been introduced early in his life. However, he is wary of strangers.

He is very trainable, excels in obedience, and can live almost anywhere. However, he requires a lot of daily exercise and can do well in an urban setting only as long as he is walked enough and has an opportunity to run in the country from time to time.

His thick, short coat is always solid black. He is an average shedder and requires brushing about only twice a week, more during the shedding season.

Health concerns include epilepsy, cataracts, progressive retinal atrophy (PRA can lead to blindness), hypothyroidism, entropion (eyelids that turn inward, irritating the eyeballs), and disintegration of the hip joint (Legg-Calvé-Perthes). For more details about these conditions, see Appendix I.

# SCHNAUZER, GIANT

**Size/Group:** Large/Working
**Breed History:** Bavaria, date of origin unknown; possibly some Great Dane and Bouvier mixed in
**Height:** 24 to 28 inches
**Weight:** 70 to 90 pounds
**Life Expectancy:** 11 years
**Daily Exercise:** 45 minutes
**Behavior Problems:** Indoor restlessness, dominance challenges to owner, stubbornness, aggression toward other dogs

This powerful herding dog was developed to get cattle to market. He requires a lot of daily exercise and enjoys a good run as often as possible. He is not well suited for city or apartment life unless there is a large yard and a family member who is able to exercise him daily. His indoor energy level is high, and he makes a great watchdog.

He is calm, affectionate, bright, and easily trained. The giant Schnauzer gets along well with children, although he may be overprotective of his "own" family. He will accept other dogs but will usually dominate them. He must be obedience-trained early in life in order to respect his owner as pack leader.

His thick, wiry coat is short and comes in all black or salt-and-pepper. He sheds very little, but should be brushed at least three times a week. His undercoat should be professionally stripped in the spring.

Health considerations include glaucoma; progressive retinal atrophy (PRA), which may lead to blindness; epilepsy; heart defects; hip dysplasia; and osteochondritis dissecans (OCD), which is a growth disorder of the joints. For more specifics about these health problems, see Appendix I.

# SCHNAUZER, MINIATURE

**Size/Group:** Small/Terrier
**Breed History:** Descended
from ancient terriers, mixed with
Affenpinscher
**Height:** 12 to 14 inches
**Weight:** 13 to 17 pounds
**Life Expectancy:** 14 years
**Daily Exercise:** 35 minutes
**Behavior Problems:** Stealing
and guarding food, excessive
barking, dominance challenges,
stubbornness

Because this little dog is so popular, it is very important to find an experienced breeder and to watch out for puppy-mill bred individuals.

The Miniature Schnauzer is good with children she has been raised with and enjoys other dogs. She was originally bred to guard the stable or yard from vermin and strangers. She is a fierce mouser and can get herself into a tight spot very easily.

She is tireless and will play endlessly. Both outdoors and in the house the miniature Schnauzer wants to be in on everything and becomes sulky if she is left out. She will take all the love and attention she can possibly get, and, with positive reinforcement, is an easily trained and obedient dog.

She is very well suited to city and/or apartment life, and is calm and happy as long as she gets enough exercise. Her urge to bark continuously must be curtailed early in life.

Her short, wiry coat comes in solid black, black and silver, or salt and pepper, sometimes with tan shading. She hardly sheds at all, but should have a weekly brushing and be clipped or hand-stripped professionally every couple of months.

Health concerns include liver disorders, epilepsy, a hemorrhagic disorder (von Willebrand's disease), pancreatitis, hypothyroidism, and juvenile cataracts. For more particulars about these problems, see Appendix I.

# SCHNAUZER, STANDARD

**Size/Group:** Medium/Working
**Breed History:** Bavaria, date unknown; name Schnauzer comes from the German word for "snout," *schnauze*
**Height:** 17 to 20 inches
**Weight:** 30 to 50 pounds
**Life Expectancy:** 12 years
**Daily Exercise:** 1 hour
**Behavior Problems:** Excessive protective behavior—guarding of food, places, people, and objects, dominance challenges

Bred as a guard dog and rat catcher, he has worked throughout history as a guard dog, as an assistant to police and armies, and as a guardian of livestock. He is also a very lively, affectionate, devoted, and bold pet. He is playful with and tolerant of children and throws himself into every situation with great enthusiasm. The standard Schnauzer is an excellent watchdog and can be kept in the city or an apartment as long as he gets enough daily exercise.

He should be firmly obedience-trained early in life. He tends to be highly inquisitive and to dart out quickly, so owners or handlers must take care that he is on lead anywhere near traffic.

His wiry, short coat comes in solid black or salt-and-pepper, and hardly sheds at all. He should be brushed about three times a week, and requires professional hand-stripping and trimming on a regular basis.

Health concerns include cataracts, cancer, hip dysplasia, and hypothyroidism. For more information about these health problems, see Appendix I.

# SCOTTISH DEERHOUND

**Size/Group:** Extra Large/Hound
**Breed History:** No known origins; believed to be related to the Irish Wolfhound, Borzoi, Great Dane, and other large breeds
**Height:** 28 to 32 inches
**Weight:** 80 to 110 pounds
**Life Expectancy:** 11 years
**Daily Exercise:** 45 minutes
**Behavior Problems:** Possible timidity, stubbornness, resistance to training

This huge dog requires a great deal of supervised exercise and a lot of space. She should never be let out loose near traffic. She was originally bred to hunt and capture deer and coyotes in huge open areas.

She is not at all territorial and will welcome anyone, intruders included. She is very good with children with whom she has been socialized, but toddlers can easily be knocked down inadvertently. The Deerhound is gentle with other animals in the family, but may very well decide that a neighborhood cat is easy prey. She should have early socialization or she may become easily frightened.

Her medium-length wiry coat can be tan, red, brindle, gray, or blue gray, sheds little, and needs brushing and combing about once a week.

Health problems may include bloat, a growth disorder of the joints (osteochondritis dissecans, OCD), cardiomyopathy, and osteosarcoma (a tumor on a bone). For more specifics about these health issues, see Appendix I.

# SCOTTISH TERRIER

**Size/Group:** Small/Terrier
**Breed History:** Uncertain, thought to be originally from Aberdeen, Scotland, in 1700 but rebred in 1800 to become the dog it is today
**Height:** 10 to 11 inches
**Weight:** 19 to 23 pounds
**Life Expectancy:** 13 years
**Daily Exercise:** 35 minutes
**Behavior Problems:** House soiling, obstinacy, escaping, aggression, dominance, excessive barking

This little dog was made famous when FDR was president and owned a "Scottie" named Fala. Originally a working terrier that hunted vermin such as foxes and badgers, rabbits and otters with a vengeance, he is fearless and hardy and can live in any kind of terrain and weather. He is extremely loyal to his master, but reserved with people he doesn't know. He is good with children, but not especially fond of toddlers.

Because of his independent and obstinate nature, housebreaking and other training can be difficult. He loves to be busy, and adding another pet may help keep him occupied. However, if you plan to do this, your Scottie must be socialized to other pets early in life. He is well suited to city or apartment life, but to siphon off some of his excess energy, long daily walks are a good idea. If he is left outside, regular fence checks are needed.

His medium-length wiry coat comes in solid black, brindle, or wheaten, and it hardly ever sheds. He should be brushed three times a week and needs professional clipping or stripping every three to four months.

Health concerns are minimal and consist of hypothyroidism and lymphoma. Prospective owners should also have their dogs checked for von Willebrand's disease (a hemorrhagic disorder). For more information about these ailments, see Appendix I.

# SEALYHAM TERRIER

**Size/Group:** Small/Terrier
**Breed History:** Developed in the mid-19th century by crossing many breeds: hounds, Basset of Flanders, Dandie Dinmont, Corgi, West Highland and wirehaired terriers
**Height:** 10 to 12 inches
**Weight:** 18 to 24 pounds
**Life Expectancy:** 14 years
**Daily Exercise:** 20 minutes
**Behavior Problems:** Guarding, dominance, aggression, resistance to training, digging

Very loyal to her family, the Sealyham is suspicious of strangers and makes a very good watchdog. She is wary of both people and animals she doesn't know. She gets along with older children who have been taught to respect her, and will tolerate other pets when socialized with them early in life. Originally bred as a vermin hunter, she chases rabbits and squirrels and will dig assiduously to capture a mole or gopher. However, she is an excellent city or apartment pet and is a good watchdog.

She loves exercise and romping and can be stubborn, so it is important for an owner to assert his leadership early on.

Her medium-length white (or white with markings) coat sheds very little, and she needs home grooming about three times a week. However, she must be professionally clipped or stripped frequently.

Health concerns include cataracts, progressive retinal atrophy (PRA can lead to blindness), glaucoma, lens luxation, spinal problems, heart defects, and deafness. For more details about these problems, see Appendix I.

# SHAR-PEI (Chinese Fighting Dog)

**Size/Group:** Medium/Non-Sporting
**Breed History:** Uncertain, may be related to the Chow Chow, because of its purple tongue
**Height:** 18 to 20 inches
**Weight:** 35 to 55 pounds
**Life Expectancy:** 11 years
**Daily Exercise:** 45 minutes
**Behavior Problems:** Stubbornness, dominance, aggression, resistance to training, territoriality, barking

A strong, agile dog, the Shar-Pei was used to hunt boar and large game in China, and as a guard dog—she is a fearless dog. She now is bred as a companion pet. Her soft skin falls in folds, giving her a falsely sad look. She is very clean, and is calm, loyal, and loves to play with young children. She is an excellent watchdog and a fine family pet.

The Shar-Pei requires considerable exercise and will thrive in an outdoor yard. Nevertheless, she will adjust well to apartment living provided that she receives regular exercise. She is very sensitive to heat, however, and should not be left outdoors without access to shade and should not be overexercised.

Her short, rough coat comes in all solid colors and sheds some. She should be brushed about twice a week.

Health concerns may include Shar-Pei fever, in which her joints are inflamed and swollen (this is a life-threatening disease); entropion (eyelids turned inward, causing irritation to the eyeballs); ear problems; skin infections (due to her many skin folds); problems in hot weather; and hypothyroidism. For more information about these health considerations, see Appendix I.

# SHETLAND SHEEPDOG

**Size/Group:** Small/Herding
**Breed History:** Developed in the late 17th century in Shetland, Scotland; probably a mix between a Collie and an extinct small breed called a Yakkin
**Height:** 13 to 16 inches
**Weight:** 14 to 18 pounds
**Life Expectancy:** 12 years
**Daily Exercise:** 30 minutes
**Behavior Problems:** Fear-biting; irritable snapping; excessive, endless barking; food stealing; timidity; phobias and touch shyness

Originally bred to herd sheep, hogs, and goats, she is now primarily a companion pet and a good watchdog. The "Sheltie" is very responsive to her owners and loves to play with children. She is an excellent urban or apartment dog as long as she gets enough daily exercise and the opportunity to run in the country now and then. She is very loyal and obedient and barely requires any training in order to behave. She watches her owner's face and seems to be able to "read" his thoughts. However, she does have an independent streak and needs to be taught early on who the pack leader is.

When she is bored or excited, she may bark excessively, a trait that must be controlled, especially in an urban or apartment setting.

Her long, silky coat has the same markings as a collie and sheds a great deal. A weekly brushing is needed, with more frequent grooming during the shedding season.

This little dog has many potential health problems, including cataracts, progressive retinal atrophy (PRA may lead to blindness), malformation of the optic nerve (collie eye anomaly), hip dysplasia, patellar (knee) luxation, a heart anomaly (patent ductus arteriosus, PDA), epilepsy, hypothyroidism, a hemorrhagic disorder (von Willebrand's disease), and dermatomyositis (inflammation of the skin). For more details about these health problems, see Appendix I.

# SHIBA INU

**Size/Group:** Small/Non-Sporting
**Breed History:** An ancient breed, brought to Japan from China 2,000 years ago; probably a mix of Chow Chow and Kyushu (an ancient Japanese breed)
**Height:** 14 to 16 inches
**Weight:** 18 to 25 pounds
**Life Expectancy:** 12 years
**Daily Exercise:** 30 minutes
**Behavior Problems:** Independence, dominance, wariness of strangers, roaming, aggression, resists training

The most common breed of dog in Japan, the Shiba Inu is very independent and dominant and should be obedience-trained early and have continuous reinforcement. He needs a well-fenced yard or a good leash, or he will be off and running.

He is good with children he has been raised with. Although he is sometimes used for hunting small game by sight and scent, he is primarily a companion pet. He is very territorial and makes an excellent guard and watchdog. Spirited and bold, he likes all weather and enjoys rolling in snow or taking long walks in the woods.

His short, thick coat is soft and sheds a little. He should be brushed about once a week, more often in the spring shedding season. He comes in solid red, black, sesame, black with tan markings, and sesame with white markings.

Health concerns include patellar (knee) luxation, hip dysplasia, and hypothyroidism. For more information about these health problems, see Appendix I.

# SHIH TZU

**Size/Group:** Tiny/Toy
**Breed History:** Developed in Peking; brought to England in 1930
**Height:** 9 to 11 inches
**Weight:** 10 to 16 pounds
**Life Expectancy:** 13 years
**Daily Exercise:** 10 minutes
**Behavior Problems:** Stubbornness; irritable snapping; touch shyness, especially in the heat; house soiling

Because of this dog's popularity, there are a number of puppy-mill individuals on the market, and they tend to be very aggressive with both other dogs and people. So be sure to choose carefully from a reliable breeder.

This popular little dog is characterized by her flowing mane of hair, hence her name, which means "lion." She is the most common pet dog in Japan. Bred to be a companion pet, she fulfills her role very well, loves people, and can be taught to do tricks. Plucky and alert, she is good with gentle children and is often used as a therapy dog because she is equally endearing to the elderly and lonely. As a matter of fact, she loves almost everything about life.

Her long, thick coat comes in all colors and sheds minimally with regular combing and brushing. Because of her thick coat she particularly dislikes hot weather and should be protected from it as much as possible. She is a perfect city and apartment dweller.

Health concerns may include autoimmune hemolytic anemia, degeneration of the kidneys (renal cortical hypoplasia), and a hemorrhagic disorder called von Willebrand's disease. For more details about these disorders, see Appendix I.

# SIBERIAN HUSKY

**Size/Group:** Medium/Working
**Breed History:** Originally from Siberia; brought to Alaska in the early 1900s.
**Height:** 20 to 24 inches
**Weight:** 35 to 60 pounds
**Life Expectancy:** 11 years
**Daily Exercise:** 1 hour
**Behavior Problems:** Stubbornness and tendency toward boredom, destructiveness when left alone, roaming, playful disobedience, howling, jumping on people, resistance to training

This very social dog wants to interact with a pack, either with people or other dogs. If he lives outdoors (which he can), he should have another dog for a companion and have ample opportunity to play with his people. The Husky is affectionate and makes good company. He is a very good pet for active, outdoorsy people, and will enjoy pulling a child in a wagon or on a sled. Because of his light weight, he can run fast and is often used in Canada and the northern United States for sled races. He is not very territorial or protective. Training is important, but it must be done with praise, patience, and rewards.

His medium-length, thick coat comes in all colors and sheds a lot. He needs to be brushed at least twice a week, and combed during the spring shedding season.

Health problems may include cataracts, corneal dystrophy (white patches on the eye surface), glaucoma, progressive retinal atrophy (PRA can lead to blindness), and hip dysplasia. For more information about these health concerns, see Appendix I.

# SILKY TERRIER

**Size/Group:** Tiny/Toy
**Breed History:** Originated in Australia, a cross between the Skye, Cairn, and Yorkshire Terriers; cousin of the Australian Terrier
**Height:** 9 to 10 inches
**Weight:** 8 to 10 pounds
**Life Expectancy:** 14 years
**Daily Exercise:** 10 minutes
**Behavior Problems:** House soiling, excessive barking, irritable snapping, stubbornness, dominance, resistance to training

Also known as the Sidney terrier, this tiny dog was originally used to kill mice, rats, and snakes on poultry farms. He is now a companion dog and thrives on attention. He is more active than many other toy breeds and needs regular exercise. He has seemingly endless energy for attention and action. He is extremely bright and demanding, and sometimes aggressive. He would really like to run the household. He is very vocal and makes a moderately good watchdog. He is highly suitable for city or apartment life. He is also good with children to whom he has been exposed early in his life.

His long, straight, silky coat is blue with tan markings, hardly ever sheds, but requires constant care. He needs damp brushing at least five times a week and an occasional professional trimming.

Health concerns include tracheal collapse, epilepsy, patellar (knee) luxation, and disintegration of the hip joint (Legg-Calvé-Perthes). For more details about these health considerations, see Appendix I.

# SKYE TERRIER

**Size/Group:** Small/Terrier
**Breed History:** The result of a shipwreck of a Spanish ship off the Isle of Skye in the Scottish Hebrides, surviving Maltese were mated with local terriers
**Height:** 9 to 10 inches
**Weight:** 20 to 30 pounds
**Life Expectancy:** 13 years
**Daily Exercise:** 20 minutes
**Behavior Problems:** Irritable snapping, overprotectiveness, picky eating, timidity and dominance combined lead to a "shy-sharp" personality, aggression, territoriality

Boss, the well-loved pet of Queen Victoria in the 1800s, was the first famous Skye. This breed originated at least three hundred years earlier, making it one of the oldest of terrier breeds. Skyes were developed to fight tough underground vermin and can get into difficulty if they follow a scent onto a busy highway or somewhere far from home. They need a secure fence or a strong leash to remain safe. They can easily break out of the best cages.

These dogs are especially tuned in to their owner's moods and are protective and loyal pets. However, they do require a patient and experienced owner because of the determination and fire still in them. They are fine with older, well-behaved children, but are not fond of other animals. They really want to be "top dog." But they can be trained not to harass cats. Smaller animals such as hamsters and gerbils must be kept out of reach.

Their long, straight coats come in various colors: black, blue, gray and silver gray, cream, and tan, often with markings on the face. They shed some and require frequent (four times a week) brushing and combing.

Health considerations include hypothyroidism, premature closing of the leg bones, and anal problems. For more particulars about these, see Appendix I.

# SOFT-COATED WHEATEN TERRIER

**Size/Group:** Medium/Terrier
**Breed History:** Popular in Ireland for hundreds of years; only recently introduced in the U.S.
**Height:** 17 to 19 inches
**Weight:** 20 to 40 pounds
**Life Expectancy:** 13 years
**Daily Exercise:** 35 minutes
**Behavior Problems:** Dominance, possible aggression, jumping up on visitors, house soiling, resistance to training, separation anxiety

In Ireland this dog has many roles. She is used for defense and guarding, leading flocks of animals, and hunting. In this country she is primarily a companion pet, suitable for city or apartment living as long as she gets enough daily exercise. Agility or obedience training (or both) also help.

Active, easygoing, and full of fun and high spirits, a Wheaten will follow people and animals anywhere if she is not fenced in. She almost never tires and is impervious to bad weather. She thrives on companionship (both human and animal) and should not be left alone for long.

Her medium-length, soft coat is always tan (or wheaten), and she hardly sheds at all. However, she does require quite a bit of regular grooming. She should be combed at least three times a week and professionally trimmed when necessary. Her soft, wavy coat tends to collect things in it, such as leaves, mud, snow, or burrs and must be checked over every time she comes indoors.

Health concerns include arthritis, hip dysplasia, cataracts, progressive retinal atrophy (PRA can lead to blindness), degeneration of the kidneys (renal cortical hypoplasia), and a hemorrhagic disorder known as von Willebrand's disease. For more specifics about these conditions, see Appendix I.

# SPINONE ITALIANO

**Size/Group:** Large/Sporting
**Breed History:** An ancient breed from Italy
**Height:** 22 to 27 inches
**Weight:** 60 to 85 pounds
**Life Expectancy:** 13 years
**Daily Exercise:** 45 minutes
**Behavior Problems:** Roaming, barking, stubbornness, resistance to training

This versatile, hearty dog can live anywhere as long as he is well fenced in and has a lot of company. Highly sociable, he likes to be within sight of his family as much as possible. He is excellent with children. He loves to travel in the car with his family. All in all, he is a very good family pet. He is an average watchdog and will bark at strangers.

Affectionate and patient, he is also courageous, robust, tireless, and obedient. When he is not being simply a companion pet, he can also be a retriever, hunting dog, pointer, and bird dog. His sense of smell is very keen. His long, thick coat provides excellent protection against the elements, and he can hunt in even the worst weather without complaint. Added to this, his leathery, oily skin means he can hunt in water without getting sick.

This long, thick coat comes in white, white with apricot, chestnut roan, and white with other markings, and it sheds little. He should be brushed about twice a week and may need to be stripped occasionally for neatness.

Health concerns are few: bloat and hip dysplasia are generally his only complaints. For more specifics about these disorders, see Appendix I.

# STAFFORDSHIRE BULL TERRIER

**Size/Group:** Medium/Terrier
**Breed History:** Developed in Staffordshire, England, in the 19th century; cross between a Bulldog and various terriers
**Height:** 14 to 16 inches
**Weight:** 24 to 38 pounds
**Life Expectancy:** 12 years
**Daily Exercise:** 45 minutes
**Behavior Problems:** House soiling, indoor restlessness, aggression, possibly dangerous to visitors if untrained, dominance challenges to submissive people

This dog was originally bred for dogfighting and bullbaiting and retains his predatory nature. Therefore, he must be under careful control around other dogs, small animals, and children whom he doesn't know.

Greatly devoted to his family and master, the Staffordshire must be socialized and obedience trained early in life. Because of his high energy level, he requires regular daily exercise in order to work off steam.

His short, thick, smooth coat comes in many colors: red, beige, black, blue, brindle, apricot, fawn, gold, or any of these colors with white markings, usually on the chest. He sheds little, except during the spring shedding season, and should be brushed with a currycomb about once a week.

Health concerns include cataracts, entropion (inturned eyelids that can irritate the eyeball), and hip dysplasia. For more information about these issues, see Appendix I.

# SUSSEX SPANIEL

**Size/Group:** Small/Sporting
**Breed History:** Developed in the early 19th century in Sussex, England
**Height:** 15 to 16 inches
**Weight:** 35 to 45 pounds
**Life Expectancy:** 12 years
**Daily Exercise:** 35 minutes
**Behavior Problems:** House soiling, howling, occasional snapping if annoyed, aloofness with strangers, stubbornness

Not very well known in this country, the Sussex was bred to hunt, track, flush, and retrieve small game. While hunting, she barks all the time. She is also a good companion pet and enjoys sleeping by her owner's feet equally as much as playing or walking in the woods. She is not happy without her people.

Very cheerful and friendly with people she knows, she likes children, especially when raised with them. She will often walk with her front legs and slide her rear end on the ground like a seal. She is wary of strangers. The Sussex is usually easily trained (although she may be quietly stubborn). She needs early socialization and gentle obedience training; harsh handling will turn her off. She can be friendly with other animals, but likes to be the boss. She is intelligent but slow, steady, and deliberate in her actions. She is a good watchdog, sounding an alarm if a stranger approaches.

Her medium-length wavy coat is always solid brown and sheds some. She should be brushed about twice a week, and needs an occasional bath and nail clipping.

Health considerations include hypothyroidism, autoimmune diseases, heart defects, and hip dysplasia. She gains weight easily, so her diet should be carefully watched. For more details about these health issues, see Appendix I.

# TIBETAN MASTIFF

**Size/Group:** Extra Large/ Working
**Breed History:** Descendants of the famous Tibetan dogs, which were used as guard dogs and protectors of flocks; perfected in England
**Height:** 24 to 29 inches
**Weight:** 140 to 200 pounds
**Life Expectancy:** 13 years
**Daily Exercise:** 30 minutes
**Behavior Problems:** Excessive barking, especially at night, aloofness, extreme protectiveness and territoriality, stubbornness

Originally bred to be a sheepdog, the Tibetan Mastiff can be a ferocious enemy of wolves or leopards. He is also used to guard entire villages and homes that are isolated in the countryside. If he is going to be living in a home, he needs a large well-fenced yard at the very least, and is best with a lot of open space. He must be carefully monitored with visitors, no matter how many previous times they have been introduced. Drop-ins are not advised. He is not suitable for urban or apartment dwelling. If he lives in small quarters, he will resort to overguarding behavior, constant barking, or both.

Those that are bred in England are close to their masters and obedient. Because he is so intelligent, protective, and stubborn, the Tibetan Mastiff must have early socialization and training to live in a household. He is very good with his own children, but his protective instincts may be a problem with playmates—early socialization and training may help alleviate this problem.

His heavy, thick, long coat comes in all black, black with gold or tan markings, brown, gold, red brindle, or blue with tan markings. He sheds a lot and should be brushed at least three times a week.

Health concerns include hypothyroidism; hip dysplasia; and painful, swollen joints and bones (HOD, hypertrophic osteodystrophy). For more details about these conditions, see Appendix I.

# TIBETAN SPANIEL

**Size/Group:** Tiny/Non-Sporting
**Breed History:** Tibet; thought to be cross between the Pug, Pekingese, and a Japanese Chin
**Height:** 9 to 10 inches
**Weight:** 9 to 15 pounds
**Life Expectancy:** 13 years
**Daily Exercise:** 45 minutes
**Behavior Problems:** Aloofness with strangers, extreme independence, snorting in the heat

This independent little dog needs strict obedience training and a lot of daily exercise. Originally used as an "alarm dog," she alerted larger guard dogs to the approach of strangers. She is a good watchdog. In the house, she will jump up onto the arms and backs of furniture in order to get a better view out the window, and will sound an alert at the approach of anyone.

She is lively, lovable, and affectionate to her family, but wary of strangers. She is good with gentle children.

Her medium-length, silky smooth coat comes in all colors, and sheds some. However, during the spring shed she loses her entire coat, leaving a trail of wisps of soft hair. At other times she should be misted with water and brushed with a pin brush about three times a week.

Because of her slightly foreshortened muzzle, she cannot tolerate extreme heat well and often snorts in an effort to get enough air. Otherwise, she is a pretty sturdy little dog, although she is prone to progressive retinal atrophy (PRA may lead to blindness), abnormally small eyes (microphthalmia), patellar (knee) luxation, congenital liver malformation (liver shunt), and disintegration of the hip joint (Legg-Calvé-Perthes). For more specifics about these health problems, see Appendix I.

# TIBETAN TERRIER

**Size/Group:** Medium/Non-Sporting
**Breed History:** An ancient breed, forebear of all other Tibetan breeds
**Height:** 14 to 17 inches
**Weight:** 18 to 30 pounds
**Life Expectancy:** 13 years
**Daily Exercise:** 35 minutes
**Behavior Problems:** Stealing and guarding food and objects, dominance challenges, house soiling, touch shyness, wariness of strangers

The Tibetan terrier is definitely not a terrier, but was lumped in with all small breeds hundreds of years ago, when small dogs were all called terriers. He is more spaniel-like, with a trace of a small Mastiff.

Originally used to herd and guard flocks, he is now primarily an affectionate and lively companion pet. He has his nose into everything and is playful and active. He can live well in an urban setting, but does enjoy a good run in the country as often as possible. He is good with well-mannered children. Although he is not overly territorial, his loud, deep bark makes him an excellent watchdog.

His long, wavy coat comes in all colors except brown and sheds into itself, and he requires grooming at least three times a week to prevent matting. During his teenage months, he sheds a lot.

Health concerns include progressive retinal atrophy (PRA may lead to blindness), cataracts, lens luxation, hypothyroidism, hip dysplasia, patellar (knee) luxation, and a hemorrhagic disorder called von Willebrand's disease. For more details about these health problems, see Appendix I.

## TOSA (Tosa Inu, Tosa Ken, Japanese Fighting Dog)

**Size/Group:** Extra Large/ Working
**Breed History:** Developed in the late 19th and early 20th centuries, a cross between a local Japanese breed (the Kochi), the Bulldog, the Bull Terrier, the Great Dane, and the Saint Bernard
**Height:** 24 inches
**Weight:** 83 pounds or more
**Life Expectancy:** 12 years
**Daily Exercise:** 1 hour
**Behavior Problems:** Aggression, dominance, wariness of strangers

Bred to be a fighting breed, the Tosa is now used as a watchdog and bodyguard. Although he is pugnacious, aggressive, and relentless in a fight, he can be trained to be a good, gentle, and loving family dog. However, he must be under strict control around strangers. Because of his enormous strength and massive build, he must have early, strict obedience training and a lot of daily exercise. He is not at all a suitable pet for an inexperienced owner. The breed is banned as a pet in the United Kingdom because of his aggressive nature. He, naturally, makes a great watchdog.

His short, thick coat comes in many colors: red, fawn, brown, black, brindle, and multicolored (often with white markings). He sheds a fair amount and should be groomed three times a week.

May suffer from bloat (gastric disorder) and hip dysplasia. See Appendix I for more details.

# TREEING WALKER COONHOUND

**Size/Group:** Medium/Rare/ Hound
**Breed History:** Dating back to colonial times, this breed is one of the most popular hunting dogs in the U.S.
**Height:** 23 to 25 inches
**Weight:** 50 to 60 pounds
**Life Expectancy:** 12 years
**Daily Exercise:** 1 hour
**Behavior Problems:** Destructiveness, excessive howling, stubbornness, dominance, some aggression

Treeing Walker Coonhounds are loving, affectionate dogs, but prefer to be outdoors and require a lot of exercise. Eschewing the life of a pampered lapdog, this breed has a one-track mind, and always wants to be working in the great outdoors. Courageous and untiring, they follow commands well.

Their coat is short and dense, and simple bathing and brushing is all that's required for this hardy breed. Special attention should be paid to the pendulous ears.

Health concerns include bloat and ear infections. See Appendix I for these health issues.

# VIZSLA

**Size/Group:** Medium/Sporting
**Breed History:** Hungary; may be a cross between two ancient breeds, the Turkish Yellow Dog and the the Transylvanian Hound, with some Pointer recently added
**Height:** 22 to 24 inches
**Weight:** 48 to 66 pounds
**Life Expectancy:** 14 years
**Daily Exercise:** 1 hour
**Behavior Problems:** Roaming, destructiveness, hyperactivity, anxious chewing of furniture when left alone, timidity and skittishness

This is an excellent hunter, with a keen sense of smell and a talent for retrieving in any kind of terrain, even in marshy land. During World War II, when Hungarians were forced out of their country, they took their Vizslas with them, so now they can be found all over Europe and in the United States.

An active, energetic dog that needs a lot of exercise, she is happiest with outdoorsy, athletic people, and is not suited for city or apartment life. She needs early, firm obedience training in order to behave indoors. She likes to live in the country, where she can run in fields. Although she loves the outdoors, she also likes to sit by the fire with her owners after a run. Because her coat is short, she does better in warm weather rather than the cold.

Her short, smooth coat is always tan, gold, or dark yellow, and it sheds a little. Usually, a weekly brushing is all that is needed to keep her neat.

Health concerns include hip dysplasia, progressive retinal atrophy (PRA may lead to blindness), epilepsy, entropion (turned-in eyelids that can irritate the eyeballs), and degenerating hair follicles and oil glands (sebaceous adenitis, SA). For more specifics about these health issues, see Appendix I.

# WEIMARANER

**Size/Group:** Large/Sporting
**Breed History:** A breed that is several centuries old, bred by the nobility in Weimar, Germany, there is a lot of controversy about his ancestry
**Height:** 22 to 27 inches
**Weight:** 65 to 85 pounds
**Life Expectancy:** 12 years
**Daily Exercise:** 1 hour
**Behavior Problems:** Excessive barking, indoor restlessness, destructiveness when left alone, possible house soiling, stubbornness

Originally bred to be a hunter, bird dog, pointer, and retriever, this dog is very obedient with strict training and a strong owner. Tireless, she can hunt for up to six hours at a time. She needs to be kept active and challenged, and is not recommended for a first-time dog owner. She is assertive, lively, and affectionate, and requires a lot of attention.

When she is well trained, she can be used as a guard dog. She is very well tuned in to her owner, and really enjoys work sessions and training. If bored, she may become destructive. She may be a bit too much dog for young children, and she can be a serious threat to cats.

Her short, smooth coat comes in either silver gray or gray and sheds little if brushed every day.

Health concerns include hip and elbow dysplasia; painful, swollen joints and bones (HOD, hypertrophic osteodystrophy); progressive retinal atrophy (PRA can lead to blindness); bleeding disorders; entropion (inturned eyelids that can irritate the eyeballs); an extra row of eyelashes causing tearing (distichiasis); torsion; throat and spinal disease; and heart defects. For more information about these health problems, see Appendix I.

# WELSH CORGI, CARDIGAN

**Size/Group:** Small/Herding
**Breed History:** Brought to England by Celts, where it was modified; thought to be related to the Dachshund
**Height:** 11 to 13 inches
**Weight:** 25 to 38 pounds
**Life Expectancy:** 12 years
**Daily Exercise:** 30 minutes
**Behavior Problems:** Excessive barking, wariness of strangers, snapping at strangers' heels, territoriality, aggression

A bit shorter than his cousin, the Pembroke, a Cardigan Welsh Corgi has a long tail and a long, sturdy body on very short legs, which makes him look as if his legs have been cut off. However, he is feisty and brave, and never backs down from a confrontation with a larger (taller) dog. He is suspicious of strangers and can make an excellent watchdog. He requires more space than his size might indicate, but does well in an apartment as long as he gets daily exercise and a chance to run occasionally. Originally bred to be an energetic sheepdog, he still does this task. However, he has also developed into a pleasing companion dog with a tendency to herd children and adults alike, often with a light heel nip. He also enjoys nibbling bare human toes. As an owner, you can either learn to tolerate this instinct, train it out of your pet, or end up wearing high sneakers or boots.

He is affectionate and lively, will play with a toy for hours, and enjoys playing tricks on his owners. Corgis crave companionship, both human and animal, and are often kept in pairs. He is good with children.

The Cardigan's coat is short and rough and comes in all colors except solid white. It sheds some (more during the spring seasonal shed), and needs a weekly brushing during the year, and much combing during the shed.

Health concerns include obesity, hip dysplasia, progressive retinal atrophy (PRA may lead to blindness), hypothyroidism, and intervertebral disc disease. For more specifics about these diseases, see Appendix I.

# WELSH CORGI, PEMBROKE

**Size/Group:** Small/Herding
**Breed History:** Brought to the British Isles with Flemish weavers in the early 12th century; descended from Spitz-type dogs and not as old a breed as the Cardigan, although there used to be a lot of inter-breeding
**Height:** 10 to 12 inches
**Weight:** 26 to 29 pounds
**Life Expectancy:** 12 years
**Daily Exercise:** 30 minutes
**Behavior Problems:** Possible manipulativeness or dominance, excessive barking, heel nipping, aggression, territoriality

Made famous by Queen Elizabeth II, the Pembroke is more active and outgoing than her cousin, the Cardigan, craves a lot of attention and is a good family dog. She loves company and is often owned in pairs. Happy and full of energy, she enjoys any activity with her people, from walking, riding in the car, playing catch, or watching TV after an active day. She has "a big dog heart in a compact body." Because of her short legs, she requires a moderate amount of daily exercise.

She can live happily in any setting, from farm to urban apartment, and is a good watchdog, although never mean or quarrelsome. Spunky, charming, hardy, and obedient, she is easily trained. She gets along well with all people and other animals, although she may try to be boss if not taught otherwise.

Her short coat comes in red or sable with white markings, or tri-colored and sheds a lot, especially during the shedding (spring) season. It should be brushed and combed at least twice a week.

Health concerns include degenerative myelopathy, obesity, progressive retinal atrophy (PRA can lead to blindness), lens luxation, retinal dysplasia, hip dysplasia, a hemorrhagic disorder (von Willebrand's disease), cystinuria (a hereditary condition due to a kidney impairment), and intervertebral disc disease. For more details about these conditions, see Appendix I.

# WELSH SPRINGER SPANIEL

**Size/Group:** Medium/Sporting
**Breed History:** Wales; bred for over 400 years from spaniel stock, especially for hunting
**Height:** 16 to 17 inches
**Weight:** 35 to 45 pounds
**Life Expectancy:** 12 years
**Daily Exercise:** 1 hour
**Behavior Problems:** Barking, occasional aggression, independence, wariness of strangers

Although not a popular breed in the United States, he has an especially nice, sunny nature and is good with children. He is able to live anywhere and is suitable for city or suburban life as long as he gets enough daily exercise. He was originally bred for hunting and retrieving and can work tirelessly for hours in the roughest terrain. He is completely oblivious of bad weather and doesn't even mind icy cold water.

He needs continuous training from six months on to keep him from wandering off the hunt field, but he is a good learner and enjoys training. He needs constant company, is devoted to his owner, and doesn't like to be excluded from any activity. He loves to wrestle and roll around on the ground with people, and is good with children and other pets.

His medium-length, silky, flat coat comes in red with white markings, and he is an average shedder, requiring weekly brushing and occasional trimming of his feathers.

Health concerns include progressive retinal atrophy (PRA may lead to blindness), cataracts, glaucoma, epilepsy, and hip dysplasia. For more information about these conditions, see Appendix I.

# WELSH TERRIER (Also called Lakeland Terrier, Black and Tan Wirehaired, Old English)

**Size/Group:** Small/Terrier
**Breed History:** One of the oldest terrier breeds
**Height:** 14 to 16 inches
**Weight:** 18 to 22 pounds
**Life Expectancy:** 14 years
**Daily Exercise:** 35 minutes
**Behavior Problems:** Threat to cats and other small animals, stubbornness, excessive barking, object and people guarding, stealing and guarding food, picky eating, touch shyness

This is a typically lively, spunky, and curious terrier. She was bred to hunt in lairs and dens, and also worked in packs with hounds. She is able to bear any weather and temperature, either on land or in the water. Now she is usually a companion pet and is able to live in any environment, including city apartments. She is an excellent watchdog and will sound an alarm at the approach of any stranger.

She is very sturdy with a lot of stamina and is always looking for fun, which may get her into trouble if her owners don't play with her enough. She needs obedience training from the very start, but may become bored if it is not varied enough. She will test her owners to the limit, especially during her "teenage" months. Praise, food, and play help in the training process. Although usually friendly with other dogs (some are natural scrappers and must be controlled around all other animals), they are death on cats and any other small animal.

Her wiry, short coat is either black or gray with tan markings and hardly sheds at all. She should be brushed with a slicker brush, and combed, about three times a week. She needs professional hand-stripping and clipping occasionally.

Health problems may include patellar (knee) luxation, lens luxation, glaucoma, cataracts, and an extra row of eyelashes causing tearing (distichiasis). For more details about these health concerns, see Appendix I.

# WEST HIGHLAND WHITE TERRIER

**Size/Group:** Small/Terrier
**Breed History:** In the mid-1800s a Cairn breeder had some white puppies in a litter. Bred to each other, they produced the Westie
**Height:** 10 to 11 inches
**Weight:** 15 to 19 pounds
**Life Expectancy:** 14 years
**Daily Exercise:** 20 minutes
**Behavior Problems:** Possible testiness with small children, irritable snapping, demanding of attention, digging, stubbornness, barking, excitability that may lead to biting

The "Westie" is a close relative of Cairn, Scottish, and Dandie Dinmont terriers, and it shares many of their attributes. Like most little terriers, he was originally bred to hunt small vermin, is still a very good mouser, and is tenacious and self-assured. He is now primarily a companion pet and can live in an urban apartment as long as he gets daily exercise and a chance to run in a small yard or terrace every day. He is a very good watchdog and warns his family of everything—even a squirrel in a tree outside the window!

Boisterous and bouncy, this little dog is busy all day. He is very demanding of attention. The Westie owner must learn to be firm and curtail excessive noisiness and overactivity. This dog especially likes to play in the snow and cold, and will bark to go out in winter weather. He also likes to dig, and will become covered with dirt. He is a good companion for children he has been raised with, but may be a bit testy with toddlers.

His medium-length rough coat hardly ever sheds, but should be professionally hand-stripped, clipped, and scissored on a regular basis.

Health considerations include Cushing's disease; cataracts; craniomandibular osteopathy (CMO)—a painful, thickened lower jaw; and disintegration of the hip joint (Legg-Calvé-Perthes). For more specifics about these health issues, see Appendix I.

# WHIPPET

**Size/Group:** Medium/Hound
**Breed History:** Developed by crossing the Greyhound, Italian Greyhound, and the terrier; the name means move quickly, or "whip it".
**Height:** 18 to 22 inches
**Weight:** 28 to 31 pounds
**Life Expectancy:** 13 years
**Daily Exercise:** 45 minutes
**Behavior Problems:** House soiling, irritable snapping, timidity, stubbornness, and phobias

The Whippet was originally bred to be a racing dog and for the sport of "gaming," which entailed chasing rabbits or squirrels in small enclosures, then killing them or snapping them up. (She was also called a "snap hound.") The Whippet can reach amazing speeds in a very short time. But because she has such a nice, happy, affectionate nature she has now become primarily a companion dog. She needs daily exercise, and the chance to run now and then—she is a natural athlete. She tends to get bored easily, and her routine should be varied with a game of chase, Frisbee, agility and racing challenges, and obedience training. With adequate daily exercise and entertainment, the Whippet is docile and can easily live in a city apartment. If she is left outdoors in a yard, there should be a secure fence.

She is a very good watchdog. Despite her delicate appearance, this is a hardy dog that hardly ever gets sick and is quite long-lived. She is excellent with children as long as they are not too rough.

Her short coat comes in all colors and sheds little. A weekly brushing with a hound glove and an occasional bath are all that is needed to keep her coat in shape.

Health concerns include progressive retinal atrophy (PRA can lead to blindness), cataracts, lens luxation, degenerating hair follicles and oil glands (SA, sebaceous adenitis), and heart defects. For more specifics about these conditions, see Appendix I.

# WIREHAIRED POINTING GRIFFON

**Size/Group:** Large/Sporting
**Breed History:** Developed in Holland in the late 1800s by breeding a Setter, Pointer, Otterhound, and Spaniel
**Height:** 20 to 24 inches
**Weight:** 50 to 60 pounds
**Life Expectancy:** 12 years
**Daily Exercise:** 1 hour
**Behavior Problems:** Possible house soiling, excessive barking, picky eating, stubbornness, independence, cat chasing, overactivity

This is a rare breed in this country. Bred to be a hunting dog, he points as well as retrieves; his primary prey are hare and quail. His wiry, harsh coat makes him impervious to cold climates, bad weather, and rough countrysides such as saltwater marshes. He has an excellent sense of smell and a passion for hunting. He requires a great deal of daily exercise and is not at all suited for city or apartment life.

He is an intelligent, good-natured, affectionate family pet. He is good with children, except that he tends to consider them equals, and they have to earn the dog's respect if they are going to be able to make him obey them.

His medium-length wavy coat comes in brown or gray and sheds a little. He requires only a weekly brushing, and occasional hand-stripping for showing.

Health concerns are few and may include hip dysplasia and ectropion and entropion (lower eyelids hanging, and eyelids turned inward), causing irritation of the eyeball. See Appendix I for more details about these conditions.

# XOLOITZCUINTLI

**Size/Group:** Toy/Rare/Non-Sporting
**Breed History:** Their likeness appears etched in ancient Aztec ruins, and Spanish traders introduced the dog to Central and South America in the early 1500s
**Height:** 16 to 23 inches
**Weight:** 20 to 31 pounds
**Life Expectancy:** 15 years
**Daily Exercise:** 45 minutes
**Behavior Problems:** Protectiveness, excessive barking, training requirement

Known as the Standard Mexican Hairless, this breed is alert, outgoing, affectionate, curious, and lively. These dogs are loving, attentive, and easily trained. Good with gentle children, they like warmth and comfort and are ideal lapdogs because they crave and need body heat.

This hairless breed has the advantage of no shedding or brushing, but one has to be careful to protect the skin. They need a coat or sweater for cold weather and sunscreen in the summer. The "Xolo" is ideal for people with allergies.

He has no known breed-specific health concerns.

# YORKSHIRE TERRIER

**Size/Group:** Tiny/Toy
**Breed History:** The Yorkie was developed by miners in the county of Yorkshire who wanted to breed a dog that would catch the rats infesting the mines, crossing a Skye Terrier, Dandie Dinmont, Black-and-Tan Toy Terrier, and the Maltese
**Height:** 7 to 9 inches
**Weight:** 2 to 7 pounds
**Life Expectancy:** 14 years
**Daily Exercise:** 10 minutes
**Behavior Problems:** House soiling, irritable snapping, incessant barking, dominance, fear-biting, unpredicted aggression, guarding behavior, touch shyness

This little dog really wants to be a pampered lapdog. But she also has the usual terrier traits; she is lively, stubborn, and spunky, affectionate with her master and slightly suspicious of strangers. She trains well, but requires firm discipline or else she will take over.

She gets along well with all other pets, cats included, and is always the dominant animal in a multipet household, despite her small size. At the same time, she doesn't mind being an "only child," and is often toted around by her owner. Care must be taken around large dogs and children, for fear that this little girl might get hurt or stepped on. She is ideally suited for city or apartment life because she has no particular interest in exercise or walks.

Her long, silky coat is black with tan or dark steel-blue when she is an adult. When she is a puppy, she is always black and tan.

Health concerns may include patellar (knee) luxation, pancreatitis, hypoglycemia, liver shunts, and abnormal lymph vessels (lymphangiectasia). For more particulars about these health problems, see Appendix I.

# WHERE TO FIND
# YOUR DREAM DOG

Once you have your checklist marked with your choices of potential dream dogs, it is now time to meet those breeds up close and personal. This will enable you to winnow the field down to your breed of choice.

An easy way to locate a dog show in your area is to contact the American Kennel Club, and they'll send you a booklet guide to all the different dog shows in your area and surrounding communities. Take the time to visit these shows. You and your family will be entertained and enlightened by the breeds you are interested in.

At the dog show, you also will have the opportunity to meet and speak to the professional breeders. Breeders are professionals who not only know the breed, but also love the breed and can educate you to what the dog is really like. However, remember that showing dogs is the breeders' work, so they do not have a lot of time to chat while they are working. But after you introduce yourself and express an interest in their breed, most breeders will be more than happy to make an appointment with you to visit their breeding kennel, at which time you can discuss the breed with them in depth.

If you can't find a dog show in your area—if it's too far away or if you just missed it and the next one is months away—the American Kennel Club will send you a list of national breed clubs in your area, and these clubs in turn will put you in contact with reputable breeders in your area.

A wealth of information on hundreds of breeders, including photographs of their dogs, is available on the Internet. The advantage here is that you can send e-mail to any breeder and receive an immediate response. Still, the most reliable way to find a good breeder is by word of mouth and personal recommendation. If you know someone whose dog you admire, ask that person to recommend his or her breeder. A satisfied client is the best recommendation of all.

Going to a breeder cuts out the middle man, which may result in large savings to you. After all, pet stores purchase from breeders and then must charge you a substantial markup on what they paid for the dog. Even more important than the financial benefits, by purchasing directly from the breeder, you are getting the guarantee of the dog's pedigree papers, which the breeder is proud to share with you.

A word of caution: For a first-time potential pet owner, an initial encounter with a breeder can backfire. A new client explained to me her experience in getting a puppy, her *tail* of woe. Because everyone told her that she should go to a breeder, she called one. Unfortunately, the breeder brusquely told her, "I don't have a puppy right now, and I'm busy, call me later." She was taken aback by his curt, unhelpful response. So she went instead to the local pet shops in her neighborhood. Some didn't have the breed she was looking for in stock, but advised her they could order it and have one for her within a couple of days. She felt that she couldn't wait, so she went to one pet shop after another until she found one with her desired breed, but was quoted an astronomical price. She finally found another pet shop with her breed of choice and bought the puppy. She and her daughter took the dog home that day. A few days later, I got a frantic call from the woman. The puppy wasn't housebroken, was barking incessantly and nipping and biting. She needed help. The friend who told her to call the professional breeder recommended she call me. I visited the household as soon as I could, and I helped her with some behavior and training modification. We were able to create the dream dog for her.

There is a veritable litter of lessons to be learned from her story. First, people who want to get a puppy in the worst way often do. Second, finding a "dream dog" requires serious education, thought, and reflection; the process can be better likened to a marathon and not a sprint. After all, you are choosing a new member for your family. As the old saying goes, "Sin in haste; repent at leisure." Third, this is a perfect example of needing a fence at the top of the cliff rather than an ambulance at the bottom. Fourth, sometimes a professional dog breeder can be more high-strung than his dogs.

Clearly, prospective dog owners need to understand the steps in acquiring a dog from a reputable, professional breeder, and breeders need to be a little more approachable in their demeanor with the novice pet owner. I often joke that getting a dog—with the commitment to love and cherish that dog for a lifetime, which can be either side of fourteen years—is a lot like getting married. If that's the case, these breeders are your potential "in-laws." They may seem a little off-putting at first, but that's only because they are passionate about their breed of choice, and the welfare of their dogs is their paramount concern.

## PROFESSIONAL BREEDERS VS. PRIVATE BREEDERS

Today's professional breeders work diligently to improve their breeds. Thanks to their dedication and careful breeding techniques, many potential genetic problems such as hip dysplasia (common in larger breeds such as Akitas and German Shepherds) are being bred out of the dogs. Good breeders are dedicated to producing the best possible dogs, grooming them into champions, and placing them in good homes with responsible owners. Understandably, before they even think of selling you one of their future champion pups, they'll want to know as much about you as you want to know about them. Don't forget, they only want the best for their loved ones—and once they accept you as the new owner of one of their cherished pups, you'll find yourself embraced in a warmly supportive extended family. Your breeder will be a trusted friend, mentor, and "nanny" to you and your dog.

Most people have pleasant experiences with breeders. Here's an example that illustrates how a professional breeder, cognizant of the specific needs of a family, directed them to a dog that was right for them. The family initially went to a professional breeder they had found through the AKC. The breeder's Portuguese Water Dogs had garnered numerous championship titles and degrees. The breeder was very nice to the family. She patiently explained that she takes her breeding program very seriously, and that she sells a dog only to people who are committed to showing the dogs and hopefully adding to the championship line. The family explained to the breeder they just wanted a family pet, and were not interested in lineage and ribbons. This effectively closed the door with this breeder. Nevertheless, she recommended they go to a private breeder she knew. The professional breeder's champion (stud) had been bred with the private breeder's female, making champion-sired puppies. This private breeder's business is to sell puppies as pets to wonderful families. The family met with the private breeder and came away with the puppy of their dreams.

A reliable breeder can do many things for the prospective owner. She will provide a litter of healthy, temperamentally sound puppies for the prospective owner to choose from, and will also help him to make the right choice. Most breeders believe it's their duty to educate new dog owners to the fine points of their breeds, and how that can impact the unwitting owner. I had a client, for example, who was at her wit's end. Her children had fallen in love with a Golden Retriever they had seen in a pet shop, and, knowing how good the breed is with children, she gave in and purchased the pup. "Goldie is great with the children," explained the exasperated mom, "but she's so badly behaved! No matter how much time we spend with her, when she's outside she gets into all our neighbors' yards and brings home their newspapers. I've tried everything to break her of this, but she doesn't seem to know how bad she is." I explained to my client that Goldie didn't know her behavior was bad, because in truth, it wasn't. As a retriever, Goldie was simply doing what came naturally—retrieving. I explained to her that a canine trait you might think is a behavior problem is in fact an instinct of a specific breed of dog. Over the centuries, dogs have been selectively bred to perform particular tasks and to behave in specific ways to meet their masters' needs (hunting, herding, retrieving, and so on). So it shouldn't be surprising when they still behave in these ways. Depending on the particular dog you choose, you may have to learn to control or modify some of your dog's inbred characteristics. This can often be quite easy and enjoyable. All Goldie really needed to learn, for example, was that newspapers were off-limits, but she could retrieve to her heart's content by playing fetch with her own toys with the children.

A breeder perceiving that the breed is not the right one for the prospective owner will caution him, explaining why it is the wrong breed for that person. Most breeders will be happy to guide the novice to a breed that is a more realistic fit for his household.

## BREEDER ETIQUETTE

Now that you have an idea of what to expect from a breeder, you are ready to meet them. Here are some etiquette tips which will make the breeder feel that you are as well bred as his dogs. Once you've compiled a list of potential breeders, begin contacting those in your community. I believe it's always best to work close to home simply because it allows you greater access to the dogs themselves and facilitates face-to-face communication with the breeder before and after you've purchased your dog. You'll find that professional breeders love to talk about their dogs, but only when they have time. Therefore, showing up unannounced at their breeding kennels is discourteous. Call and make an appointment. Tell them what you (think you) are looking for; then listen carefully to what they have to say. They will answer any questions you have on temperament, inherent breed problems, diet, or grooming care. Explain your lifestyle to them—whether you're married or single, whether you work or are at home all day, whether you have kids, live in the city or country. Basically, you'll have a chance to recite to the breeder the notes in your Dream Dog Notebook. These facts will tell the breeder whether her breed is the right one for you. In fact, you might just learn that the dog you thought you wanted may not be as suitable as another similar breed. Breeders are able to articulate the fine nuances that differentiate what seems to the uninitiated layman very similar, almost identical breeds. And if the breeder determines that his breed and similar breeds are the wrong breeds for you, she can suggest alternative breeds better suited to your wants and lifestyle, and direct you to the appropriate breeders.

Even if the breeder finds that his breed is the right breed for you, be prepared to be interviewed in depth, because the breeder also wants to make sure that you are the right owner for his dogs. For instance, as we have seen, many breeders are interested in preserving their championship lines. If you don't plan to show your dog, the line stops there. They may say they're not interested in selling for pet purposes. Please don't feel rejected. This isn't personal; it's simply the business in which he has invested years of work, and the choice is his to make. On the other hand, you should ask him to refer you to another breeder with quality dogs. Occasionally however, a "show-dogs-only" breeder may have a pup that, by a quirk of fate, isn't show quality. It happens in the best of kennels and in no way reflects the quality or reputation of the kennels. Even two top champion dogs may produce a litter that just isn't up to the show ring—the bite, say, isn't up to the breed's standards, or the nose shows a bit of pigmentation where the standards permit none, or perhaps the runt of the litter is a bit too small to make the championship grade. In cases like this, even the most show-oriented breeder will be willing to sell his dog as a pet. It doesn't hurt to ask, and you may wind up with your dream dog. And, before you say you want "just a pet," check out the dog show information in chapter 6. I have clients who originally were interested only in having a loyal canine companion and afterward became so proud of the beautiful dog they owned that they decided to go into the ring themselves.

Most breeders won't even consider selling to someone they haven't "flushed out," like a retriever who "flushes out" game in the field. Expect the breeder to interview you thoroughly and to ask questions that you may consider somewhat nosy. It's not meant that way, but each breeder is extremely concerned with the fate of her dogs and wants to be certain that you're the right owner. I have one client who was interviewed three separate times by her prospective breeder and says it was the toughest job interview she'd ever had. That's good. It shows the breeder's concern for her dogs. If a breeder is eager to sell you a dog, no questions asked, you might want to consider a different breeder.

The breeder is interested in knowing the following: How will you be able to provide for the dog? Are you able to give the dog the time it deserves for play, for grooming, for exercise, and for just plain loving? Where and how do you live? In a city apartment or a country house? If it's an apartment, will you be responsible for seeing the dog is walked four times a day? If you can't walk it yourself, will you invest in a dog walker who will? If you live in the country, is your yard fenced? If not, will you commit to fencing it? Are there children in your family? If so, how old? (Breeders know when their breed is not especially good with children, and they'll be quick to warn you away from that particular choice.) Have you ever had dogs before? What breed? Have you a dog now? What's its age? If it is an older dog, what will its response be to a puppy? (If it's a laid-back older dog, that's usually fine; an aggressive older dog means no sale.)

One breeder has told me that these questions often make a prospective buyer rethink the project entirely. Some people come to realize that they have grossly underestimated the time and money needed to maintain the dog properly and they cannot or do not want to commit that much time or money. Others come to realize that bringing a new puppy home to an old and ailing dog would be unfair and might cause injury to the puppy. Some prospective owners had no idea that bringing home a canine baby is just about as much work as bringing home a real one. Remember that the breeder's primary interest is in the future welfare of the dog and that his questions are being asked for that reason only.

Similarly, you need to feel comfortable with, and confident in, the breeder. The condition of a breeder's kennels can go a long way toward instilling confidence or undermining it completely. If the kennel is a spotless state-of-the-art facility with happy, healthy-looking dogs, you are on the right track. If you see anything less—smelly kennels, dirty cages, nervous dogs—then turn and head for the door fast. As in any marriage, it's better to change your mind at the altar than to spend a lifetime regretting it.

If at the end of the interviewing process, you remain convinced that a particular breed is for you and the breeder likewise thinks that you are right for her breed, she will let you know when a litter is due and when you can visit your puppy-to-be. (Usually it's about six weeks.) Even though you won't be allowed to take your pup home until it's at least eight weeks old and weaned (though occasionally breeders have older pups that are "ready to go"), most breeders will ask you to reserve your pup at the first visit or risk losing out. Having the entire litter together in one place offers the perfect opportunity for choosing the pick of the litter using the Five-Point Temperament Test we described in chapter 1.

## THE CONTRACT

Finally, when you've chosen your dog-to-be, sign a contract. It will save a great deal of trouble if something should go wrong down the line. The contract should spell out clearly that if you get the dog and decide you don't want it or can't keep it for any reason, the breeder will accept its return. Good breeders readily agree to this provision because they always want to control the fate of their dogs. Indeed, good breeders not only will accept the return of the dog (and repay the purchase price less shipping), but will require that you return the dog rather than give the dog to someone else. After all, that new person has not undergone the stringent interview process with the breeder.

As an extra precaution, ask the breeder for a veterinarian certificate showing that the dog has been X-rayed and does not have hip dysplasia. (As you learned from chapter 3, this is especially important for large breeds with a genetic tendency to the problem.) If you get a dog with serious defects such as epilepsy or hip dysplasia, even when those problems don't show up for a period of time, the breeder will usually be willing to take the dog back and return your money. Of course, by that time you may not want to part with your friend and companion regardless of the health problems.

If, on the other hand, the dog first arrives at your door looking sick, take it to a veterinarian at once to determine the problem. If it's been shipped, it may only be a case of jet-lag and nothing more serious. But if a real medical problem is discovered, telephone the breeder and, in your most diplomatic way, say, "I'm sure you didn't know this, but this is a very sick dog." More likely than not, the breeder did not knowingly sell you a sick dog and will want you to return it promptly.

## RESCUE GROUPS

Another terrific way to get a purebred dream dog is through breed-specific rescue groups. Almost every breed has such a group, which usually is associated with the national breed club and works closely with shelters to find homes for purebred dogs who've lost theirs.

Again, the American Kennel Club can provide you with the address and telephone for the breed club of your choice, which in turn will put you in touch with that breed's rescue group. This is a wonderful way to give a needy and deserving dog a good home, as well as getting a high-end dog at a low-end price.

These breed-specific rescue organizations, or "leagues" are a loose-knit network of caring breeders who save pedigreed dogs who have lost, or are in danger of losing, their homes. Perhaps the dog's long-time owner has died, or become ill and unable to continue caring for it. Or, someone ended up with a purebred and abandoned it. Responsible breeders, of course, are always concerned about making sure this doesn't happen to their dogs, but occasionally one slips through the safety net. That's when this professional community goes into action. The Greyhound Rescue Organization, for example, probably the most visible and well-known to the general public, has done an outstanding job in finding homes for older racing dogs, who, before this group stepped in, were being routinely put down once age or infirmity diminished their racing speed.

Rescue organizations also work closely with the staff at regular animal shelters, who often telephone these groups when a purebred turns up at their facilities. As a rule, rescue organizations place rescued dogs in foster homes until permanent homes can be found. Dogs placed by these organizations usually have been checked by a veterinarian. The only cost the new owner will incur is the reimbursement of any medical fees or expenses to the organization.

You'll not only get the breed of your choice—which means you'll have some inkling of its genes—but you'll be saving a life, as well. I can think of no more gratifying way to acquire a purebred dog. Knowing the characteristics of the breed will make the period of adjustment somewhat easier for you both. But one sad fact remains: The dog has been given up. It's feeling lost, lonely, and confused and needs every bit as much love and attention as the shelter dog. Your understanding of its heritage will give you a valuable head start on making it feel secure again.

## PET SHOPS

As a rule, unless I know the owner of a pet shop, I recommend breeders rather than pet shops because, as tempting as those innocent, furry little puppies may be, many pet shops buy their stock from "puppy mills"—breeding factories run by unscrupulous people more interested in making a quick buck than in breeding a good dog. Many of these dogs suffer from serious genetic flaws that are often undetectable at first, but surface much later, when it's too late to return the dog. Of course, not all pet shop puppies are flawed, but it's almost impossible to know which pet shops deal with puppy mills. And while pet shop dogs come with papers (American Kennel Club registry), many of these puppies grow up bearing little resemblance to the breed they supposedly represent. True, many of these puppies can be loving and lovable pets, but the risk of buying from a pet shop can be both costly and heartbreaking.

One current trend is the so-called "new breeds" which are a combination of two favorite breeds. For example, people like to combine the best qualities of the Poodle, which is hypoallergenic, with the personality and habits of the Labrador Retriever, resulting in a medium-size dog that has the characteristics of a Labrador with the allergy prevention of the Poodle. They call this a "Labradoodle." The problem with this mixed breed is that it lacks having the years of responsible selective breeding necessary to make it a purebred. So do not be fooled by those who proclaim this is a new breed. You may have heard of or seen other so-called new breeds like Schnoodles (a mix of Schnauzer and Poodle), Cock-a-poo ( a mix of Cocker Spaniel and Poodle), Peek-a-poo (a mix of Pekingese and Poodle) and a Westy-poo (a mix of West Highland White and Poodle). You may be led to believe that these are new breeds, but in reality people are simply mixing breeds and charging high prices for the mixed breed while touting them as a new breed. Mixed breeds are not new breeds, and the acceptance of them as such is a fad. Some people fancy these mixed-breeds, and more power to them, for the dogs may be loving. But to those who fancy them as purebreeds, I suggest that without years and years of selective breeding they should be viewed more properly as passing fancies.

## SHELTERS

Many clients of mine have adopted dogs from shelters, and they've found them to be the best dog they've ever owned. Maybe it's because these shelter dogs know they've been rescued, their lives have been saved, and they're grateful and give you their undying devotion. I also have had great experiences adopting from a shelter. Many of the dogs in my family came from animal shelters. And, almost invariably, when I was doing a tremendous number of commercials and movies, the dogs who appeared in these commercials and movies were "shelter" dogs, usually of that renowned breed known as the Great American Mutt, dogs whose lineage is, so to speak, questionable and varied. For instance, I adopted Chelsea, the cutest dog imaginable, with over one hundred different breeds in her, from a shelter. She really was a treasure and one of my most requested dogs in the entertainment industry, shooting countless television shows, commercials, and print ads. (Her résumé includes commercials for Mounds, Almond Joy, and Cheerios.) But I was equally (if not more) proud of Chelsea's wonderful work as a pet therapy dog. Her incredible personality made many of my early pet therapy programs a success. (You can read more about pet therapy and how you and your dog can be involved, in chapter 6.)

On the other hand, with shelter dogs the likelihood of emotional "baggage," which manifests in behavioral problems, is much greater than with dogs from a reputable breeder. Frankly, oftentimes the reason dogs end up in shelters in the first place is because of behavioral problems. Shelter personnel will be happy to give you as much information as they have on the dog's history and lineage, but quite often they have very little information to give.

With training applied with patience and persistence, these behavioral problems can often be solved. But, being a professional, it's easier for me to resolve these problems, so if you're thinking of getting a shelter dog, seek out professional trainers or behaviorists to help you. Many shelters nowadays retain trainers on staff to address these potential problems and to be sure that adopted dogs will be well behaved and able to adjust to their new homes, thus breaking that sad cycle of pet abandonment, recycled dogs and overpopulation.

Occasionally, you can find purebred dogs in shelters, as well. This is frustrating because oftentimes these are perfectly good dogs but not a good match for their owners. Often, the owners have given the dogs up to the shelters because of their unfamiliarity with breed-specific traits, instinctive traits that the owners perceive as bad behavior.

One final word in favor of those Great American Mutts that predominate in shelters. Cross-breeding often creates a stronger gene pool, resulting in fewer genetic problems. It can also create adorable one-of-a-kind dogs (just look at Benji), which is why the mutt remains a popular favorite in films, television, and commercials. And, since mixed breeds tend to be savvy and street smart, they can often be easily trained. Many clients who have always owned purebreds, but for one reason or another ended up with an adopted pet, swear that a dog rescued from death row is the most devoted, affectionate, grateful pet on the planet. It's a gratifying experience to take an animal into a new and loving home—and also an inexpensive way to acquire a really great dog.

## MALE OR FEMALE?

No matter where you ultimately find your dream dog, you still need to choose the right sex and age. For many people, the choice of whether to get a male or a female dog is as perplexing as the choice of a breed itself. For sex does influence behavior in a number of predictable ways. Giving thought to a dog's sex as well as its breed can take much of the guesswork out of the question of what a puppy's behavior will become as it matures into an adult.

I always recommend that people choose a female puppy or dog. Females are more apt to be "homebodies"; that is, they adapt more readily to living with a family and are happy to be part of it. Although male dogs certainly make wonderful pets, they often need more training, firmer discipline, and greater direction than females. Just as in a wolf pack, where the males are always more dominant than the females, many male dogs continually battle for dominance with their owners. In general, male dogs tend to display higher activity levels, are more aggressive toward other dogs, are more territorial, and play rougher than females. Females, on the other hand, tend to be more obedient, easier to house-train, and demand more affection. So, in general, female dogs tend to be "easier." If, for example, you've decided your dream dog is a breed of high energy and territorial instincts, such as an Akita, choosing a female might reduce the impact of these strong behavioral characteristics. However, if you choose a more mellow breed, like a Labrador or Spaniel, for example, which do not have tendencies toward aggression and territorial instincts, you can feel more free to choose a male, since the breed is low in this trait to begin with. In general, a dog's sex affects all the characteristics listed in the breed profiles except the tendencies toward excitability, excessive barking, and watchdog barking. For these three traits, the difference in sex is negligible. As a basic rule of thumb, I suggest that in choosing your dream dog, first choose a breed that approximates the profile you like, then choose a male or female to enhance the traits you desire or to reduce the less desirous traits.

Finally, if you're not planning to professionally show or breed your dream dog, I recommend spaying or neutering. First, this safe procedure prevents cancer of the reproductive organs in both males and female. Second, it makes for a happier, healthier, and more compliant pet. Especially in males, it significantly reduces sex-linked behavior: scent marking, roaming, and territorial aggression. Third, and most important, it greatly helps to control the pet population.

So, to sum up,

1. Choose your Dream Dog first on the basis of your dreamed-of breed profile. (Consult your Dream Dog Notebook.)
2. Choose sex based on how it will influence behavior.
3. Think of neutering as a means of further shaping the behavior of males, if necessary.

## WHAT AGE?

Finally, age needs to be considered. The majority of people who want a dog as a family pet choose a puppy rather than an adult animal. They feel raising a puppy is not only more fun, but is educational if they have children. A puppy will become bonded to them more readily than an adult dog. If you want a puppy, you should select one that's neither too young nor too old. The ideal age is somewhere between eight and twelve weeks, after it's completely weaned and used to being away from its mother almost all the time. A puppy that's taken away from its mother too soon will miss a necessary developmental stage with its littermates. Even though a six-week-old puppy is usually weaned and can get along perfectly well without its mother from a physical standpoint, important elements of behavior can be learned only through interaction with its siblings. Through play and play-fighting with its brothers and sisters, each pup gradually develops its own personality and learns how to respond to others. Just as in the wolf pack, a hierarchy emerges within a litter of pups, and each individual eventually assumes a particular role.

Getting an older dog can be a little bit like flying blind—there are more uncertainties. If, for example, a pup is not adopted by the time it's three months old and is transferred to a pet shop, gaining its trust and bonding with it can be more difficult. If the puppy's been handled by a number of different people, it may be confused. Little or no previous interaction with other living creatures can cause such a puppy to become unsociable. It can be fearful and suspicious if it hasn't had a chance to become accustomed to normal household noises and activity. Also, an older puppy that has remained with its litter too long can have many of the same problems bonding with people, or become so strongly bonded with one person it becomes a "one-man dog." Still, an older dog may turn out to be a well-adjusted dog. And, adjustment problems or not, having an older dog may turn out to be a very gratifying experience.

With older puppies and adult dogs, I strongly recommend retaining the services of a professional dog trainer to help you over the rough spots.

One final word on this subject: The older dog will have settled into a calmer, more adult lifestyle. So a mature dog is a terrific choice and a wonderful companion for older people who may not have the patience or the stamina to train a puppy. As noted earlier, sometimes a breeder may have kept a dog intending to show it, but the dog turns out not to be suitable. When it reaches maturity, the breeder may be willing to sell it.

This alternative can work out very well for some people. A client of mine, a doctor who works in a home office, wanted a dog, but didn't want to have to go through all of the initial training steps involved in puppy ownership. She contacted several good breeders and discovered one of them had just such a dog—a lovely Golden Retriever that had been raised in the breeder's own home and had already been socialized and obedience-trained. It turned out to be a perfect choice, and both owner and dog are extremely happy.

Now that you know where to find your dream dog, the search is over—but the dream has just begun. In chapter 5, you'll discover how to make your dream come to life.

# Part III

# FROM DREAMS
# TO REALITY:
# STARTING RIGHT

Now that you've found your dream dog, it's time to prepare for the homecoming. And *prepare* is the key word here. Just as new parents make their home "baby friendly" in anticipation of baby's arrival, so you need to make your home "puppy friendly." But as new puppy parents, what you put into your head is just as important as what you put into your house. I never talk politics with my clients, but one thing I'm absolutely rabid about is the importance of being "PC." No, I don't mean politically correct—I mean puppy correct!

While first-time parents often find themselves stymied when trying to figure out the needs of a baby, imagine the dilemma of first-time puppy parents—they need to divine the needs of a vulnerable infant from a totally different species. I don't mean to be flip, but the advice I give my clientele is co-opted from an age-old precept: Do unto your dog as you would have done unto you.

With this in mind, the first thing you have to remember when getting a puppy is that she is coming to a new home and also leaving the only home she has ever known. Just imagine how a puppy feels, being taken away from her mother and littermates. They are all the love and home she has ever known. I know you love your new puppy, but sometimes love just isn't enough. Remember the stories in chapter 2 of abandoned children being raised by wolves? Reportedly, she-wolves nurtured these children as lovingly as their own litters in the dens—but they were still wolves, and the children were human. Other than basic survival, these wolf mothers—despite their "love"—couldn't possibly provide adequate care to meet human children's needs.

To think PC, imagine how you would feel if you were leaving your family to go live with a wolf family. Think of it as a kind of interactive species-exchange program to foster better understanding between people and their dogs. Aside from missing your own family—and being bewildered and overwhelmed by your new wolf family—you'd probably be pretty darned uncomfortable in a dark and drafty den. When you can articulate what you would need to live comfortably in a wolf den, and then transpose that to what your new puppy will need in his new home, then you're ready to bring your new baby dog home.

The first issue is this: You need to relieve yourself. But where? Everything in the den is so foreign. Let's face it, even in a three-star hotel room, the first thing we humans look for is decent bathroom facilities. You can be sure that's just what your new puppy will need. *Be certain to have Piddle Pads down for puppy.* Also, you're probably hungry and thirsty. You'll want your own dishware, and you'll want nutritious and familiar food. Hopefully, the she-wolf will keep you on the same diet you had back home. (That raw elk carcass would wreak havoc on your digestive system.) *Keep puppy on the balanced diet your breeder has weaned her on.* You'd also like a nice room with a comfortable bed to fall safely asleep in. *Make sure puppy has her own crate or kennel cab.* With good food and water, bathroom facilities, and a room of your own, you're definitely starting to feel better—albeit a little bored. *Treat puppy to toys and chewies.* Now that you're starting to feel at home in the den, it might be fun to do some sightseeing. What would make it even better is if your adopted wolf family would go out with you. *Make certain your puppy has a properly fitting collar and leash.* This is primarily for her safety, but it will also strengthen her bonds with you as you take her out on each new day's adventure.

Just as you wouldn't think of bringing home a new baby without a crib and a good supply of bottles, formula, and diapers, so, too, you must plan wisely for your new puppy. And part of this is remembering that unlike a new baby, a new puppy is very mobile.

Part of making your home puppy-friendly is making it puppy-proof. This chapter will teach you how to crate-train your puppy, and I always recommend pressure gates or expandable playpens to cordon off puppy-safe zones. When it comes to puppies, I strictly adhere to the Boy Scout motto: Be prepared. Certain plants, for example, are poisonous to dogs (check with your veterinarian), and all household-cleaning supplies should be removed or carefully stored away. Never underestimate a puppy's ability to find trouble. I cannot stress this enough.

Now that we know that love alone is not enough for your new puppy's well-being, we need to remind ourselves that love is still job number one. You are your puppy's mother, guardian, pack leader, and caretaker all rolled into one, and he will be dependent on you for all his needs.

# COLLAR

Buying the right collar is probably the most important initial purchase you will make for your new arrival. The collar will have your pup's identification attached to it, which will help ensure the pup's safety. Many people buy a collar that is too large, expecting the puppy to grow into it. An ill-fitting collar puts the puppy at risk for slipping out of it—a dangerous situation indeed—and will make correcting the puppy during training much more difficult. Although I recommend the chain-link control collar as a valuable training accessory for dogs, for most puppies, especially the very young or small, I recommend a simple soft leather or nylon buckle collar. Young puppies can be quite fragile, and for the initial "getting to know you" phase, this gentle collar is just what the puppy needs. A collar should be snug but not tight. You know you have the right fit when the collar fits comfortably without being able to slip over the pup's head. A good measure for a good fit is being able to slip two fingers between the collar and your new pup's throat. Don't forget, your new pup may be intimidated by many things you find perfectly harmless, and like a wolf pup, its instincts will be to freeze. If your pup puts on the brakes and you try to coax it forward, your pup, even unintentionally, can slip right out of its collar. Also, don't forget that collar is your pup's safety harness—its first line of defense in its new big wide world. Just as toddlers seem to outgrow T-shirts and diapers before you know it, so puppies will go through several collar sizes and changes. Keep a sharp eye out for a collar that's in danger of getting too tight. A good rule of thumb is to remember the "two digit doggie" rule: every now and then when you bend down to give a cuddle or a scratch behind the ear, try to wiggle two fingers under its collar.

Another choice in collars is the show lead, which is a combination of collar and leash. Then, at about three to five months old, a pup can graduate to a nylon control collar, or slip collar. This works exactly like the traditional chain-link control collar. It tightens and releases as the owner pulls or loosens the leash, and helps to familiarize and prepare the pup for future training.

## LEASH

I always advise getting a four-foot to six-foot leash. This can be either nylon or leather, but I usually recommend nylon, simply because it's washable, lightweight, and generally more comfortable to handle. And comfort is the key. Hopefully, you and your new buddy will be sharing this leash a great many times, and you both will want to be comfortable. This is why I never recommend a chain-link leash. The metal is too heavy to swing down near your friend, and too hard on your hands when you're grasping for extra control. Of the two lengths, I prefer the six-foot leash. The four-foot leash can be a little too confining, but anything longer than six feet gives your pup too much freedom and can be dangerous. Six feet is just right, which is why it is used for training. It keeps your dog comfortably within your control. Just like boisterous children, puppies need your guidance and feel safer within the parameters you set for them.

## CRATE OR KENNEL

Within even the happiest of homes, each family member needs a place of his own: a place to study, play a video game, read a book, or just hang out. That peaceful solitude, or downtime, is important to the health and well-being of all of us.

Just as the collar and leash provide security when your new puppy is outdoors, so the crate or kennel provides security when your new puppy is indoors. I can't tell you how many times I've heard people who don't know any better protest that they could never keep their dog in a cage. But the problem with that attitude is that the wolf cub within their little puppy craves a den of his own. Den behavior is one of the essential components of pack behavior and is very much alive in all domestic dogs. A den is vital to having a happy, flourishing dog. Just as you wouldn't put a baby to sleep unattended in an adult bed or left to play without the parameters of a playpen, so you wouldn't leave a pup unattended and vulnerable to danger—not to mention leaving your house vulnerable to mischievous disaster! A crate or kennel is the only way to keep your pup, and your household, under control.

There are two types of crates: the traditional metal "cage" crate and the kennel cab, which is the pet carrier that meets official airline standards for transporting your pet. As a daily den, I personally prefer the traditional wire crate, because it gives the dog a 360-degree view of the outside world. Being in visual contact with his family allows him to feel safe and secure in his den without feeling alone or cut off from his pack family. At the same time, it allows you, his alpha guardian, to keep an eye on him. And for those times when your dog truly needs quiet—if he's recuperating from surgery, for example—draping a towel or blanket over the crate allows that extra measure of quiet and privacy.

Speaking of quiet and privacy, the kennel cab was designed specifically to increase your pet's safety and to decrease stress. Totally enclosed on three sides, the kennel cab decreases visual stimuli, thus providing the nervous dog with the added comfort and security she needs. Choosing a kennel cab as your dog's den also has the added benefit of preparing your dog for air travel. If your dog must travel, simply being separated from you will cause some anxiety, especially when that separation is compounded by unfamiliar sights, sounds, and smells. But if her traveling kennel cab has also been her home den—then that measure of security will be, quite frankly, immeasurable. For this reason, while for the average dog I recommend a "cage" crate, I strongly urge clients whose pets will be flying to substitute her regular wire crate with her traveling kennel cab as her den for at least a few days prior to the plane trip. Your dog will transfer her feelings of safety and security to her new kennel cab, and that will be one less worry for her as she embarks on her great adventure.

Equally important in your choice of crate or kennel is the correct size. A grown dog should be able to lie down comfortably inside the crate or carrier, yet it shouldn't be overly roomy. A too-large kennel cab would be dangerous for travel, as the dog could be tossed about in transit. At home, too much space negates the kennel cab's effectiveness as a cozy and safe den, and is counterproductive for housebreaking training, which relies on your dog's natural unwillingness to soil the area he sleeps in. So if you're planning on using a kennel cab for travel, then you must purchase the proper fit at the time of the trip. Just as with your pup's collar, the kennel cab is for his safety, and you cannot buy a larger one and have him "grow into it." This is another reason I recommend a wire crate as your pup's permanent den, and purchasing the kennel cab only when you first need it. Not only will it ensure being the right fit at the right time, but in the long run it will save you money. To be sure of the proper size, don't hesitate to ask for guidance at your pet supply store.

As for a crate, it is extremely versatile, since it can be fitted with dividers to "customize" its size. Some styles are collapsible for easy moving or storage; others have side doors, allowing usage with station wagons or vans. And, unlike the kennel cab, this ability to grow with your puppy's needs allows you to purchase, right from the start, the size crate your puppy will need when she reaches adulthood.

Whichever "den" you choose for your puppy, it should be cushioned with comfortable padding. Pads are made to fit all crate and kennel sizes, and you can also create your own mattress out of towels or a pillow. Remember, even a real wolf wouldn't choose to sleep on cold steel or hard plastic.

## BOWLS FOR FOOD AND WATER

The choice for your dog's food and water bowls depends on you. I have one client who feeds her dog from a priceless antique porcelain bowl, and another who uses a sentimental ceramic dish that has served generations of her family's dogs. But whatever your choice in doggie dishware, you have to keep it as clean as you would for your own dishware. Always make sure that there is fresh water in your dog's water dish. This is especially important in hot weather, and ice cubes in the water dish is a simple and effective way to quench thirst and cool your dog's body temperature quickly. Don't forget, his temperature normally is already 102 degrees, so he will more readily feel a blistering heat wave.

I can never remind my clients enough that a dog's water dish is his only source of water, so, again, it is vital to monitor and replenish his water! If you don't, you really can't blame your dog for drinking from the toilet bowl. As funny and unappetizing as that sounds, drinking from the commode is no joke. In fact, it can be deadly. Common household products designed to freshen the toilet bowl (and that includes fresheners used in the tank) can poison your dog. So never, ever use chemicals in the toilet.

## FOOD

Making sure your little one is getting all the nutrition she needs is vital to keeping her healthy. Undoubtedly, your breeder has started your pup on a good regimen, and you should stick with it. Puppies tend to have rather delicate digestive systems that are sensitive to abrupt changes in diet. It's always best to keep your puppy on the breeder's current selected diet, unless your veterinarian indicates otherwise. That diet will, of course, change over the years. As your dog matures and her body changes, so her nutritional needs will change, as well. With an incredibly wide variety of dog foods available—from supermarket brands to high-end premium quality (including special diets to address diabetes, kidney disorders, food allergies, and even cancer)—your veterinarian is the best person to prescribe the right diet for the right time for your dog.

## PRESSURE GATE OR EXPANDABLE PLAYPEN

If you plan on making an area of the house puppy-friendly, you'll need to section this designated area off from the rest of the house. The area you choose may be a small room, such as an extra bathroom or pantry, or it may be an area of the kitchen or living room. Any of these options will work because, like your puppy's den or crate, having a separate puppy area is safe but doesn't seem separate to your newest family member. If you are simply cordoning off a small room, a simple pressure gate—which comes in many styles—is more than adequate for the job. My preference is a wire-mesh gate, with openings small enough to retain even the tiniest pup. However, if you're planning on having your pup share a room with you, such as the kitchen or living room, then an expandable playpen is ideal and gives you many options. Again, when making your choice, keep in mind that a squirming and determined puppy can wriggle through the smallest of openings.

## THE BASHROOM

The "BashRoom" is the perfect fixture for your puppy's "powder room." These wee ones (pun intended) need to focus and "do their business," and my BashRoom encourages this with minimum fuss and optimal results. For some dogs, traditional Wee-Wee Pads by themselves aren't enough. Although the pads are infused with a scent that stimulates pups to urinate, the pads can get bunched up as puppies scratch and circle as part of their "business" procedure. But with the BashRoom fixture, the pads remain fixed in place, allowing dogs to remain concentrated on doing their business as well as containing spillovers and leakage.

Basically, the BashRoom provides a litter box for dogs. Begin with a box-framed tray, which can be purchased at the same pet stores where you buy your Wee-Wee Pads. They can also be found in kitchen, bathroom, or storage solution areas of any home or department store. Or, if you prefer, you can quite easily construct your own by building a wooden frame (18 by 24 inches and approximately 2 inches high). Once you have your base, simply fill it with a layer of waterproof plastic topped by newspapers or Wee-Wee Pads or both.

## BRUSH AND COMB

A proper daily brushing is integral to every dog's well-being, and not every brush and comb is right for every dog. The coats of different breeds differ so dramatically, from long to short, silky to coarse—and that doesn't take into account a coat like a Cairn Terrier's, which has a rough, wiry outer coat and a second, soft inner coat. Since it is so important to get the right brush and comb for your dog, your breeder can recommend the preferred choice. You may also want to check with your local grooming shop, as well. Also, I recommend professional grooming on a regular basis, once your dog is about six months old and after he has had all his shots.

I do not recommend regular professional grooming in lieu of your dog's vital daily brushing. So don't get lazy! Regular grooming appointments can, however, be a strong adjunct to your dog's home health care regime. Not only will grooming appointments make your dog's daily upkeep easier, but a professional can spot and treat potential problems that the most well-intentioned but unskilled owner cannot.

## TOYS AND CHEWS

Just like babies, puppies go through their teething stage. This happens about the same time they begin to exhibit the exploratory nature of their wolf ancestors, and is bound to keep you on your toes. They will chew on just about anything they find, and they love to carry their exciting discoveries about with them. They'll resist your best efforts to have them relinquish their precious finds, so unless you want your pup chewing on your sofa or hiding your best pair of shoes, provide her with some preapproved doggie delights. Just as with babies, choose toys that are safe. Puppies explore by putting everything into their mouths, so never choose anything small enough to be swallowed. For extra caution, you may want to consult your veterinarian about appropriate toys for your pup, but in every case let common sense and safety be your guide. Chews need to be chewy enough to satisfy your pup's natural chewing instinct, and if any toy gets torn apart, take it away immediately—as she may swallow the smaller parts—and replace it with a sturdier toy. Finally, as with toddlers, this is an age when you really need to keep an eye on your inquisitive pup, because you never know what she has her eye on.

# PUPPY'S ROOM

Before you bring your new puppy home, you need to choose the place that will become his nursery. Here is where your puppy will learn to adapt to a strict schedule of eating, sleeping, and relieving himself. Your puppy wants and needs parameters, and this will keep everyone in the household—your puppy included—happy.

A puppy's nursery needs to be a small and confined space. It can be an extra bathroom cordoned off with an expandable pressure gate (so he doesn't get lonesome) or playpen set up in the kitchen. Try to pick a room with easily cleaned floors. Wee-Wee Pads aren't 100 percent waterproof, and to puppies, expensive rugs and carpets are just oversize Piddle Pads. I stress the need for a confined space, because it promotes the fastest, least stressful, most efficient housebreaking, and, equally important, your puppy will be happier. Once he understands what you are asking him to do through your efforts to housebreak him, he will be happy to please you. Also, what we view as confinement, he sees as cozy. The house is overwhelming for a young puppy, and giving him the run of it would be the wrong thing to do. What a puppy needs most, at this tender age, is a small, simple, and secure environment where he feels completely safe. Here too is where your pup will learn the basics. I call this "microtraining," since it reduces the pup's world to the simplest elements.

Microtraining is facilitated by microsizing your pup's nursery. The nursery should be a space no more than double the size of the crate or kennel you've chosen as his sleeping space. Within this small nursery should be the "crib"—your pup's den—the "BashRoom," food and water bowls, and, of course, his chews and toys. This microenvironment meets all the puppy's nursery needs—a place to sleep, eat, relieve himself, and, of course, play. As your puppy masters his microenvironment, he can graduate from this nursery school to the macroenvironment of your world. He can have the run of the house, and you won't have to worry about bad behavior, soiled carpets, or chewed furniture, because puppy will already have learned his ABC's in nursery school:

1. Who the **A**lpha leader is
2. Where to go to the **B**athroom
3. What he may and may not **C**hew

## CHOOSING YOUR VETERINARIAN

How do you find the right veterinarian for your new puppy? The same way you would go about finding a competent physician for yourself or beloved family member: research, research and more research! Word of mouth from satisfied clients is a good place to start, so begin by asking your dog friends which veterinarians they use. You might also ask about the doctor's rates, her office hours and location. Your veterinarian's location is more than a question of convenience; it can mean a real difference in an emergency. Certainly, you want the best possible veterinarian for your precious puppy, but if your dog is in a serious accident or terribly ill, even the most brilliant vet will be unable to help if she's fifty miles away.

If you don't know anyone with a dog, contact your local Veterinary Society, and they will provide you with a list of veterinarians in your community. Although all vets are qualified, many veterinarians, like so many medical doctors nowadays, have chosen specialties, with board certification in areas such as ophthalmology, dermatology, and surgery. With your brand-new, healthy puppy, you shouldn't need any specialists just yet. What you need is a reliable, all-around good vet— a general practitioner.

Once you've compiled a list of the most likely candidates, make appointments to interview every vet on the list. A good client-veterinarian relationship is integral to your puppy's health and well-being. Your dog has no voice himself, so you have to ensure that he will get the basic care that leads to good health. He is utterly dependent on you to get him the medical attention he needs, so it is vital to have open and constructive communication with your veterinarian. A good veterinarian will listen carefully to what dog owners report. As one vet told me, "The owner knows his dog better than anyone, and the information he gives me can help me arrive at a correct diagnosis." You and your vet are allies in keeping your precious pup healthy, so choose a vet with whom you feel comfortable. Since you won't have your new puppy with you during this initial getting-to-know-you interview, you will have to make a judgment based on the vet's interaction with you. If, for some reason, your personalities just don't seem to click, then interview another veterinarian. Remember, although skill is the most important requisite, kindness, compassion, and empathy with you, as well as with your pet, are vital parts of this equation.

Once you have decided on your veterinarian, schedule an appointment for two to three days—but no longer—after puppy's homecoming. Unless you have a specific reason or recommendation from your breeder to stop at the veterinarian before taking puppy home, doing so can add too much stress to the little guy's already bewildering day. It's far better to take the little one directly home to his new surroundings, and get him comfortable and settled in as quickly as possible. Plus, having the new baby home for two to three days before his initial visit gives you a chance to observe his behavior, which will allow you to be better able to provide your veterinarian with a base-line picture of his health. Is he eating and drinking? If so, does it seem about right, or is he perhaps just picking at his food, or maybe drinking water excessively? Does he seem to be relieving himself in accordance with his food and water intake? Is he as playful as you would expect, or does he seem lethargic? These are all questions your veterinarian will ask, so observe the puppy carefully. Also, bring a stool sample to puppy's first vet visit as well. A marble-size sample of your puppy's bowel movement will be all your vet needs to test for any common (and easily treatable) parasite your puppy may have. Having puppy home for forty-eight hours before his first trip to the veterinarian will make it as productive and stress-free as possible—and make puppy more willing to return for his second doctor's appointment.

## PREPARE YOUR SUPPORT SYSTEM

It takes a village to raise a child, and the same can be said for raising a happy and healthy puppy. Once you've found the right veterinarian for your dog, you need to once again examine her needs and your ability to fill those needs. Most of my clients find that, next to choosing their veterinarian, it is crucial to find the right groomer and dog-walker or -sitter. This will depend largely, of course, on the breed of your dog, as well as your lifestyle and where you live. For example, ask yourself these questions: Do you have a Poodle, Lhasa Apso, or Komondor? These are breeds with high-maintenance coats that require proper and regular grooming to promote good health and well-being. Or, do you have a German Shepherd, Labrador Retriever, or Border Collie? These are high-energy dogs, and they require a great deal of exercise on a regular basis. How compatible is your schedule with your new dog's schedule? Do you work in the home or outside the home? Are you away for long hours or can you come home at lunchtime? Finally, do you have the time and talent to handle everything yourself? If not, then to ensure you raise a happy and healthy puppy, you should seek out the help of some local "villagers."

If you cannot always meet your puppy's needs as well or as often as you would like, you need to do the next best thing: hire the people who will consider your dog's needs as important as you do.

### Groomer

I always cringe when I hear people say that professional grooming is only for "show dogs or Poodles with fancy haircuts." Nothing could be further from the truth. Whether you do it yourself or have it done professionally, regular grooming is essential to the health, well-being, and, yes, happiness of your dog. Basic grooming such as brushing and combing should be a daily routine for you and your dog, and you obviously don't want or need a professional groomer for that. Plus, the occasional bath after a romp in the country or a roll in something foul-smelling is easily handled by yourself. But for those of you who are new to puppy "parenting," I wouldn't advise grooming the dog yourself. First, with scissors and other sharp instruments, you could end up hurting yourself or your dog, making your dog less inclined to hold still for the second grooming session. Also, it's not as easy as it looks. I had one client—a professional hair stylist to the stars, no less—who tried valiantly to give his Lhasa Apso a proper haircut. It was a lot more difficult and frustrating than he imagined, and no amount of good intentions could make up for lack of know-how. He finally gave up and took his dog to a good groomer to do damage control. Because my client is so wonderful with his celebrity clientele, he shall remain nameless to save him from embarrassment—but he should be jailed for inflicting a very bad hair day on an innocent dog!

Above and beyond the basics, the groomer is a professional who is often the first line of defense in guarding your dog's good health. Regular professional grooming can control and prevent fleas and ticks and the potential hazards they pose to your dog's well-being. Flea allergies can cause serious skin problems, and ticks can infect a dog (and his family) with Lyme disease. The professional groomer will also clean your dog's ears. Some breeds seem predisposed to ear infections. The ears of breeds like Labrador Retrievers, for example, which are lopped or folded over, tend to retain warmth and moisture. This, combined with buildup of everyday dirt and grime, can unwittingly create a perfect breeding ground for infection. And if, like a Labrador, you have a dog that does a great deal of swimming, you need to be on guard against ear infections. With proper ear care, these infections can be prevented or treated before they get out of hand. They can be serious, however, and your groomer can alert you that your dog should be seen by a veterinarian. Ears are a very delicate part of the anatomy, and the groomer is a skilled professional with a deft touch. By the same token, your groomer will clean in and around your dog's eyes, especially important for the health of dogs such as the Pekingese, Old English Bulldog and Shar Pei. Having your dog's nails professionally clipped is equally important. If your dog's nails are too long, or long hair is growing between his pads, walking and exercise will be painful for her. A good eye and steady hand are important for proper nail clipping. If not done properly, you risk cutting into the "quick" of the nail. It's not fatal, of course, but it does get messy (it will bleed quite a bit), and, more important, your dog will be in pain, and thus very resistant the next time you try to clip her nails. Finally, if you or your dog has any allergies (the Bichon Frise, for example, can sometimes be allergic to grass), your groomer—along with your veterinarian and allergist, of course, can help provide the proper treatment.

Your breeder and veterinarian can probably make a recommendation for a groomer in your area, but you may also ask at your local pet shop. Word of mouth is always good. If you see someone on the street with the same breed as your dog, don't hesitate to ask where she gets her dog groomed.

One final tip: Dogs are generally far more agreeable to a professional grooming than the often clumsy but well-intentioned attempts by their owners. In fact, most dogs come to enjoy a visit to the groomer's. Like us, dogs find it feels good to get dirty hair washed, tangles combed out, and skin soothed. Not only do the dogs feel better and know they're being cared for, but like all pack animals, they also enjoy the hustle and bustle and interaction with the groomers and the other four-footed clients.

### The Dog-Walker or Dog-Sitter

We would like to be all things to our dogs at all times. As your puppy's primary caregiver, that's a natural and commendable desire, but sometimes it's not realistic. Unless you are a celebrity or own your own business or command a *Fortune* 500 company and can take your dog everywhere with you, you probably have to work outside the home, and you have to consider secondary caregivers. You may be lucky enough to have a five-minute commute to work, and therefore can return home on a lunch break to walk your dog. Still, I recommend finding a reliable dog-walker or -sitter even if you do not foresee an immediate daily or regular need for one. In the event of an emergency, or an occasion that takes you out of town unexpectedly, you don't want to be left holding the leash. Finding someone to entrust with your puppy is not a decision to make at the last minute. You wouldn't do that with your children, and you shouldn't do that with your dog.

Due to two-career families and ever-lengthening commutes, the need for dog-walkers and -sitters has increased dramatically, and the services offered to meet those needs have flourished. Indeed, a number of associations have formed to monitor the quality of the services provided. Many dog-walkers and -sitters are bonded and insured. Where you live will affect your choices. Obviously, large cities have a plethora of pet services to choose from. But whether you choose a professional or hire the part-time college student living next door, your standards should be equally high.

First and foremost is your dog's safety and well-being. You and your dog-walker should be in total understanding of the parameters of your dog's needs, from the amount of exercise to when and what he eats, and to when and where he is walked. As with a baby-sitter, your dog-sitter should have your veterinarian's phone number as well as where you can be reached. Finally, if you can trust your pet-sitter with your dog, you can certainly trust her with the key to your home. Don't forget, she'll be of no use to your dog if she can't reach him.

The best place to begin your search is with your veterinarian. She will probably have several listings of a variety of pet-related services. Don't hesitate to ask your veterinarian if she can personally recommend someone for the job. Oftentimes, health care professionals working in veterinary clinics provide these services on the side. It certainly pays to check. Your groomer and local pet shop should also be helpful in this area, and, once again, don't hesitate to ask other dog people whom they use.

## WHAT TO NAME PUPPY

Your new puppy won't care what you call him—he just wants you to love him. You may already have a name in mind—whether it's from a character in a book or movie, or paying homage to sweet old Aunt Sadie. I advise two guidelines when choosing a name. First, remember that the most important criterion is that your dog immediately recognizes his name, so he can respond to it. This will not only help in training, but, more important, such instant response is vital to your pup's safety. Dogs respond best to short, snappy words with sharp consonants, such as Buddy, Duke, Jenny and Lady. Don't give a dog a complicated name with too many syllables, like Samantha or Beauregard. Dogs communicate, wolflike, in sharp, staccato yips and barks, and that's what they'll respond best to. If you must have Beauregard, shorten it to Bo. If you have your heart set on Rebecca of Sunnybrook Farm or Mr. Bojangles, then shorten them to Becky and Bo. Deciding on puppy's name can be lots of fun, but don't spend too much time deciding. Once you've got a feel for that special little personality, pick a name to match. Once you decide on puppy's name, use it uniformly (don't start mixing in nicknames, it will just confuse him) and often, and always with love and approval. This will guarantee that he will look up to you whenever you mention his name.

## BRINGING PUPPY HOME

Now that you've completed all your preparatory work—you've made your house puppy-friendly, puppy-proof, and you've lined up your veterinarian and support staff—it's time to pick up your newest family member.

Naturally, everyone will want to go along to pick up baby, but that may be too much excitement for the little guy. It's always wise to ask the breeder and then act accordingly. You don't want to overwhelm the puppy, so it might be wise to leave the children at home. Their disappointment can be placated by reminding them that they'll have plenty of time to play with the puppy for years to come. And, if they are old enough, you can make them feel included in this very special journey by leaving them with an assigned puppy-related task, such as making sure the puppy comes home to a fresh bowl of water and an assortment of puppy-friendly toys.

When bringing baby home, remember just that—that she is a *baby*. Never just dump a puppy in the backseat. It's not only dangerous, but would terrify her, as well. Don't forget, she's leaving all the family and home she has ever known. If two of you are picking up the puppy, make sure to take along a couple of soft towels to cradle the puppy in. She will probably be frightened and wet on the way home. The towels will keep dampness contained, diaperlike, and wrapping her in them and holding her close to you will reassure her.

If you're traveling alone, however, make sure you have a dog carrier. I recommend the Sherpa Bag, which is soft and cushioned, and the next best thing to being held by you. Keep the puppy in the bag in the seat next to you, and speak to her frequently in calm, soothing tones along the ride home. If your ride is longer than thirty minutes, take along a doggie baby bottle filled with water. Take a break midway to give her water, but be sensible. Give her only enough water to wet her mouth. Too much water, combined with the motion of the car, may make her throw up. Remember, puppies have delicate tummies to begin with, and this is her very first car ride.

When the puppy arrives home and meets more family members for the first time, be careful not to overwhelm her. Everyone wants to greet her and hold her, of course—she's just so cute!—but tender and quiet greetings are best, and, for the moment, should be kept to a minimum. Too much of anything—even affection—can be detrimental right now. She'll probably have to relieve herself, so start her off on the right paw by taking her immediately to the Wee-Wee Pads. This will give the puppy a chance to get her bearings, sniff out this new strange place, and to assimilate all the new smells, sounds, and voices surrounding it. And once your puppy relieves herself, she will be marking your home as her own.

# HOUSEBREAKING

I always recommend that my clients try to schedule a puppy's homecoming during a time when they can be home to give their new baby their undivided attention. If you work outside the home, a long weekend or holiday is ideal. This will allow you to spend as much time as possible with the puppy during this all-important bonding and early initial training time. Since a dog's lifetime, averaging fourteen years, is so much shorter than ours, think of these early weeks and months as his "formative years." You'll want to be with him as much as possible. The time you spend with your puppy today will shape the kind of dog he will grow up to become. Quality time spent with your puppy at the very beginning of your life together really pays off in the long run. These first few weeks are a positive investment toward a successful and rewarding long-term relationship with your dog.

With housebreaking, as with everything else puppy-related, you must again think PC. But now, we take it a step further. If you really want your puppy to mind you, then you must mind your *P*s and *C*s.

When potty-training your puppy, as with all training, it is vital to use your *P*s: *Patience, Persistence,* and *Praise*; and your *C*s: *Compassion, Care,* and *Concern.*

Remember, just bringing the puppy home is a big adjustment for the little one. Even though he is a domestic dog, try to think of him as a tiny, wild creature that is confused and frightened. It is unrealistic to expect a very young animal to understand immediately what it's supposed to do and not to do. You cannot really expect too much of him in the way of orderly behavior. At the very beginning, your job is simply to make sure he is comfortable and secure, while at the same time letting him know where he may and may not go to the bathroom.

But don't be afraid to gently but firmly "show him the ropes." All dogs are pack animals, just as wolves are, and this means that no matter how young your puppy is, he requires order and structure in his life to be happy and function successfully. He needs a pack leader—you—to comfort him, protect him, and teach him, just like his real mother would. I did this with Mariah, and you can do this with a puppy. And make sure to establish your leadership role with puppy from the beginning. All puppies, like children, need boundaries in their lives. Otherwise, your dog, left to his own devices, will take leadership into his own paws and begin to run things his way. And although your puppy has been born with certain genetic instincts that shape his personality and behavior, your puppy will eventually become the kind of adult dog your alpha "parenting" skills make him.

Whether you want your new pup paper-trained or completely housebroken is up to you, your puppy's breed, and your lifestyle. Obviously, a large breed should be trained to relieve himself outdoors. Large dogs need plenty of exercise and really do have to be walked, so it would be cruel to try to paper-train one. Being outside keeps both you and your dog physically fit, and gives you both a chance to socialize with other dogs and their owners, and helps to reinforce that special bond between you and your dog. In fact, because of these added benefits, I recommend outdoor housetraining whenever possible.

Still, in some cases this just isn't possible. People who have medical problems or mobility constraints, people who are elderly or fragile, mothers with infants, or merely those whose demanding jobs keep them working 24/7, find paper-training the only option. In-house training can be done quite successfully without detriment to the dog's health, well-being, or socialization. In fact, many of my celebrity clientele prefer this method. Mariah Carey and Jennifer Lopez, for example, love to take their Toy dogs everywhere with them, including to recording studios and movie locations, so this method works perfectly for them. Another celebrity client pair of mine, two high-profile movie stars, went through a very public, very messy divorce. For two years the paparazzi camped outside their home, recording their every move. To salvage at least a shred of privacy, I retrained their already older, outdoor dogs to go to the BashRoom indoors. This benefited both my clients and, more important, the dogs. The often unruly paparazzi, along with hordes of gawking onlookers jostling for a glimpse of the stars, was unsettling, to say the least, for the dogs. After the divorce, when things quieted down, I had to retrain the dogs to once again do their business outside. But that's another story. All I can say is, thank heavens dogs put up so patiently with our foibles and frailties.

But right now, as you're house-training puppy, *you* must put up with his foibles and frailties with *patience, persistence,* and *praise,* and *compassion, care,* and *concern.*

Remember, your puppy is a baby. His ability to follow your house-training schedule will rely on his ability to understand what you want him to do and on his physical ability to follow through. Puppies' bladders are small, and veterinarians caution that asking a dog to hold his urine longer than six hours may be taking a chance with his health. Kidney damage could result. However most dogs, even puppies, can sleep through an eight-hour night, as long as you don't give unlimited water before bedtime. A good rule of thumb is, what goes in must come out, so feeding and watering time is strictly scheduled and should be strictly adhered to.

## INDOOR AND OUTDOOR SCHEDULE FOR
## A PUPPY UP TO FOUR MONTHS OLD

This schedule will work for both paper-training and outdoor training, but whichever method you choose, training will be greatly facilitated if you continue to keep puppy's sleep time and downtime safely confined in her den (crate or kennel cab). Plus, the times of day for each activity can be adjusted according to your own timetable. What's important to remember here is that the lapses of time between each activity should remain constant.

6 A.M.
  You and the puppy wake up.
  Immediately put her on paper or take her outdoors.
  Give her food and water.
  Put her on paper or take her outdoors.
  Socialize and play with her for as long as possible.
  Put her back into her crate.
7 to 7:30 A.M.
  Go to work, do errands, or keep appointments.
10 A.M.
  Wake the puppy up if necessary.
  Put her on paper or take her out.
  Give her water.
  Put her on paper or take her out.
  Socialize and play.
  Put her back into her crate.
1 P.M.
  Wake the puppy up.
  Put her on paper or take her out.
  Give her food and water.
  Put her on paper or take her out.
  Socialize and play.
  Put her back into her crate.
4 P.M.
  Same as 10 A.M.

7 P.M.
  Same as 1 P.M.
10 to 11 P.M.
  Wake the puppy up.
  Put the puppy on paper or take her out.
  Socialize and play.
  Give her a biscuit or snack and an ice cube.
  Put her on paper or take her out.
  Put her to bed in her crate.

Between the ages of four to six months, you and your puppy will graduate to a new phase in your path to successful housebreaking. If you have chosen a small breed and paper-trained her for in-house housebreaking only, then she is probably ready to graduate from her microenvironment to a designated "puppy-friendly" area of the house. Here, she will still have her den (crate) to sleep in, but she will have the freedom to move about and play with her toys, because she has learned, whenever nature calls, to return, by herself, to her "BashRoom."

## OUTDOOR SCHEDULE FOR A PUPPY BETWEEN SIX AND NINE MONTHS OLD

At this age a puppy can be fed two meals a day, as long as she is eating a highly nutritious diet. If your puppy is eating a less densely nutritious, commercial diet, she will probably still need three meals a day. Check with your veterinarian.

6 A.M.
  Wake up.
  Take the puppy outdoors.
  Give her food and water.
  Take the puppy outdoors.
  Socialize and play.
  Put her back into crate.
11 A.M. to Noon
  Wake the puppy up, if necessary.

Give her water.
Take her outdoors.
Socialize and play.
Put her back in the crate.
4 to 5 P.M.
Same as 6 A.M.
8 P.M.
Give her water.
Take her outdoors.
10 to 11 P.M.
Give her a snack or biscuit and an ice cube.
Take her outdoors.
Put her to bed in the crate.

Under ideal circumstances, at about nine months of age, your puppy should be able to last without needing to go out for up to five or more hours during the day, depending on her size, breed, and degree of maturity. Puppies from shelters or pet shops may need longer due to lack of early socialization.

## INTRODUCING A PUPPY TO THE LEASH

Whether you plan to housebreak your puppy indoors or outdoors, proper puppy leash behavior is a must. Your puppy's leash is his lifeline. You are his parent, his alpha leader, and he will feel more secure in the big, wide world knowing he is firmly attached to you and your guidance. In fact, the leash is his first line of defense in any unforeseen occurrence. Like a safety harness for a car ride, the leash is a safety belt for a walk.

Even if you have a fenced-in yard, it's a good idea, when housebreaking, to take your puppy on his leash into the yard to do his business. This practice isn't forever, of course, but for housebreaking it's a good idea. Too often puppies who have simply been "let out" on their own to do their business will be too confused to do their business, when necessary, on a leash. Make certain you have a four- to six-foot leash. That gives you control over your puppy, but also allows him the freedom to engage in what I call the "poo-poo dance." That's the all-important signal to watch for to facilitate housebreaking. After eating and drinking, your puppy will begin to sniff and circle, scratch, and run back and forth (all within a two- or three-foot space) before squatting or lifting his leg.

Remember, this is not formal leash training, but it lays a good foundation by familiarizing your puppy with the leash.

# LIVING THE DREAM: ADVENTURES IN CANINE COMPANIONSHIP

Once your dream dog settles in and is feeling secure in her new environs with her new family, you may notice something you find peculiar. At times, when your dog is sleeping on her side, you may see her legs moving as though she was running. You are mystified. What's going on? you wonder. It's simple. Your dream dog is . . . dreaming. She is in that stage of sleep known as REM (rapid eye movement—or should I say, rapid leg movement) during which most dreaming occurs.

Okay, that's one mystery solved, but one remains. What, you wonder, is your dog dreaming about? Well, to quote, Dr. Sigmund Fido, who was never known to bark up a wrong tree: "I don't know," at least not for sure. However, I think that it is a good bet that your dog is dreaming about adventures she and you have shared, and about adventures yet to come. "What adventures?" you ask. Well, just consider the following wide variety of adventures you and your dog can share.

The first is basic training, because good behavior is the passkey that will open doors to all sorts of ways of life you probably never dreamed of. Visit me at my Web site (www.pawsacrossamerica.com), where I'll show you how to find the best trainer and individual or group classes in your area, as well as all my books and videos to guide you. You'll find that in-tandem training truly is an adventure in and of itself. It's a great deal of fun, and it strengthens that special bond you and your dog share.

## BECOMING A CANINE GOOD CITIZEN

Once the two of you have mastered basic training, you should consider having your dog tested for Canine Good Citizen (CGC) certification. This program is open to all dogs, not just purebreds. CGC certification announces to the world that your dog has demonstrated that he is well mannered and well behaved. CGC certification is gaining increasing recognition throughout the world, opening doors which previously had been closed to dogs.

For example, a client of mine wanted to move into a luxury building in New York City, but was experiencing substantial resistance from a co-op board notoriously adverse to accepting people with dogs. I appeared before the board to attest to the dog's good behavior. I explained to the board that the dog was CGC-certified and demonstrated that the dog immediately responded to commands. The board was so impressed that it not only accepted my client and his dog, but also decided that in the future, potential residents with dogs would be given a leg up (so to speak) in the approval process if the dog was CGC-certified. Not only that, but more than one board member was heard to mumble, "If they only had a similar behavioral certification for children."

The CGC program was started over a decade ago by the American Kennel Club. The AKC's then Director of Obedience, Jim Dearinger, offered me the opportunity to help create, promote, and test-market the CGC's premier program. The program and the dogs have come a long way since those early pioneering days. Mr. Dearinger, now retired, became the AKC Secretary and Administrator of the CGC, and under his watch the CGC certification became increasingly accepted as the standard for responsible pet behavior, not only across the nation, but also in many other countries, including England, Australia, Japan, Hungary, Denmark, Sweden, Canada, and Finland.

In addition to opening doors to places previously opened only to service dogs (Seeing Eye dogs, hearing ear dogs, and the like), CGC certification serves as a requisite for dogs receiving training to become a pet therapy dog, a humane education dog, a volunteer search and rescue dog, or an animal actor. Indeed, a CGC certification is fast becoming a required credential.

## PET THERAPY DOG

Once your dog is a certified Canine Good Citizen, you may decide to go to the next level: certification as a therapy dog. It is now a well-accepted fact that dogs have a unique healing ability.

Nursing homes, hospices, and hospitals across the country increasingly utilize pet therapy. We've come a long way, because it wasn't always so. Back in 1985, I was instrumental in influencing then Bronx Borough President Stanley Simon to proclaim Pet Therapy Week in the Bronx—the first such proclamation in the United States. The following year, New York City Mayor Ed Koch proclaimed a citywide Pet Therapy Week, and a subsequent statewide pet therapy program was developed under the direction of the Center for Pet Therapy in New York City, of which I was a director.

Pet therapy dogs give the kind of unconditional love that only a dog can give. They give touch contact, so missed by individuals who are removed from loved ones, and they are nonjudgmental in their acceptance of people. What's more, they often bring a person who has lost his sense of reality back to the present. And, in tandem with her handler, the therapy dog acts as a social catalyst and provides a common ground for conversation and communication. It sounds simple, but sometimes proves to be near-miraculous, as I discovered when my Chihuahua, Goldie, and I paid one of our regular visits to a nursing home in New York City. Most of the residents knew my dogs and me quite well (the pet therapy program was a hit from the start), but that day there was a new resident in the group. The facility's recreation director informed me that the woman was suffering from a severe case of Alzheimer's disease. She was unable to remember anything, and hadn't spoken in months. The patient's husband, who was visiting her, confirmed this, adding that his wife had once been a very active and accomplished woman. She had been a concert pianist, an eye surgeon, and had been fluent in six languages. He told me how pleased he was that I had brought Goldie, because his wife had always loved animals.

Armed with this information, I brought Goldie over to the woman. As I stood in front of her, I asked her husband what languages she knew. He told me she had been born in Greece. Having grown up in Europe myself, I speak a little bit of a lot of languages, so I spoke to her in the language of her childhood. I said, *"Te kanis,"* which means "hello" in Greek. While stroking Goldie, she looked up at me and gave me the most beautiful smile. *"Te kanis,"* she whispered. Her husband was shocked, and all the health professionals rushed over.

As Goldie leaned closer to the woman, I tried another language. This time it was French. *"Desirez-vous le chien?"* ("Do you want the dog?") I asked her. As she gently cuddled Goldie, her eyes grew radiant, *"Oui, je desire le chien!"* With that, her husband could contain himself no longer, and shouted, "Look! She's talking!" Everyone, including the health-care professionals, laughed and clapped.

A door had been opened. Goldie had done her job superbly. Now it was time for the professionals to take over. With therapeutic reconstruction (working from her childhood on, by using the languages she had learned when she was young), they were able to rebuild her ability to communicate.

This illustrates perfectly what pet therapy is all about. Sometimes the touch or loving attention of a pet therapy dog—combined with an intuitive handler (that would be *you!*)—can create a means of communication that has been long forgotten. This can cause a person to relax, forget the stress or infirmities of his present circumstances, and open up an avenue of memory and feeling that can build a bridge back to the present.

I was so happy Goldie and I had been part of the team of professionals that facilitated this lovely woman's "miracle" journey in recapturing her life. This happened many years ago, and strengthened my resolve to bring pet therapy into the mainstream. Toward this end, I served as a board member of the Delta Society, an international organization dedicated to improving human health through service and therapy animals. During my years there I had the opportunity to promote the therapeutic use of pets in nursing homes and schools. I also helped develop and promote their Pet Partners Program, where both owner and pet can become certified pet therapists.

To learn more about how you can become involved in pet therapy—and all the other adventures you will read about in this chapter—please consult Appendix II, the "Directory of Dog Organizations."

## HUMANE EDUCATION DOG

The idea of Humane Education was first championed by Eleanor Roosevelt. While her husband valiantly led America during the dark days of World War II, the indomitable First Lady led the conscience of the nation on domestic issues. With courage and conviction, she worked to promote the twin causes of child abuse and animal welfare, and the heartbreaking link between the two. A woman ahead of her time, she worked diligently to bring humane education into our schools, and for legislation to enforce and maintain such important education. In fact, one statute actually required schools to provide thirty minutes of humane education per week. Unfortunately, humane education never really took off the way Eleanor Roosevelt had envisioned, and in the boom years following World War II, much of this good work fell by the wayside and the humane education statutes languished unnoticed and unused.

But with the Canine Good Citizen certification becoming a kind of doggie "passport" to all kinds of public facilities formerly off-limits to dogs—and with the advent of today's high-profile pet therapy dogs—humane education is making a comeback.

Of course, for many dedicated and caring professionals and volunteers alike in the animal welfare community, humane education has always been a way of life. In fact, I even had my wolf, Mariah, volunteer for a stint in humane education. It is designed to promote understanding and humane treatment of animals, and I usually toured schools and libraries with my show dogs, shelter dogs, and a variety of other critters. Mariah, however, had even more to offer the students. Her gentle and well-socialized demeanor was such a direct contrast to the widely held misconception of the "big bad wolf" that she helped to promote interspecies understanding. When Mariah and I gave an endangered species seminar at the Horace Mann School in New York City, the young students were floored—literally—when, in demonstrating wolf cub play behavior, they were allowed to sit on the floor with Mariah and pet her as she gave them her trademark "play bow."

## SEARCH AND RESCUE DOG

Search and rescue dogs have been highly trained to use their keen senses of smell and hearing to locate people who are missing in the wilderness, help the police to find homicide and drowning victims, and find disaster victims who may be buried under rubble after an earthquake or a building collapse.

These incredible dogs also use what I call an extra-special sense-thermal sensitivity. Wolves and dogs share the ability to sense a person's or animal's body heat inside their noses and pinpoint a hidden source of odor. I once watched Mariah as she sniffed along the surface of freshly fallen, untracked snow. Suddenly, she stopped and began to dig. Soon, she unearthed a mole that had been hiding under a rock. In the wild, wolves use this sense to survive in snowy, icy winters. Over the years, Saint Bernards have used this sense to find people trapped below many feet of snow.

For you and your dog to become a search and rescue team, the two of you have to undergo an intensive—but very exciting—training program. Although because of their size, thick double coats, and physical strength, German Shepherds are the traditional breed of choice for this work, dogs of other breeds, especially the Labrador Retriever and Border Collie, have also become successful search and rescue dogs. Even a mixed breed, if it is up to snuff, will be accepted into the program. The earmarks of a good search and rescue candidate are a dog's receptiveness to training and his relationship with, and responsiveness to, his handler. This is especially important because of the nature of the work. A great deal of search and rescue work is conducted in wooded areas, and since search and rescue dogs always work off-lead, they must never be distracted by game (rabbits, deer, squirrels, for example) in the woods. This gives German Shepherds a big advantage, because they are not hunting dogs and therefore not distracted by game.

Ideally, although there are no age requirements, training should begin when a dog is young. After his initial socialization, a puppy slated for search and rescue work is taught to further develop his strong sense of smell. Through an elaborate hide-and-seek game in which the owner-handler hides, the puppy is trained to use his nose to locate people by means of airborne scent. Later, as the dog matures, he goes through advanced obedience training to learn to work entirely off-leash under voice command only. As the dog hones his tracking ability, all-important agility feats are developed, and his stamina is built up. Agility is very important, as search and rescue dogs must circumnavigate all sorts of terrain with treacherous footing, tunnels, caves, cliffs, and the rubble of collapsed buildings and earthquake-ravaged cities.

After all of this intensive training, a search and rescue dog and his owner-handler are ready to join the team. As with pet therapy and humane education, search and rescue is an extremely rewarding adventure. (For more information on this training, consult Appendix II).

## ANIMAL ACTOR

How many times have you watched a dog in a commercial, television show, or movie and thought, "My dog can do that"? Or maybe you've flipped through a magazine and spotted an especially appealing little pup and exclaimed, "That looks just like my dog!" Every day people just like you call me or visit my Web site (www.starpet.com) to ask whether their dogs have what it takes to succeed in the entertainment industry. And you know what? Very often these dogs do have what it takes—and so might yours. It's not that big a leap from "Sit! Come! Heel!" to "Lights! Camera! Action!"—or should I say, "Lights! *Canine!* Action!"

My dogs have worked in every medium in the entertainment industry—Broadway, motion pictures, television series, commercials, and print ads—and I can tell you that even the most critically acclaimed "four paws up" performance is simply an extension and refinement of a lesson learned in basic on-lead and off-lead obedience.

Of course, there is more entailed in these performances. Once in the studio, and the director barks, "Quiet on the set!" the cameras will be rolling and your dog will have to perform with just a hand signal from you. Since you have to remain out of camera range, your dog has to have the ability and concentration to stay focused on you, interpret your signals from a distance, and act on them immediately, undistracted by the milling about of assorted cast and crew members.

Still, dogs are intelligent, sociable, loving pack animals. They love to learn, they love a challenge, they love to work, they love to please, and they love to be around people. My dogs thrive on this. They love to perform, and they especially love the praise and attention that follows a terrific performance. And the entertainment industry loves dogs. You may have noticed recently that advertisers have been using dogs in all sorts of commercials for products that have absolutely nothing to do with dogs. Why? People love them, and they sell. In fact, casting calls for dogs have tripled in the last few years.

To meet this demand, I've expanded my StarPet animal talent agency to include open casting calls and workshops. One of my long-time clients (a hardworking and fairly successful actress) began working with her mixed breed she rescued from the streets. The dog was so successful that her own acting career had to take a backseat to her dog's career.

But don't let success frighten you. If your career should begin to take a backseat to your dog's, then Fido is probably doing quite nicely for you. For most of my StarPet clients, "show business" is not a vocation, but an avocation. It's a fun and exciting adventure. Indeed, most of my StarPet dogs enjoy the occasional work in print ads and soap operas *(The Edge of Night, Guiding Light, One Life to Live)* for precisely the same reason their human counterparts do—it allows them to have a private life.

If your dog is talented and enjoys learning performance tricks, but you don't want to go the show biz route, your dog can remain a private Canine Good Citizen by volunteering to entertain children and adults in schools, libraries, hospitals, and nursing homes.

So whether your interest is professional or personal, learning performance arts with your new pup (or old dog) is an adventure in and of itself.

# AGILITY

Since dogs love to work almost as much as they love to play, a play experience that combines the two is ecstasy for a dog, and the exciting sport of agility has taken the world by storm. Today, there's an increasing number of interesting and challenging places for dogs and their people to play and practice agility—from doggie playgrounds with agility courses to dog parks and runs. In New York City in 1998, my Pets, People & Parks campaign, in tandem with the Friends of Van Cortlandt Park and the New York City Parks Department, premiered the world's first dog playground. Sporting both an agility course and a grassy "free play" area, then New York City Parks Commissioner Henry Stern made history by launching the world's first government-sanctioned dog playground. As Commissioner Stern, with his dog, Boomer, at his side, christened the park Canine Court, news agencies from around the world, including CNN, covered this historic event.

Canine Court's main attraction is its obstacle and agility course—with hurdles, hoops, tunnels, crawl spaces, seesaws, slides, and fences—which is self-contained within the playground. The playground also features an enclosed free-play dog run with trees and grass, as well as benches for people. Dogs are allowed unobstructed playtime both on the obstacle course and in the free-play area. Canine Court has served as a prototype for similar playgrounds in other city parks and across the country, forever changing park signage from NO DOGS ALLOWED and PLEASE KEEP OFF THE GRASS to DOGS DEFINITELY ALLOWED, PLEASE PLAY ON THE GRASS and NO ADULT ADMITTED WITHOUT A DOG!

Agility is a way for both dogs and their people to have fun, keep physically fit, and bond. I love to see dogs work on agility courses. When you see their delighted expressions as they work the maze, climb the seesaw, crawl through the tunnels, and leap triumphantly over the final jumps, you'll understand how important play is to your dog.

If you and your dog have a competitive streak, check out the American Kennel Club's Agility trials. This field is growing rapidly, and many dogs have earned progressively more difficult titles. For the supreme title of Master Agility Champion (MACH), which judges both speed and accuracy, the points the qualifying dog earns (750) is based upon the *speed of sound*.

# DANCING WITH DOGS

If you liked the movie *Dances with Wolves* but you're a city slicker who prefers Manolo Blahnik and a night out at the Copacabana to moccasins and a night out camping, then the intriguing, inventive, and downright irresistible Canine Freestyle Dancing with Dogs should fill your dance card nicely.

Canine Freestyle Competition is a little bit theater, a little bit sport, all rolled into an engaging dance in which the dog and her owner move in tandem through a set of choreographed steps accompanied by the music of their choice. The dance moves in freestyle do not need to be elaborate, and aficionados advise that the music should be chosen by your dog (sounds and rhythms that your dog seems to like and naturally get her moving). What at first blush seems like fun and games actually requires a great deal of skill. It's like tipping your hat to Ginger Rogers in acknowledging that she had to do everything Fred Astaire did, only backwards and in heels.

The choreography is based on a series of steps derived from standard obedience, such as heel. But dancing is much more demanding, as you have to teach your dog how to heel on both sides, not just on the handler's left side, as traditional obedience training demands. And (like Ginger Rogers) your dog will have to learn to walk backward in a straight line, and how to pivot in place and how to sidestep.

Still, dance in freestyle doesn't have to be elaborate, and you can be creative and playful, encouraging pivots, spins, leaps and play bows. The dance, like the music, should be based on what your dog lets you know she's enjoying. There are as many styles and outlets in the World of Canine Freestyle as there are breeds in the dog world. Musical freestyle, whether it's country, jazz, balletic, or ballroom, is a showcase that truly and artistically demonstrates the joys and fun of bonding with your pet.

Plus, freestyle canine competition is a wonderful intergenerational, worldwide way to have fun. Everyone, young or old, who wants to have fun with his dog—any breed and any age—is eligible. And the only "equipment" you need is you, your dog, your favorite music—and your imagination. Children especially enjoy the artistry, teamwork, costuming and athleticism of the sport, and 4-H Clubs around the country now offer both Musical Freestyle, as well as Heelwork-to-Music, which incorporates traditional dog obedience with the art of dressage.

## AKC CONFORMATION

If you're a traditionalist and your dog is a purebred, you may want to consider showing your dog at AKC-sanctioned shows. While the AKC sanctions many field trials and performance events, the most competitive one, and the one most of us think of when we hear the words "dog show," is Conformation. After being examined by a judge, dogs are placed according to how well (in the judge's opinion) they measure up to their breed standard.

There are three types of dog shows: specialty, group, and all-breed. Specialty shows are limited to dogs of one breed, and group shows are limited to a particular AKC group. All-breed shows, as the name indicates, are open to all AKC breeds.

Many of my clients have bought their dream puppies thinking they wanted only a loving loyal canine companion, and then afterward became so proud of their beautiful "babies" that they took them right into the show ring themselves. They had to admit it was pretty thrilling to see their precious puppy walk away with a blue ribbon.

Aside from the conformation and competition, the dog shows open up an ever-widening social network for both you and your dog. While the dog world is large in size, the show circuit is considered by many to be a family. It gives fanciers from all walks of life and from all levels of participation an opportunity to ask each other what's happening in their everyday lives, their social events, and comings and goings. In fact, my clients often make a point to meet their dog's littermates on the show circuit. It makes for a fun family reunion.

Most important, you're sharing the experience of a lifetime with your canine companion. You only have to watch these dogs in action to know that, for them, this is the stuff dreams are made of.

## AKC OBEDIENCE

Obedience training is the foundation upon which all canine activities are based, whether it be conformation, agility, tracking, search and rescue, service dogs, therapy dogs, theatrical dogs, fieldwork, and the like.

In 1933, when AKC Obedience competition began, the concept of obedience training was to develop a very close working relationship between people and their dogs, while demonstrating the usefulness and enthusiasm of dogs. This time-honored concept remains as important and relevant today as it was in the program's infancy. There are several levels of long-standing obedience classes, and newer titles have recently been added, continually raising the bar in the AKC's uncompromising standards of excellence.

## AKC TRACKING

AKC Tracking events are the competition form of canine search and rescue. These tracking events provide training for dogs and their handlers in finding lost humans or other animals, as well as demonstrating the extremely high level of scent capability that these dogs possess.

Tracking is a wonderful event to watch even if you're not participating. We've all seen movies with dogs following the trail of an escaped convict through the swamps, for example. Well, the AKC's Tracking Team will demonstrate at these events the dogs' ability to recognize and follow human scent.

A dog earns his Tracking Dog status by following a track up to five hundred yards long with up to five changes in direction. The track (scent) is laid by a human track layer, and is then "aged" for up to two hours before the dog begins scenting. As impressive as this is, it is merely a warm-up for some of these impressive dogs. The next level is Tracking Dog Excellence (TDX), and this is earned by following an "older" track (laid up to five hours before the dog begins to follow it), and the course is up to a thousand yards with seven directional changes.

Finally, there is the Variable Surface Tracking (VST). Because in the real world dogs often track through urban settings as well as through wilderness, a VST dog has to demonstrate its ability to master a challenging five-hour-old track through streets, buildings, and other areas devoid of vegetation.

If you're participating, the vigorous outdoor activity is terrific for your dog and for you.

# AKC EARTHDOG

Earthdog trials are some of the most popular AKC events, probably because they involve the antics of some of the most popular and engaging breeds of the AKC, the terriers.

These trials are for the "go-to-ground" terriers—the smallest of the Terrier Group, such as the Cairn Terriers, Jack Russell Terriers, and Dachshunds. These dogs were all originally bred to go into dens and tunnels after their quarry, which ranged from rats to badgers.

The object of the test is to give the dog an opportunity to display its ability to follow game and to "work" (to show interest by barking, digging, and scratching) the quarry (game). At these trials, the quarry is usually an artificial substitute, which is located behind a barrier, properly scented, and capable of movement. I call this the Santa Claus quarry. It's not real, but the little terriers don't know that, and the fantasy provides a great deal of fun. And don't worry if you go to an Earthdog trial that happens to use real rats. These adult rats are always caged and adequately protected from the dogs.

As with many AKC events and trials, Earthdog trials also include a junior class level for handlers.

## AKC HERDING

Another lively and colorful AKC trial—both for onlookers as well as participants—is Herding. AKC Herding Trials and Tests are designed to allow a dog to demonstrate its ability to herd livestock under the direction of a handler. Stock used at these trials are sheep, cattle, goats, and ducks. In herding tests, dogs are judged against a set of standards, but they also compete against other dogs for placement. This is where advanced titles and championships are earned.

However, if you're just starting out, there are also noncompetitive herding clinics and instinct tests given by AKC clubs all across the country.

## AKC LURE COURSING

If your dream dog is one of the breeds known as a Sighthound, such as a Basenji, Greyhound, Afghan, or Whippet, you may be interested in Lure Coursing. In this competition the dogs follow an artificial lure (think of the old "carrot on a stick" cliché) around a course in an open field. The description is matter-of-fact, but the event is anything but that. It is exciting and beautiful to watch. Coursing dogs are scored on speed, enthusiasm, agility, endurance, and their ability to follow the lure.

Coursing is a great way to keep your hound physically and mentally fit. If you've had the opportunity to see the event, you may be interested but a bit daunted. Don't be intimidated by the grace and beauty and competence of these dogs. As with so many AKC events, many AKC affiliated clubs offer noncompetitive Lure Coursing clinics for the novice.

## AKC FIELD TRIALS

AKC Field Trials literally take the dog out of the show ring and into the field. They offer practical field demonstrations of a dog's ability to perform what it was historically bred to do. Field Events are open to Pointing breeds, Retrievers, Spaniels, Beagles, Basset Hounds, and Dachshunds. Beagles, for example, are judged primarily on their accuracy in trailing rabbits. The Pointing breeds, such as German Shorthaired Pointers and Gordon Setters, demonstrate their ability to find, point staunchly, and retrieve birds. The Retrievers, such as the Chesapeake Bay, Golden and Labrador, and Irish Water Spaniels, are tested for their ability to remember ("mark") the location of one or even multiple birds, and return to their owners. Finally, the Spaniels are judged on their ability to hunt, flush, and retrieve game both on land and in water.

Field trials are exciting to watch. The dogs compete individually against one another for placement and points toward their championships; they also compete, not just one on one, but as pairs and in groups. For example, the Pointing breeds run in pairs (braces), and the Beagles are run in braces of two or three, as well as being divided into packs of seven.

## AKC HUNTING TEST

AKC Hunting Tests evaluate a dog's hunting abilities on different elements of pointing, retrieving, and flushing. The dog's ability to perform is judged against a standard of perfection established by the AKC regulations, and the AKC assures competitors that, theoretically, every dog can be a winner.

## COONHOUND EVENTS

As exciting, colorful, and invigorating as all these AKC trials and events are, the Coonhound Events are truly in a class by themselves. I'm always at a loss to explain them to laymen. To those of you in the general public who are not fanciers, Coonhound Events can best be likened to the popular Renaissance Festivals of medieval fans, and the Civil War re-creations of history buffs. Steeped in the history and tradition of the breed (think of the acclaimed children's classic book,

*Where the Red Fern Grows*), Coonhound Events re-create all that the Coonhound was bred to do, which was to tree raccoons. Since raccoons are nocturnal, these field events take place at night, and can last anywhere from three to five days.

So, there you have it. How to discover your dream dog, where to find him, how to nurture the dream to reality, and how to live the dream, with all the many adventures you can share. So perhaps it's appropriate that we close the book with the adventures of the Coonhound, a breed of dog that lives his dream at night, doing what he was bred to do, and that comes to life in a children's bedtime story.

Good night, and sweet dreams, Dream Dog. Tomorrow is another day, and new adventures await you.

# Appendix I

# YOU AND YOUR DOG: PARTNERS IN HEALTH CARE

In chapter 2, "From Wolf to Dog," we learned about the origin of the breeds and discovered that man's history with the wolf dates back to well over four hundred thousand years ago. In addition, our alliance with the dog has endured over fourteen thousand years. Talk about long-term relationships! As I often tell my clients, acquiring a dog is like entering into a marriage. You are committing to a relationship that, ideally, should be "for better or for worse, in sickness and in health, till death do you part." And the best way to ensure a happy and healthy life for your dog is to become an informed partner in his health care.

Just as chapter 3, "Basic Guide to Dog Breeds," introduced you to the basic natures, temperaments, strengths, and potential weaknesses inherent in the many varied breeds from which you may choose your dream dog, this appendix will help you to understand the language of the many health issues and treatment options which a dog of a particular breed may be faced with at some point in her lifetime. Having a basic working layman's knowledge of both generic and breed-specific health concerns will help you to foster a strong foundation of viable communication between you, your breeder, and your veterinarian, and will make you a valuable adjunct in safeguarding your dog's health and well-being.

There has never been a more exciting or gratifying time to be a part of your dog's health-care team. Several top-flight canine health foundations, such as the American Kennel Club Canine Health Foundation—whose mission is to improve the quality of life for dogs and their owners through the promotion of greater understanding of canine genetics and the development of new diagnostic and therapeutic options for treating canine diseases—have sponsored breeders and veterinary hospitals in groundbreaking canine health research. This research has resulted in many innovative treatments and cures for canine diseases.

In fact, because of the genetic similarities between dogs and people, this research is providing leads to the development of new treatments and cures for human diseases as well—proving once again that, as we enter a new millennium, the dog is still man's best friend. For instance, recent advancements in gene therapy have successfully restored the vision of blind dogs. Blindness in dogs, it has been discovered, has many genetic similarities to blindness in humans. With insights gained from gene therapy for blind dogs, scientists may glean the road map to developing a similar gene therapy for blind people. Then it may be truly said that a "seeing-eye dog" has led the way!

For example, when it comes to curing blindness in children, the lovable French herding dog, the Briard, may well be the dog that guides human research. A diagnosis of blindness seems especially tragic in puppies and babies, who are just beginning to discover and explore the world around them. But thanks to the vision, generosity, and medical finesse of a host of dedicated professionals, puppies (and hopefully, someday, babies) will enjoy the gift of sight. Working in tandem with the Briard Club of America and the American Kennel Club Canine Health Foundation, Dr. Gustavo Aguirre of the James A. Baker Institute for Animal Health at the Cornell College of Veterinary Medicine has discovered that the molecular genetic basis for congenital stationary night blindness (CSNB), which can be found in Briards, is similar to the gene responsible for severe retinal degeneration and blindness in children. Building on this breakthrough, and in collaboration with researchers from the University of Pennsylvania and the University of Florida, veterinary researchers have successfully restored vision to afflicted three-month-old puppies. Through selective breeding, the genetic disease can be eliminated entirely in dogs, which will obviate the need for gene therapy to restore vision in dogs. But this successful gene-therapy procedure for blindness in large animals offers hope that a successful gene-therapy procedure may soon be developed into an accepted treatment for children.

Because our dogs are our best friends, we walk together through all that life has to offer—both good and bad—and some of the greatest strides we've made together are in surviving or living with cancer. In fact, the most common form of bone cancer in dogs is also the most common form of bone cancer in people: osteosarcoma. But while in the past such a diagnosis often meant amputation (the traditional treatment for bone cancer), recent dramatic inroads in veterinary medicine now offers patients the encouraging alternative of limb-sparing surgery, which effectively saves the afflicted leg. This innovative procedure involves removing the affected segment of the dog's bone while preserving as much of the surrounding nerves, muscles, and blood supply to the limb as possible, allowing the dog to resume a fully functioning pain-free use of the affected limb.

This medical advancement not only offers hope to dogs with a diagnosis of bone cancer, but it can also be used successfully for dogs with bones destroyed by trauma or infection. And in some cases the affected bone of the limb is replaced with an entirely new segment of healthy bone. But as daunting as it may sound, this aspect of the surgical procedure is relatively risk-free, as stored bone is a nonliving structure, so there is no risk of tissue rejection. There is no need, as there is in organ donation, to match a donor to the recipient. Any dog can receive a bone graft from any other dog. Still, this is a technically demanding surgery, requiring highly trained veterinary surgeons. However, recovery from this surgery is no more involved than recovery from a simple bone fracture. Generally with rest, limited activity and tender loving care, your dog will soon be up and around on all fours, ready to romp and frolic once again.

The vast majority of dogs will require only routine veterinary care during the course of their lifetime. It is comforting to know, however, that such incredible advances are being made in treating catastrophic trauma and disease. Veterinary science continually makes advances in improving the health and lengthening the longevity of dogs. So approach your dog's health and well-being as you would your own. If your dog exhibits a physical symptom, don't assume the worst. Usually it is not indicative of anything serious. Similarly, when reading the possible "side effects" of doggie medicines, don't be alarmed. Like the possible side effects noted for human medicines (indeed, even those listed on the side of a bottle of simple aspirin can be off-putting), the chances of your dog experiencing such side effects are quite remote. If there is a problem, more often than not, as with people, there is a solution, a treatment, an option—most of which you will read about in this appendix. In any event as noted in chapter 5, "From Dreams to Reality: Starting Right," if you have any questions and concerns about your dog's health, call your veterinarian. This appendix is designed to promote better, clearer, and more effective communication between you and your dog's veterinarian.

By fostering a better understanding of the inherited breed-specific traits of our own dogs' health and well-being, we can help to ensure the best possible health and well-being for future generations of dogs. My clients often ask me what they can do, on a personal level, to assist canine health research, and for those clients who have purebred dogs, I recommend they get in touch with the American Kennel Club Canine Health Foundation. The average person and her dog—without even stepping outside their community and day-to-day schedule—can be the key to vital veterinary research progress. The core for all genetic research is DNA, and DNA samples are obtained by your veterinarian simply drawing a blood sample or taking a cheek swab. In fact, there are even home kits available now for cheek swabs. Think of it: a few short moments for a simple, pain-free procedure can contribute to an incalculable difference in the lives of dogs. Some of the extraordinary research ordinary dogs have contributed to include studies to eradicate deafness in Dalmatians and English Setters, and forms of cancer in a wide variety of breeds.

The immeasurable benefits that will be gained through this research will lead to the prevention and treatment of canine diseases and new therapies and treatments for human afflictions, as well. Together we can vastly improve the quality of life for both dogs and their people. Dogs, especially purebreds, are an ideal species for studying genetics. Among the species of veterinary and comparative medical importance, the dog has over four hundred known inherited diseases that are akin to those in people and, when identified at the molecular level, they can serve as prototypes for conquering human diseases as well.

So just as canine genes allow us to "dance" with our dogs (dogs walk on their toes, rather than their feet, facilitating running, jumping, and "dancing") and to play Frisbee (dogs have better peripheral vision than people, and the placement of their eyes allows better wide-angle vision, enabling them to snag a Frisbee gliding sideways)—these same canine genes allow us to leave a legacy of good health and long life, free from disease and pain, for future generations of both dogs and people.

Many dog breeds have genetic tendencies toward various congenital defects, diseases, or disorders. Before you choose your new pet, it is a good idea to go to dog shows and talk to owners and breeders of the type of dog you are considering. You should also talk to at least one veterinarian about the common congenital defects or disorders your potential pet may have. We suggest talking to more than one veterinarian.

The knowledge that the breed or breeds you want could have potential problems may not affect your decision to go ahead and choose the dog you like anyway. But at least you will then be prepared and know what signs of illness or disorder to look for in your pet.

**Addison's disease:** This ailment was first described in dogs in 1953. It is an endocrine (related to hormones) disease that occurs when the adrenal cortex does not make enough cortisone and aldosterone, and the dog becomes very ill. Symptoms include weakness, vomiting, and loss of appetite. It is diagnosed by a blood test, and a large percentage of dogs with Addison's disease are young females. The disease is easy to treat by the replacement of the deficient hormones, and the prognosis for a properly treated dog is good. Breeds with a predilection toward Addison's disease are the Bearded Collie, Portuguese Water Dog, and West Highland White Terrier.

**Allergic skin diseases:** Dogs are prone toward many allergic skin diseases. All result in severe itching. Dogs with allergic skin diseases are usually face rubbers, foot lickers, or armpit scratchers. Among the kinds of allergic skin diseases dogs can have are the following: *Atopic* *dermatitis,* which is caused by inhaled allergens. This condition worsens as the dog ages. It may or may not be seasonal. It is treated with cortisone and intradermal skin testing to identify the allergen so a process by which the allergen is made into a vaccine can begin. This latter process is performed at only a few of the larger veterinary institutions in this country. Breeds prone to this disorder are Belgian Tervurens, Cairn Terriers, French Bulldogs, Rhodesian Ridgebacks, Staffordshire Bull Terriers, Vizslas, Welsh Terriers, and West Highland White Terriers. *Allergic contact dermatitis* is rare and usually affects sparsely haired skin, such as the stomach area, in "contact" areas. It also may or may not be seasonal. It is diagnosed by means of isolation and provocative exposure (that is, trial and error), and is treated accordingly. *Food allergies* are nonseasonal and are not always associated with the introduction of a new food. A dog may suddenly become allergic to a food he has eaten all his life. They are sometimes treated with cortisone, but diet testing is the preferred treatment to determine what particular food the dog is allergic to. Ibizan Hounds are often very food sensitive, resulting in vomiting and diarrhea. *Insect hypersensitivity* is usually associated with fleas, and it may simply be fleabite dermatitis rather than an allergic reaction. It is usually treated with rigorous flea control, sometimes with the addition of oral cortisone. Ibizan Hounds often have severe reactions to insect bites. *Drug eruptions* can mimic all the other skin diseases. It is rare, usually itchy, and often does not respond well to steroids. Diagnosis usually involves discontinuing the offending drug and watching to see if the dog recovers. Therapy involves discontinuing the drug, avoiding any similar medications, and prescribing new medication. Breeds that are particularly susceptible to allergic skin diseases are American Cocker Spaniels, American Water Spaniels, Bichon Frises, Black and Tan Coonhounds, Boston Terriers, Briards, Shar-Peis, Chow Chows, Clumber Spaniels, English Springer Spaniels, Irish Water Spaniels, Pointers, Scottish Deerhounds, and West Highland White Terriers.

**Arthritis:** This is a joint inflammation of which there are several medical types: degenerative arthritis, idiopathic immune-mediated arthritis, infectious bacterial arthritis, rheumatoid arthritis, and systemic lupus erythematosus arthritis. Collies, Samoyeds, and Soft-Coated Wheaten Terriers are particularly susceptible to arthritis.

*Degenerative arthritis:* This is a degeneration of cartilage (a connective tissue between two bones) in older dogs. It is a result of wear and tear and comes with aging. Fissures and erosion initially develop in the articular (of or pertaining to a joint) cartilage, leading to inflammation and joint pain. It may also develop as the result of injury or illness such as fragmented medial coronoid process (FCP)—the fragmentation of one of the forearm bones at the elbow of the dog. This is a condition that usually surfaces between the ages of five and nine months and is common in Retrievers, Rottweilers, and other large breeds. Signs are foreleg lameness or stiffness, which is worsened by exercise and is usually noticeable after a dog has rested. It may be accompanied by osteochondritis dissecans (OCD)—see page 341. The outcome of treatment depends on early diagnosis, surgical removal of the bone fragments, and the degree of degenerative arthritis that develops.

*Idiopathic immune-mediated arthritis:* This common canine arthritis disorder occurs when immune system antibodies are either deposited or formed within the joint, causing reaction to the joint lining and fluid production. The exact cause of the disease is unknown. Signs include depression, loss of appetite, fever, lameness, general limb stiffness, and joint swelling. Diagnosis is based on orthopedic examination, X rays, and blood tests. It has to be differentiated from other forms of arthritis. Treatment involves the use of steroids alone or in conjunction with immunosuppressive drugs. Prognosis is good, but recurrences may occur after the drug therapy is discontinued.

*Infectious bacterial arthritis:* This condition results from the presence of bacteria within a joint. Bacteria may arise by a penetrating injury such as a bite wound, from bacterial septicemia (blood poisoning), in which bacteria in the bloodstream are carried into the joint, and as a complication of joint surgery. Diagnosis is made by examination of the joint and aspiration of joint fluid, followed by microscopic examination and culture to confirm the particular type of bacteria. X rays may show the extent of joint damage and help establish a diagnosis. Treatment with appropriate antibiotics for several weeks is needed. Surgery may be needed to drain and flush the joint and assess the amount of damage. Complications of infectious arthritis may include spread of the infection to adjacent bones. Prognosis depends on the number of joints involved, how quickly the joint infections are treated, the amount of damage to the joint, the particular joint involved, and the dog's size and activity level.

*Rheumatoid arthritis:* This is a deforming, painful joint disease that produces multiple joint swelling and lameness in dogs. It may resemble systemic lupus erythematosus, except that it is generally seen in older dogs. If the disease has gone on long enough, X rays will show characteristic bony changes. There is also a blood test for the presence of rheumatoid factors. Sometimes a biopsy is also performed. Treatment is supportive and directed at pain relief. Often, corticosteroids and perhaps other immunosuppressive drugs and pain relievers such as aspirin are given. It is possible to alleviate the pain and lameness and slow down the inevitable process of bone change with proper management, but in general the disease is not considered curable.

*Systemic lupus erythematosus arthritis:* This arthritis often involves multiple joints and is one of the conditions associated with systemic lupus erythematosus. Diagnosis is based on orthopedic exams, blood tests, X rays, and microscopic examination of aspirated joint fluid. Treatment with immunosuppressive drugs (corticosteroids) is needed. With proper drug therapy the disease can usually be controlled.

**Ataxia:** This is a term that means "lack of coordination." It is manifested by a dog's inability to sense the position of his limbs. Typically, he will cross his limbs so that he cannot walk right; walk on the top side of his paws; move his limbs away from the center of his body, or walk with an overlong gait. Aging German Shepherds are especially prone to a neurologic disease known as degenerative myelopathy, in which their rear limbs slowly and progressively become weak, causing ataxia. The cause is unknown, although degeneration of the spinal cord is usually observed. The dog is not in pain, and there is no cure. Near complete paralysis occurs over time. Jack Russell Terriers often suffer from this disease.

**Aural diseases and disorders:** See **Ear problems.**

**Autoimmune diseases:** An autoimmune disease is one in which the body attacks itself in a number of different ways. It can occur when antibodies form against tissue or body organs. It can occur when antigen-antibody complexes form and attack different tissues and organs. And it can also occur by the direct attack of the immune-defense cells (cellular attack). The causes of autoimmune diseases are not known, but are closely related to the causes of cancer and can have a genetic, viral, or environmental basis, or a combination of any of these. Autoimmune diseases are diagnosed by blood tests for specific antibodies and, in the case of systemic lupus erythematosus and the pemphigus group, biopsies of the affected organs. In general, autoimmune diseases are treatable but not curable. Canine autoimmune diseases include autoimmune hemolytic anemia, immune-mediated thrombocytopenia, systemic lupus erythematosus, rheumatoid arthritis, and the pemphigus group. Breeds that are prone to this disease are the American Cocker Spaniel, American Staffordshire Terrier, American Water Spaniel, Belgian Malinois, Belgian Tervuren, Bearded Collie, Curly-Coated Retriever, English Cocker Spaniel, Field Spaniel, German Wirehaired Pointer, Italian Greyhound, Pembroke Welsh Corgi, Portuguese Water Dog, Rottweiler, and Skye Terrier.

**Autoimmune hemolytic anemia:** In this disease, a dog's body destroys its own red blood cells, leading to anemia. Symptoms include lethargy, pale mucous membranes, and possibly dark-colored urine. It is diagnosed by a special blood test called the Coombs test. Therapy consists of immunosuppressive corticosteroids and a blood transfusion. If the dog is not responsive to these procedures, other immunosuppressive medications or a splenectomy may be suggested. The prognosis is fair. It is more optimistic if the dog responds well to the steroid therapy. The American Cocker Spaniel, the Clumber Spaniel, and the Flat Coated Retriever are all prone to this disease.

**Axonal dystrophy (AD):** The Ibizan Hound Club of the United States first commissioned a study of this fatal disease more than ten years ago to determine the mode of inheritance and the nature of the disease. It turned out that this is a recessive trait, and many dogs were identified as carriers during this study. Reputable breeders are now taking steps to ensure that they do not have puppies with this illness. The symptoms are a "drunken gait," that is first seen at about six weeks of age and never goes away permanently. It is degenerative and eventually fatal. There is an AD analysis that can be done by a professional on any animal considered for breeding. Potential owners should always ask about this rating.

**Bladder cysts:** A cyst is a cavity or sac that contains a liquid or semi-solid material.

**Bladder stones:** This term refers to a mass of hard and unyielding material found in the bladder (vesical calculus) that causes pain, especially when a dog is urinating. They can occur alone or in more than one place at the same time. In addition to the bladder, they can be in one or both kidneys and in the urethra after passing through the kidney(s). The most common type of stones found in dogs are triple phosphate. The cause of urinary tract stones is unknown, but may be caused by a urinary tract infection, an impeded urine outflow, hereditary factors, and diet. Symptoms include frequent urination (polyuria), straining to urinate (stranguria), an unusually large amount of red blood cell in the urine (hematuria), an unusually large number of white blood cells in the urine (pyuria), and eventually uremia—which is manifested by increased water intake, increased urine volume, loss of appetite, vomiting, depression, lethargy, and anemia. Bladder stones are treated by controlling any infection present, increasing urine volume, dietary management, and urine acidification. Surgical removal is often recommended, followed by an analysis of the stones so that the proper drugs to prevent further formation of stones can be prescribed. Dalmatians and Bichon Frises are especially prone toward bladder stones.

**Bleeding disorders:** Bleeding or hemorrhaging from any part of a dog's body can be an emergency if the bleeding is profuse or if it is at a slow pace and continues for a long time. An owner can assess the seriousness of the bleeding by checking for pallor and other signs of shock.

*Nasal or oral bleeding:* This can be life-threatening if it is profuse. Ice packs or cold compresses over the nose or mouth may help slow the bleeding, but it can be very difficult to get a compress over the affected area. There is, therefore, very little an owner can do except get the dog to a veterinarian as fast as possible.

*Skin or surface bleeding:* Cuts, or any kind of wounds can cause bleeding. Usually, wounds on the surface of the skin cause little bleeding. The exception is a deep wound that involves a vein or blood vessel beneath the surface. This is most likely to occur in the neck area, where the jugular vein is, or with cuts on the dog's legs or feet. If there is significant skin bleeding, manual pressure should be used in places that cannot be bandaged. With a clean cloth apply pressure beside the wound until the bleeding stops. Use a compression bandage (a tightly wound bandage) in areas where it is possible. Do not use a tourniquet. Tourniquets are dangerous and may even cause the loss of a limb due to a prolonged interruption of the blood supply.

*Bleeding on the feet and legs:* Bleeding from the legs, and especially the feet, is a problem for dogs. Foot pad lacerations tend to bleed a lot. Because foot pads are very spongy, bleeding will continue every time the dog walks. If this continues for too long, there can be significant blood loss. Foot pad lacerations should be bandaged with a compression or pressure bandage and held in place with a sock. There is a small but significant artery just behind the foot pads. This is a prime spot for a dog to cut if he steps on broken glass or some other sharp object, causing arterial bleeding in which the blood spurts or pumps out. This is a serious condition, and must be treated with a compression bandage around the entire foot—again, a sock can help hold it in place. *Do not tie a constricting band over the cut; this will cut off circulation to the rest of the foot.* If you must bandage the lower part of a dog's leg, bandage the entire lower part to avoid swelling. Bleeding that occurs higher on a dog's leg can be significant if superficial veins or arteries are injured. A soft-padded compression should be used, in general.

*Vomiting blood:* If fluid is being vomited, vomiting is frequent, and the extent of bleeding is specks or streaks of blood, it is not a life-threatening emergency. But if there is a lot of blood thrown up, or if there are blood clots, it can indicate bleeding in the stomach, and veterinary attention should be sought quickly.

**Bloody diarrhea or stools:** If the blood is only flecks or streaks with a normal stool or with diarrhea, it is not an emergency. If, however, the stool becomes pools of dark, foul-smelling blood and that is all that is passed, it may be *hemorrhagic gastroenteritis (HIG),* which is a severe and life-threatening emergency. A small dog can go into shock very quickly with HIG; it will take larger dogs longer. A lot of water will be mixed with the blood, and this can lead to a specific kind of shock, called *hypovolemic shock,* which is caused by the loss of too much fluid from the bloodstream. Emergency veterinary care is a must.

**Blood in the urine:** Blood may also drip from the penis of males. This is usually a sign of a urinary tract infection or a bladder infection, and is usually not a significant emergency. The dog may also show signs of straining to urinate, and passing urine in small amounts. Carbohydrate-loading for work dogs has shown that it may lead to blood in the urine, and is not recommended. If there is significant bleeding and the urine becomes very dark, or there are blood clots, it requires immediate veterinary attention.

**Spontaneous bruising:** This may be hard to see through a dog's coat, but it can be significant. Large purple splotches on the skin, especially the abdomen, can indicate a bleeding disorder. Little purple or red spots on the insides of a dog's ears or his gums may indicate a low platelet count, rat poison, or some other type of bleeding disorder. Dogs can also bleed into areas such as the brain, which can cause acute problems. Any of these types of bleeding should be considered medical emergencies.

Blindness: Dogs are very good at adjusting to gradual vision impairment. A dog that is blind in one eye, for instance, usually acts like a perfectly normal dog. Even a dog that suddenly goes completely blind will usually do well after a brief adjustment period to the environment and will use his other senses to adapt. The exception to this is in very old dogs who also have some loss of hearing. They may take longer to adjust. Even completely blind dogs usually function well in familiar surroundings, and an owner may be completely unaware of a sight loss until the dog is taken to an unfamiliar environment. Blindness in a dog may be caused by a number of different factors. It may be due to a genetic malformation of the eyes (see Collie eye anomaly, page 314), disease, or trauma.

**Bloat (Gastric dilatation/torsion complex):** Sometimes called twisted stomach, this is a severe emergency that usually affects large-breed barrel-chested dogs that weigh over sixty pounds. Signs include nausea and frequent attempts to throw up, usually followed by a swelling of the stomach as it becomes filled with gas, and difficulty breathing. As the stomach swells, it puts pressure on all the other internal organs, including the diaphragm. Pressure on the veins returning blood to the heart traps blood in the dog's back end and keeps blood from returning to the heart to be repumped. Eventually the dog will go into shock from lack of blood. He will become confused and weak, will collapse and have a rapid heart rate and pale mucous membranes. Immediate veterinary help is needed. Dogs most often afflicted with bloat are Akitas, Black and Tan Coonhounds, Bloodhounds, Borzois, Briards, Chow Chows, Collies, English Foxhounds, German Shepherds, Gordon Setters, Greater Swiss Mountain Dogs, Greyhounds, Irish Wolfhounds, Komondors, Samoyeds, Scottish Deerhounds, and Weimaraners.

**Blood Problems:** There can be many problems with a dog's blood itself, which can only be determined by a blood test. All breeds have a red blood cell volume (hematocrit) of forty to forty-five, except for racing Greyhounds, whose red blood cell volume is sixty, probably due to their greater oxygen requirements.

*Aplastic anemia* is a condition of bone-marrow suppression and may be caused by a malignancy, *autoimmune disease,* which may be induced by estrogens, other drugs, or an unknown cause. Therapy is supportive and symptomatic, involving blood transfusions and attempts to stimulate normal bone-marrow function with several drugs.

*Immune-mediated thrombocytopenia (IMT),* or low platelets, is caused by antibody destruction of the dog's platelets—components of the blood necessary for normal blood clotting. In some cases IMT may be associated with, or traced to, recent vaccinations or drug therapy. Signs include pale mucous membranes, bruises, bleeding from the nose or urinary tract, or bloody diarrhea. Diagnosis is made with blood tests, bone marrow aspiration, and a special platelet antibody test. IMT is initially treated with corticosteroids. Blood transfusions are sometimes needed if the problem is severe. Prognosis is variable, but often long-term control is possible.

**Bone disease (marrow disease, tumors, cancer):**

*Bone marrow disease (aplastic anemia)* is a condition of generalized bone marrow suppression. It is characterized by a low white blood cell count (neutropenia), a low platelet count (thrombocytopenia), and anemia (low red blood cell count). A dog may show signs of bleeding tendencies, infections, lethargy, and pale mucous membranes. It may be caused by a malignancy, autoimmune disease, or induced by estrogens or other drugs, or the cause may be unknown. Therapy is supportive and symptomatic, and may involve blood transfusions and attempts to stimulate normal bone marrow function with drugs.

*Tumors:* The incidence of cancer in dogs is approximately the same as in humans. There are two basic types of canine tumors: liquid, or *hematopoietic tumors,* such as *leukemia* and *lymphosarcoma,* which involve blood-forming elements; and solid tumors, or masses, which may be internal or external. There is no single cause for cancer, either in humans or dogs. There are always environmental influences such as diet or radiation, and there are also genetic predispositions toward cancer and infections or viral causes of cancer.

The most commonly held theory of cancer is that basically there is a combination cause in which certain genetic predispositions are influenced by either environment and infection (or both) to cause either a malignant growth or leukemia. An older and widely held theory is that cancer is caused by a failure of immunosurveillance. That is, all living bodies have mutant, abnormal cells that arise either intermittently or continuously and that a normal immune system recognizes them and destroys them—in the case of cancer, it does not. Cancer would then arise from one of the two causes. Immune system failure could be an aftermath, rather than a forerunner of the disease. The activation of the oncogene could then cause an immune system failure that would cause cancer.

In dogs, the most frequent types of cancer are skin tumors, mammary gland tumors, and hematopoietic tumors. Giant breeds are prone to *bone tumors*, while highly pigmented dogs such as Scotties, Black Labradors, Black Poodles, Black Cockers, and Kerry Blue Terriers are susceptible to *melanomas* of the mouth and skin. *Mast cell tumors* are frequently seen in Boxers and Boston Terriers, and *hemangiosarcomas* frequently appear in German Shepherds.

In general, all dogs can develop cancer in all parts of the body. Other types of cancer in dogs range from *digestive system tumors, histiocytomas, lung cancer, oral tumors, perianal adenomas, sebaceous gland adenomas, testicular cancer, transmissible venereal tumors,* to *urogenital tumors.*

**Breathing problems:** It should be considered a severe emergency whenever a dog is having severe problems breathing. Breathing problems can be caused by *congestive heart failure, severe pneumonia, or a traumatic chest injury,* any of which can result in fluid in the lungs, fluid in the chest cavity around the lungs, or air in the chest cavity around the lungs (pneumothorax). The dog will expand his chest in order to try to get more oxygen and will often be cyanotic (a bluish discoloration of the mucous membranes and skin), as well. Immediate veterinary help is needed to draw the air and excess fluid out of the dog's chest cavity.

Dogs that have breathed in smoke in a burning building may develop serious respiratory problems. This may not be obvious until several days after the exposure. Again, veterinary help is necessary.

Brachycephalic breeds (those with pushed-in faces, such as Pugs, Boxers, and Boston Terriers) may often have nasal obstructions, congenital defects of the nose (stenotic nares, in which the nasal openings are too narrow—see entry, page 348), or soft palate disorders that cause them to become short of breath and make them seem to struggle to get enough air. A veterinarian can assess the problem and provide help when needed.

**Cancer:** See bone disease—tumors/cancer, pages 310–11. Breeds that are especially susceptible to cancer (except hemangiosarcomas, histiocytic sarcoma, lymphosarcoma, mammary cancer, mast cell tumors, osteosarcoma, and squamous cell carcinoma) are the Akita, American

Eskimo, Belgian Malinois, Bernese Mountain Dog, Bloodhound, Boston Terrier, Boxer, Briard, Borzoi, Curly-Coated Retriever, English Foxhound, Flat-Coated Retriever, German Shepherd, German Wire-haired Pointer, Golden Retriever, Great Pyrenees, Greyhound, Irish Water Spaniel, Mastiff, Otterhound, Pembroke Welsh Corgi, Portuguese Water Dog, Pharaoh Hound, Rottweiler, Soft-Coated Wheaten Terrier, and Vizsla.

**Cataracts:** A cataract is any clouding of the normally clear eye lens. Almost all dogs with diabetes (see page 318) will eventually develop cataracts because of the abnormally high concentration of glucose bathing their lenses. A cataract can be anything from a microscopic dot on the lens to complete clouding of the lens. Cataracts can progress slowly or extremely fast. A dog with this condition should be observed regularly by a veterinarian. It is very difficult to perform cataract surgery on dogs because their lenses are much larger than human lenses; therefore, the cataract is much larger and more difficult to remove. Dogs' eyes are very sensitive to surgery and become badly inflamed, which may result in scarring and lead to blindness. Thus, cataract surgery is usually reserved for dogs that are totally blind in both eyes. Small cataracts do not need surgery. If you are thinking of cataract surgery, be sure that your dog has a complete medical workup to be sure he is a good risk for anesthesia. Also, the tissue of the dog's eye behind the lens itself should be evaluated to be sure that the retina and optic nerve are in good condition. Breeds that are at risk for juvenile cataracts are the Boston Terrier, Siberian Husky, and Staffordshire Bull Terrier. Breeds at risk for cataracts at any age are the Alaskan Malamute, American Cocker, Bichon Frise, Black and Tan Coonhound, Cairn, Havanese, and Samoyed.

**Cardiomyopathy:** This is a cardiac disease that affects large and giant breed dogs that weigh more than fifty or sixty pounds. It is an acquired heart disease that usually affects young to middle-aged males. It causes the heart muscle either to become flabby, dilated, and weak or to become thickened and stiff. It will eventually lead to *congestive heart failure.*

**Cleft palate:** Normally, the hard palate closes completely before birth. But in some cases the two sides of the hard palate do not close, which leaves an abnormal opening between the upper and lower chambers of the pharynx. Food and other foreign matter may pass through this opening in the mouth and into the nasal cavity, which leads to chronic nasal inflammation and discharge. Conversely, excess nasal secretions may enter the back of the throat and be aspirated into the lungs. Affected puppies will have difficulty sucking and eating and will not grow normally. Diagnosis is made by visual inspection and the problem can usually be corrected with surgery. Brittany Spaniels and French Bulldogs have a propensity toward this disorder.

**Colitis:** This is a general term meaning inflammation of the colon. Symptoms include straining to defecate, bloody diarrhea streaked with mucus, and an increased frequency of bowel movements. The most common cause of colitis in dogs is *intestinal parasites,* such as hookworms or whipworms, but it can also be the result of an *ulcerated colon,* or other nonspecific causes. Treatment includes worming, antibiotics, other anti-inflammatory medication, and dietary therapy in the form of additional roughage and bulkier foods to stimulate the colon and aid in the absorption of water in order to add form to the stools. Sometimes bone splinters can lodge in the colon, causing pain when the dog defecates and causing him to become constipated. In this case the dog must be hospitalized so the bone fragments and hardened stool can be removed.

**Collapsed trachea:** This is a congenital problem associated with small-breed dogs. It is a condition in which there is insufficient rigidity in the tracheal rings that keep the tracheal tube open; the rings flatten and the tube collapses inward, narrowing or closing the opening through which air passes. It is a condition that may be present at birth or it can develop over time with wear and tear. Sometimes it can be a congenital condition in which the entire trachea is incompletely developed at birth. It can be diagnosed with external palpation, X rays, dye studies, or tracheoscopy. Usually there is little that can be done when there is a complete tracheal collapse, although surgery is performed at some large veterinary universities. Norwich Terriers, Yorkies, and Toy Poodles are especially susceptible to this problem.

**Collie eye anomaly:** This is an infrequent condition in which the optic nerve is malformed. There is a large pit at the head of the optic nerve tissue, which can lead to severe visual problems or even a detached retina (see page 318). In mild cases there may be no noticeable visual problems. When severe, it can lead to blindness (see page 308).

**Congenital liver malformation:** This is a condition in which the liver is not formed properly at birth. It results in an inability of a dog's body to store and filtrate the blood, secrete bile, and to perform numerous other essential metabolic functions. It will lead to *cirrhosis* of the liver, which may be fatal.

**Corneal ulcers:** Corneal ulceration is very common especially among small breeds with exposed or protuberant eyes. In particular, the brachycephalic breeds such as Boston Terriers, Boxers, Bulldogs, Lhasa Apsos, Pekingese, and Pugs are susceptible to this disease. The top of the cornea is about ten layers thick and, along with the flushing action of tears, serves to protect the eyeball. If this cell layer is weak or damaged because of constant dryness, or an injury to the tissues such as a foreign body or scratch, the eye can quickly become infected. As bacteria grow they can enter the inner layer of the cornea and begin to eat this layer away. At worst, so much of the thickness of the cornea will be lost that the innermost corneal layer will be pushed outward and appear as a small bubble on the eye surface. This is a serious *emergency* and underlines the importance of immediate veterinary care in the case of any eye injury. Even very deep ulcerations or lacerations can often be helped with intensive medication or surgery.

**Craniomandibular osteopathy (CMO):** This is a bone disease characterized by a bony overgrowth of the jaw and surrounding skull bones. Onset usually occurs when a dog is between four and eleven months of age. Signs include swelling of the jaw, drooling, inability to open the mouth, and pain if the mouth is manipulated. X rays are needed to confirm the diagnosis and the cause of the disease is not known. Treatment is symptomatic, and most dogs are more comfortable when they are given steroids or aspirin. The disease is usually self-limiting, and although many dogs may continue to have impaired mouth function, they are usually able to eat. CMO is most commonly seen in Scotties, West Highland White Terriers, and Cairns, although it is sometimes seen in Boxers, Great Danes, Doberman Pinschers, and Labs.

**Cruciate ligament rupture:** A tear (or rupture) of the knee ligaments to which Akitas, American Staffordshire Terriers, Bulldogs, and Mastiffs are especially prone.

**Cushing's disease (syndrome):** This is the most common *endocrine* disease that occurs in dogs. It is the result of an overproduction of cortisal by the adrenal cortex, or *hyperadrenocorticism*. In a large percentage of cases it develops because the pituitary gland produces too much adrenocorticotropic hormone (ACTH), which causes the adrenal gland to enlarge. This is known as pituitary-dependent Cushing's disease. Adrenal tumors may also account for a small number of dogs with this disease. In either case, symptoms are increased appetite, thirst, urination, lethargy, muscle weakness, abdominal swelling, mild to severe hair loss, and absence of the estrous cycle in females or testicular atrophy in males. It usually surfaces in middle- to old-aged dogs and affects both sexes equally. Blood tests are used to diagnose it, and the cause of the disease determines the treatment. If an adrenal tumor is the cause, it must be removed. If the disease is pituitary-dependent, it can be treated with medication. The prognosis for a dog that is properly treated is fair to good. If left untreated, Cushing's syndrome leads to death within two years. There is a breed predilection toward this disease among Bostons, Boxers, Dachshunds, and Poodles.

**Cystinuria:** An hereditary condition consisting of persistent excessive urinary excretion of cystine and other amino acids (lysine, ornithine, and arginine) in the urine, due to a kidney impairment causing a lack of tubular reabsorption of these amino acids. Symptoms include the formation of urinary cystine calculi, making it difficult for a dog to urinate. It should be treated by a veterinarian. Bulldogs are especially prone to this disease.

**Cysts:** A cyst is a simple saclike cavity that develops within the skin and usually contains fluid or a semisolid cheesy or doughy material. They are often solitary and firm or slightly movable to the touch. Partial hair loss may occur over the cyst. Cysts come in several varieties: follicular (or epidermoid), dermoid, apocrine, and sebaceous duct cysts.

Proper treatment oftentimes consists of surgical removal of the cyst. However, some cysts are harmless and better left alone, but watched. You and your veterinarian are the best judge.

Norwegian Elkhounds and Rhodesian Ridgebacks are prone toward bodywide cysts.

*Follicular cysts* are often wrongly called "sebaceous cysts," and are common in dogs. They originate in hair follicles in any part of a dog's body. Occasionally multiple and recurrent cysts appear, probably due to a developmental abnormality.

*Dermoid cysts* are rare developmental abnormalities that may either be single or multiple lesions resembling follicular cysts. They often develop along the back (as in Rhodesian ridgebacks), but may be found at other sites.

*Apocrine cysts* are caused by obstruction of the sweat gland ducts. They usually occur singly, but it is possible for multiple cysts to be present. They have a characteristic blue tinge when viewed through the thin overlying skin. They develop mostly on the head, neck, and upper areas of the trunk.

*Sebaceous duct cysts* are rare lesions involving the ducts leading from the sebaceous glands to their associated hair follicles, and can occur anywhere in a dog's body.

**Deafness:** Owners often misinterpret deafness as deliberate misbehavior on their pets' part. If a dog does not respond to a command or directive he may be mistakenly thought of as being stubborn or unheeding. In truth, he may not be able to hear his owner's wishes. A profoundly deaf dog will not respond to the doorbell ringing or to the quiet arrival of a visitor if he doesn't see her. A deaf dog may bark at inappropriate times (when there is nothing to bark at). There is no clinical test for deafness, and an owner is the best judge of this disorder. Many dogs' hearing diminishes or fails with age. There is no treatment for hearing loss in dogs. Dalmatians, in particular, have an inherited tendency towards deafness, which may surface even when they are pups. Other breeds that are prone to deafness are Boston Terriers, English Cocker Spaniels, English Setters, Havanese, Miniature Bull Terriers, and Tibetan Terriers.

**Dengerative myopathy:** This may lead to balance or coordination problems. It is a disorder of the muscle fiber. German Shepherds and Pembroke Welsh Corgis are prone to this disease.

**Dental disease:** See **Mouth disorders.**

**Dermatomyositis:** This is an inherited skin disease that causes skin inflammation affecting the face, ears, and lower limbs of a dog. Bony areas such as the muzzle and around the eyes and ears are usually affected first; as the disease progresses, lesions may also appear on the tip of a dog's tail and ears, nail folds, and over bony areas of the legs. It may also result in muscle lesions in the chewing and limb muscles and can progress to crusted erosions and ulcers early in the course of the disease (usually by six months of age). Severe, chronic lesions may produce scarring. When muscles are involved, it may not be noticeable at first, but may cause atrophy of some facial muscles with the result of difficulty chewing and swallowing. The cause is unknown. Severely affected dogs may have stunted growth, an enlargement of the esophagus resulting in chronic regurgitation *(megaesophagus,* see page 336) lameness, muscle atrophy, and infertility. They often have cyclic recurrences over a lifetime. Diagnosis is based on the history, clinical features, skin and muscle biopsies, and examination of the electrical activity of muscles and associated nerves (electromyography, EMG). Therapy is only supportive. Dogs with this disease should not be bred, because this is an inheritable trait. Dermatomyositis affects Collies, Shetland Sheepdogs, and their related crossbreeds almost exclusively.

**Dermoid sinus:** This is a tubelike cyst in the spine of a dog.

**Detached retina:** The retinal tissue of a dog's eye gets its nutrition from the blood vessels in it and from the choroidal (the middle covering of the retina) blood circulation just beneath it. Sometimes a dog's retina becomes detached from its nutrient bases because of fluid that accumulates between the choroid and the retina. If this is allowed to continue, the dog may go blind. It can be the result of a birth defect, which is common in English Springers and sometimes Labs. It may also be caused by a viral infection such as distemper or an eye tumor. Treatment depends on the severity and cause of the condition. If there is a small area of detachment caused by inflammation, it can be reduced with medications, and will probably reattach. If, however, the detachment covers a large area, little can be done except with laser therapy, which is performed only in conjunction with a human hospital at an institution such as a university with a veterinary clinic.

**Diabetes:** Diabetes mellitus is an endocrine disease that results from a deficiency of a dog's pancreas to produce the hormone insulin. Insulin eases the entry of blood glucose into tissue cells. When there is a deficiency, the glucose is not able to move into tissue cells and builds up in the bloodstream. When the blood glucose levels rise to a certain point, the glucose overflows into the urine. At the same time, the dog's body tries to compensate for the lack of glucose-produced energy by using up stored proteins and fats. This leads to weight loss, weakness, and excessive hunger, thirst, and urination. If left untreated, strong acidic ketone bodies accumulate in the dog's blood as a by-product of fat metabolism in the liver. The result is called *acidosis,* which can cause weakness, appetite loss, vomiting, coma, and eventual death. The cause of diabetes in dogs is usually not known, but is often developed in conjunction with other conditions, such as *Cushing's syndrome.* It occurs most often in older dogs, and is more common among unspayed female dogs. Juvenile-onset diabetes occurs rarely and is mostly seen in Keeshonds and Golden Retrievers. Diagnosis for both types is made with blood and urine tests. Dietary control by itself is almost never successful in dogs, and the disease is usually treated with insulin injections. Successful treatment involves an owner who is willing and able to test a dog's urine and administer daily injections. Two serious complications that can occur in insulin-treated dogs are *hypoglycemia* (see page 328) and *cataracts* (see page 312). There is a high incidence of this disease among Poodles.

**Dilated cardiomyopathy:** This is an acquired heart disease that usually affects young to middle-aged male dogs. It causes the heart muscle to become flabby and weak and will lead to congestive heart failure. Boxers, English Foxhounds, Portuguese Water Dogs, Scottish Deerhounds, and Standard Schnauzers suffer from this disorder.

**Dilated esophagus:** See **Megaesophagus.**

**Distichiasis:** An extra row of eyelashes that grow along the lid margin, turn toward the eyeball, and rub against a dog's eyes, causing them to tear from the irritation. It may be an inherited tendency and is common among Cockers, Golden Retrievers, and Weimaraners.

**Dry eye:** A deficiency of tear production is a very common dog eye problem. Two glands are responsible for the watery part of tears: the gland of the third eyelid and the lacrimal gland. Many different situations can cause damage to these glands. Some viral diseases, drugs used to control diarrhea and urinary infections, and an autoimmune disease can harm these glands with the result of decreased tear production. Tear deficiency can lead to gradual haziness of the cornea, and an acute loss of tears may result in an *ulcerated cornea.* Treatment involves removing any toxic influence to the glands such as drugs that are being used to treat other problems, trying to stimulate remaining glands to produce more tears, and artificial lubricants to keep the cornea as moist as possible. In extreme cases, where none of the above works, two of the dog's eight salivary gland ducts can be surgically transplanted beneath the facial skin. Thus, when the dog salivates some of the moisture goes to the eyes. Even though there may be some problems with this procedure, it is preferable to allowing the eyes to become completely dry.

**Ear (aural) problems:** Problems with dogs' ears are usually confined to the *outer ear* (pinna, or ear flap), the *middle ear* (the tympanic membrane or eardrum, and the auditory ossicles [tiny bones that transmit vibrations of the eardrum to the inner ear]), and the *inner ear* (the semicircular canals and the cochlea [a curled bone that contains the organ of Corti, the actual organ of hearing]). Middle ear problems affecting balance are considered to be neurological disorders (see *ataxia*, page 304).

Dogs' ears have a unique anatomy. Their narrow ear canal is composed of a long, vertical tube that angles downward and then runs horizontally toward the skull. This unique anatomy can often conceal ear disease from the owner, and may make it difficult for a veterinarian to diagnose and cure. This two-directional ear canal decreases the ear drum's vulnerability to injury, but it also encourages wax, dirt, and infectious material to collect at the base of the canal. These materials cannot be shaken out by the dog and can cause swelling of the canal, allow moisture to accumulate, and lessen the exposure to air—all of which create an ideal environment for infection. Added to this, many dog breeds have thick hair growing in their outer ears, which further serves to prevent air circulation, as do floppy ears. Dogs that swim or are bathed often may have water left in their ears, yet another basis for potential ear problems. Black and Tan Coonhounds and Irish Water Spaniels are especially prone to ear infections.

In addition, allergies, external parasites, abnormal thyroid or sex hormone levels, tumors, ruptured eardrums, middle ear infections, and some skin diseases such as seborrhea can all contribute to ear disease. Many generalized skin diseases may migrate into the ear canal. If this is the case, the underlying skin disease must be treated before the ear disorder can be cleared up. A dog may be allergic to certain foods, and this may cause ear and skin disease. Dietary testing and management may help in these cases. Flea allergies can also be the culprits— appropriate flea control is needed if this is the case. Rarely, contact with certain medications such as neomycin and propylene glycol (a common component of many ear medicines) are to blame.

If a dog is prone to chronic ear disease, an owner should establish a regular ear care program with a veterinarian to prevent ear infections and halt their progress early.

Ear disease can be recognized by many signs: continuous shaking of the head and ears; scratching at one or both ears; a foul odor from the ear; a discharge from either ear; inflammation of the earflap or opening of the ear canal; obvious pain when the dog is touched on or near the ear; head tilting; lethargy, depression, or hearing loss; swelling of one or both earflaps; and stumbling or circling to one side. If an owner sees one or more of these signs, immediate veterinary help should be sought. Diagnosis is made by use of an otoscope to inspect the ear canal (Note: if the ear is too painful, the dog may require anesthesia); while the dog is under anesthesia, the veterinarian may insert a catheter to flush the ear out, or use a curette to remove any foreign objects lodged in the ear.

*Aural hematomas* are blood-filled swellings in the dog's ear flap (pinna). These can be caused by trauma, allergy, or excessive ear scratching or shaking by the dog for various underlying reasons (see above). This condition must be treated surgically by removing the fluid, stitching the ear and bandaging both sides of the ear flap for several weeks to prevent the vessels from refilling and forming scar tissue. If possible, the condition that caused the hematoma to form should be sought and removed.

**Ectropion:** Ectropion is a hanging lower eyelid. This condition can cause injury and irritation because of the increased exposure of the conjunctiva (the white part of the eye) and the cornea to the elements. This condition usually develops spontaneously during a dog's lifetime. If conjunctival or corneal disease results, surgery is needed to correct the problem.

**Elbow dysplasia:** This is a crippling disease of a dog's elbow. It has the same description as *hip dysplasia* (see page 327), and is usually confined to large dog breeds. The Greater Swiss Mountain Dog, Labrador Retriever, Mastiff, and Rottweiler are prone to this problem.

**Elongated soft palate:** An overlong soft palate can obstruct a dog's airway and may cause him to chronically make squeaking noises when he breathes, snores, or snorts, and have problems inhaling. If the problem is not severe, it may be left alone, but if it becomes severe, it should be surgically corrected. French Bulldogs and Norwich Terriers are especially susceptible to this disorder.

**Enlarged heart:** A dog's heart may gradually become enlarged as the result of any congenital or acquired heart disease. Sometimes there is an excessive layer of fat deposited in and around the heart muscle. If left untreated, *congestive heart failure* may result. Drug therapy may help; ask your veterinarian.

**Entropion:** This is a turning inward of the affected eye margin, which causes irritation and injury because of the increased exposure of the conjunctival and corneal surfaces. It usually affects the lower eyelid(s). Some dogs are born with this problem, and some develop it later in life. If it is severe and leads to secondary eye disease, surgical correction is usually needed.

**Epilepsy (seizure disorders, ictus, "fit"):** This is a very common canine disorder. The term *seizure* refers to an involuntary paroxysm in a dog's brain. Seizures may be due to a congenital disorder, or may have a number of other causes: infection, stroke, neoplasias (any new or abnormal tissue growth), trauma, liver disease, or kidney failure. There are a number of types of seizure. The most often seen is a *generalized grand mal seizure* which may be preceded by restlessness, anxiety, overly affectionate behavior, a blank expression, or other behavioral abnormalities. During the seizure there is a usually sudden increase in muscle tone and rhythmic contractions, stiffening and running motions, chomping and facial twitching. Sometimes there is also urination, defecation, hypersalivation and eye pupil changes. The dog will eventually become still and lose consciousness after the seizure. Afterward the dog may become blind, suffer from *ataxia* (see page 308), confusion, depression, tiredness, and have other behavior changes. This phase may last anywhere from minutes to days. A veterinarian should be consulted if there is persistent change in behavior, gait, or vision.

*Partial or focal seizures* may occur on their own or along with a grand mal seizure. Partial seizures are usually short, but will occur more often than grand mal seizures.

Seizures are most commonly caused by hypoglycemia (see page 328), canine distemper in puppies, and idiopathic epilepsy, which usually surfaces when a dog is anywhere between one and three, especially in Toy breeds. Any seizure should be treated promptly by a veterinarian. Diagnosis is made with a thorough history and physical exam. Often a neurologic exam is also performed. History and clinical findings will determine what tests should be taken. Symptomatic treatment with anticonvulsants is often prescribed on a trial basis, because each dog's needs differ or may change suddenly. An owner needs to work closely with the veterinarian through careful observation and by keeping a log of each seizure event. Large-breed dogs often have seizures in clusters. A seizure can become an emergency if a dog has cluster seizures, or a series of seizures for a prolonged time. A dog may die during these seizures, become hypoxic (have an abnormally low blood oxygen level), and suffer from permanent brain damage. The only thing an owner can do during a seizure is to protect the dog from harm by removing heavy objects in the area. Never put your fingers in a dog's mouth during a seizure—contrary to some beliefs, dogs do not swallow their tongues when seizing, and you may be badly bitten. There are many breeds that are prone to seizures: the American Cocker Spaniel, American Eskimo, American Water Spaniel, Belgian Malinois, Belgian Tervuren, Border Terrier, Brittany Spaniel, Collie, Curly-Coated Retriever, Dachshund, Dalmatian, English Foxhound, English Springer Spaniel, Field Spaniel (late onset), German Shorthaired Pointer, Great Pyrenees, Greater Swiss Mountain Dog, Havanese, Ibizan Hound, Irish Setter, Irish Wolfhound, Italian Greyhound, Miniature Pinscher, Norwich Terrier, Otterhound, Pekingese, Petit Basset Griffon Vendéen, Pharaoh Hound, Pointer, Portuguese Water Dog, Scottish Deerhound, Shetland Sheepdog, Siberian Husky, Standard Schnauzer, Welsh Springer Spaniel, Welsh Terrier, Vizsla.

**Fanconi syndrome:** A degeneration of the kidney tubes seen in Basenjis.

**Gangliosidosis:** This is a recessive autosomal (paired chromosomes), inherited disorder seen in German Shorthaired Pointers, caused by a defective enzyme that allows lipids (fats) to accumulate in the brain. Onset usually occurs at about six months, and puppies exhibit nervous behavior, clumsiness, partial blindness, and deafness. Afflicted pups usually die by the time they are two years old.

**Glaucoma:** *Glaucoma* is a general term that refers to increased pressure within a dog's eye(s). It is rare in dogs, but is an emergency if it occurs. It happens when the fluid (aqueous humor), which is constantly manufactured, circulated through the eye, and drained out, fails to drain due to scarring or inflammation of the drainage area (the iridocorneal angle, which extends 360 degrees around the outside of the eye). *Lens luxation* (see page 332) may block the flow of fluid in a dog's eye. If this happens, pressure builds up within the eye and damage can be done to the optic nerve within twelve to eighteen hours, permanently impairing vision. Symptoms include extreme discomfort, squinting, red eyes, widely dilated pupils, and a hazy blue cast of the cornea. Treatment consists of trying to reduce pressure as fast as possible, before damage is done. There are a number of medical and surgical techniques designed to accomplish this. If treatment is not successful and a dog's vision is lost, he may often remain in pain and further treatment will be necessary to make the dog more comfortable. American Cockers, Basset Hounds, Petit Basset Griffon Vendéens, and Welsh Terriers are especially prone to this problem.

**Globoid cell leukodystrophy:** Global cell leukodystrophy is the abnormal development and/or function of certain types of white globoid cells in the brain.

**Glycogen storage disease:** Glycogen is an animal starch: a complex carbohydrate that is usually stored in a dog's liver and muscles and broken down into sugar (glucose) molecules whenever they are needed in the body. A recessive trait causes glycogen storage disease. Breeds prone to this disease include the Japanese Spaniel, the German Shepherd and the Pomeranian.

**Heart disease:** Heart, or cardiac, diseases in dogs fall into several categories. *Congenital heart diseases* are the result of an abnormal embryo development and signs are often noticed when a dog is still a puppy. *Acquired heart diseases* are more common and frequently involve the heart valves. *Valvular heart diseases* most often affect small breeds, although any breed may be affected, and signs may not show up until adulthood. Acquired disorders of the heart muscle are called *cardiomyopathies,* and generally affect large and giant breeds. *Heartworm disease* is a mosquito-transmitted parasite, easily prevented by appropriate medication. Signs of heart failure are similar no matter what the cause. Shortness of breath, persistent coughing, breathing difficulty, and progressive lethargy should all be suspected as signs of heart disease and a veterinarian should be consulted right away. Untreated heart disease may eventually result in *congestive heart failure.* The first step in diagnosis of heart disease is a thorough general physical exam, which begins with an evaluation of a dog's heart and lungs with a stethoscope, and often goes on to an electrocardiogram (EKG) and a chest X ray. Treatment depends on the nature and seriousness of the problem. With early detection, most canine cardiac patients can be treated, and often a good prognosis for an improved quality of life is possible. Surgery may be needed in some cases of congenital heart disease.

*Cardiomyopathy:* Cardiomyopathy causes the heart muscle either to become dilated, flabby, and weak, or to thicken and become stiff. It will eventually lead to *congestive heart failure.* Large and giant breeds that weigh more than fifty pounds are most often affected. This is an acquired heart disease that usually affects young to middle-age males.

*Complete heart blocks:* Sometimes a disease will cause a dog's heart not to contract or beat as it should. The heart rhythm may become dangerously slow. Sometimes a pacemaker is used successfully. Only a veterinarian can decide if this is a suitable treatment.

*Congenital heart disease:* (existing at birth): A new puppy should immediately be evaluated for heart disease before you get attached to him, because a breeder will usually allow substitution of a healthy pup, especially in the case of *heart murmur.* If a puppy does not thrive, fails to gain weight, breathes heavily, coughs persistently, or tires easily, it should be suspected of having heart disease. If a heart murmur is not detected until a dog is over three and he has been able to lead a normal life, he may not need treatment and the problem can be managed medically if problems arise.

*Congestive heart failure:* This is the end result of any cardiac disorder in which the heart fails to pump enough blood. Symptoms include fatigue, coughing, exercise intolerance, weight loss, rapid and difficult breathing, and sometimes abdominal distention. There is often fluid buildup (effusion) in the stomach and chest, and in the lungs themselves (edema). Fluid in the lungs or chest is always suspected with rapid breathing. A dog will often extend his neck and head in an effort to get more air and he will appear distressed as he gropes for air. *This is a serious emergency,* and immediate veterinary help must be sought. Treatments differ with each dog and may consist of diuretics and digitalis. If treated immediately and properly, prognosis is favorable.

*Enlarged heart:* A dog's heart can gradually become enlarged due to a congenital or acquired heart disease. If left untreated, *congestive heart failure* may result.

*Heart murmur:* Heart murmurs commonly accompany many heart diseases in dogs. Treatment is not directed at the murmur itself, but at the underlying cause of the murmur, when needed.

Many breeds are susceptible to various types of heart disease. They include American Staffordshire Terrier, American Water Spaniel, Black and Tan Coonhound (murmurs), Bloodhound, Border Terrier, Borzoi, Brittany Spaniel, Chihuahua, Curly-Coated Retriever, German Shepherd, Irish Wolfhound, Mastiff, Papillon, Pekingese, Petit Basset Griffon Vendéen, and Rottweiler.

**Hemolytic anemia:** Any of a group of acute or chronic inherited or acquired anemias characterized by the destruction of red blood cells.

**Hernias:** There are two types of hernias that occur in dogs: *diaphragmatic* and *perineal.* A hernia is a protrusion of an organ or tissue through an abnormal fissure (cleft or groove). A *diaphragmatic* hernia occurs when the diaphragm ruptures and allows some of the abdominal contents into the chest cavity. Surgery is required to repair the rupture. In a *perineal* hernia the wall of the rectum protrudes through the pelvic muscles and becomes impacted with feces. Castration may help, but there is no evidence that it will prevent a recurrence of the problem. French Bulldogs are prone to hernias.

**Hip dysplasia:** Although this developmental disease is recognized in most breeds, it tends to occur most often in large, fast-growing breeds. Joint looseness is one of the first signs of hip dysplasia, and changes in a dog's normal gait often appear before limping or stiffness are noticed. Young dogs with loose hips may develop episodes of lameness, especially after strenuous exercise. There are several causes for the disease, and they include environmental, dietary, and genetic factors. There are noticeable differences in the severity of signs, the age of onset at which signs appear, the degree of pain and associated lameness, and the rate of disease progression. Diagnosis is made with the use of X rays and pathologically (by observing structural and functional manifestations of the disease). Over time, *degenerative arthritis* develops, causing added pain and discomfort. Treatment is mainly symptomatic and varies with the stage of the disease. Rest, proper exercise, restriction of activities which bring on attacks, and analgesic drugs are all used to help the dog. When degenerative arthritis develops, anti-inflammatory drugs such as steroids and other analgesic-type drugs may be used. There are several surgical procedures that may help improve this situation. Many breeds are prone to hip dysplasia. They are American Eskimo, Bearded Collie, Belgian Malinois, Black and Tan Coonhound, Bloodhound, Boxer, Brittany Spaniel, Clumber Spaniel, Curly-Coated Retriever, English Foxhound, English Setter, Field Spaniel, German Shepherd, German Wirehaired Pointer, Gordon Setter, Greater Swiss Mountain Dog, Komondor, Labrador Retriever, Mastiff, Norfolk Terrier, Otterhound, Pembroke Welsh Corgi, Pharaoh Hound, Pointer, Pug, Rottweiler, Samoyed, Shetland Sheepdog, Staffordshire Bull Terrier, and Welsh Springer Spaniel.

**Hypertrophic osteodystrophy (HOD):** This is a bone disease that affects the area of bone adjacent to the growth plate of young large and giant dog breeds. Dogs with this condition have mild to moderate swelling of the ends of the radius, ulna, or tibia. Signs include depression, fever, limping, and loss of appetite. Onset usually occurs anywhere from three to seven months, and is diagnosed by X rays and physical examination. Treatment is aimed at controlling the fever and reducing the pain. Most dogs recover spontaneously, but in severe cases permanent bone deformities may occur. Irish Setters and Weimaraners are particularly susceptible to this disease.

**Hypoglycemia (abnormally low blood sugar levels):** This is a condition usually seen in small dogs and is caused by a lack of enough calcium in the diet during late pregnancy and nursing. It is also seen in hunting dogs at the beginning of the hunting season. Hunting dogs should be fed stress-working diets high in calcium for several weeks before the hunting season begins. Older dogs can develop the disease due to an insulin-producing abdominal tumor that secretes large amounts of insulin periodically. Also, a dog with *diabetes* (see page 318) on insulin treatment that either receives too much insulin, or receives a normal amount of insulin and doesn't eat right, will also develop hypoglycemia. Symptoms include weakness, confusion, restlessness, trembling, high fever, muscle spasms, and eventually convulsions. This is an *emergency* that requires immediate veterinary care. Chihuahuas are especially apt to develop hypoglycemia.

There is another form characterized by an acute onset of seizures or convulsions. The dog will roll on his side, make rapid jaw movements, salivate profusely, urinate and defecate, and shake his limbs violently. If this goes on for too long, seizures and eventual coma are inevitable. Brain damage may occur even after proper treatment.

First aid treatment may help. If a puppy that hasn't been eating properly starts to get confused or weak, some honey, sugar water, Karo brand corn syrup, or anything containing sugar (except chocolate) may help to reverse the problem. However, if the condition has continued for long, home treatment may not help. Giving sugar to an older dog with an insulin-producing tumor while he is still awake may help. Oral sugar given before seizures or collapse is also very helpful for a diabetic dog that has overdosed on insulin. Dosage depends on the size of the dog—a tablespoon for a small dog, several for larger animals.

**Hypothyroidism:** This is the most common *endocrine disease* of dogs. It is the result of a deficiency of thyroid hormone. It can appear at any age, but is most often seen in young to middle-aged animals (from two to six years old). It is usually caused by the destruction of the thyroid gland, either from an immune-mediated process, atrophy, or cancer. Signs of the disease vary, but usually include lethargy, fatigue, mental dullness, exercise intolerance, loss of alertness and excitability, a propensity to gain weight without a corresponding increase in food intake, and increased sleepiness. It can also produce skin and coat changes including hair loss on the trunk and tail, scaling of the skin, bacterial infections and sometimes a dark pigmentation of the skin, atrophy of testicles, lack of libido, low sperm counts, seizures, a "drunken" gait, circling, head tilt, and facial nerve paralysis. Diagnosis involves a number of tests, including an assessment of the history, physical and clinical findings, and serum cholesterol and thyroid hormone concentrations. Hypothyroidism is treated with synthetic thyroid hormones, usually given orally two times a day and must be continued for the rest of a dog's life. With appropriate therapy, the signs should resolve and the prognosis for recovery is excellent. Breeds with a propensity towards hypothyroidism include Afghan Hounds, Airedales, Beagles, Boxers, Brittany Spaniels, Chow Chows, Cocker Spaniels, Dachshunds, Doberman Pinschers, English Bulldogs, Golden Retrievers, Great Danes, Irish Setters, Irish Wolfhounds, Malamutes, Miniature Schnauzers, Newfoundlands, Pomeranians, Poodles, and Shetland Sheepdogs.

**Invertebral disc disease (ruptured/slipped spinal discs):** When a dog suddenly or gradually becomes unable to get up from a lying position, it is an *emergency,* and veterinary help should be sought immediately. The cause is rarely known, so there is little that an owner can do. Usually, this condition is caused by ruptured discs in the spine, and usually occurs in Toy-breed dogs, or in long-bodied dogs, which carry too much weight on their backs. There are two types of rupture. In one, the dog has pain in his back, shakes, trembles, hides, and acts as if he is in discomfort but continues to walk, even though his rear legs function poorly. In the other, the dog lets out a scream or groan and his back legs collapse. He may still have control of his front legs and can drag his back end around with them. Some disc ruptures damage the spinal cord badly and, within minutes after the rupture, the spinal cord is already damaged permanently and the dog is paralyzed. The sooner a veterinarian sees a dog with a slipped·disc, the better the dog can be evaluated and the more likely rear limb function can be restored. Breeds that are susceptible to this disorder are Basset Hounds, Beagles, Dachshunds, Clumber Spaniels, French Bulldogs, Pekingese, and Skye Terriers.

**Juvenile cataracts:** Cataracts in general have been covered earlier in this chapter. Juvenile, congenital cataracts may or may not be inherited and generally do not progress to blindness, although in puppyhood, they may present a visual handicap. As the puppy's lenses age and enlarge, his increased lens size relative to the cataract will diminish the vision-impairing effect of a congenital cataract. Successful surgical extraction using the newest lens-removal techniques and replacing the removed lens with a clear plastic intraocular lens is now often performed.

**Kidney (renal) diseases and disorders:** Just like humans, dogs have two kidneys, located in their abdomens. These kidneys act as filters for waste materials in the bloodstream, eliminating toxins from the blood. They also regulate the dog's body-to-fluid composition and volume and aid in the production of certain hormones, which, in turn, regulate the production of red blood cells and assist in the formation of bones. The *nephron* is the functional unit of the kidney. A dog has approximately a million nephrons, each of which consists of a *glomerulus* (a tuft of tiny blood vessels, or capillaries) that filters blood and a *tubule* that modifies the filtrate formed by the glomerulus to formulate urine. Urine is then transported from the kidneys to the urinary bladder via the ureters. It is then stored in the urinary bladder, which contracts when full to empty itself. The urine travels through the urethra to the outside, via the vagina in females and the penis in males. Male dogs also have a prostate gland located outside the urethra and connected by tiny tubes to the urethra.

If only one kidney is damaged or rendered incompetent by disease, bacterial infection, trauma, or congenital malformation, the remaining kidney is usually able to take over and perform the necessary renal functions. However, if both kidneys become incompetent, a dog will suffer from *renal failure,* and *uremia* will result.

Kidney damage can occur from birth. It can also be the result of a bacterial urinary tract infection, such as *pyelonephritis,* or from an invasion of the kidneys by an outside parasite. The kidneys can also be damaged by kidney stones, renal cysts, and tumors. Kidney diseases can be of unknown origin. Signs of kidney disease vary, depending on the severity of the disorder and the degree of kidney involvement. Many signs are possible but are not necessarily present. There are a number of tests and studies available to veterinarians to help diagnose kidney disease. Treatment varies widely and depends on the severity of the disease and the kidney damage already sustained by the dog, but it almost always involves parenteral (intravenously injected) fluids and supportive care. Depending on the disease, antibiotics and diet may also be used as therapy. The prognosis for a dog with kidney disease also varies widely. (See also *urinary stones.*) Breeds that are especially susceptible to kidney disease are Gordon Setters, Miniature Bull Terriers, Norwegian Elkhounds, and Shetland Sheepdogs (juvenile).

**Laryngeal paralysis:** Normally, the vocal folds open during inhalation and partially close during exhalation. Many puppies born with severe congenital problems of the larynx will not survive. In laryngeal paralysis the vocal folds move out of time with the phases of respiration, remain closed all the time, produce a very weak, hoarse bark, and cause the dog to breathe very stridently. One or both of the vocal folds may be affected. This may be a congenital disorder in Bouvier des Flandres, Siberian Huskies, and Dalmatians. It may also be an acquired disorder in large-breed, older, long-nosed dogs, such as Labrador Retrievers. It probably occurs as a component of a more serious inflammatory disease involving the neurologic system, the muscular system, or both. Signs develop gradually and depend on the severity of the paralysis and the resulting obstruction to airflow through the larynx. The earliest sign is usually a change in a dog's bark. Dogs with this disease tire easily, are sensitive to heat, and pant a lot. In severe cases, it may be life-threatening. Affected dogs should have a thorough neurologic evaluation, and confirmation of the diagnosis can be made by direct visualization of the vocal folds under light anesthesia. Treatment is similar to that for laryngitis or laryngeal edema.

Surgical correction may be attempted, but it predisposes a dog to aspiration of foreign bodies and even food and water into the lungs. The prognosis depends on the progression of the underlying inflammatory disorder.

**Legg-Calvé-Perthes disease:** This is a noninfectious necrosis (cell death) of the head and neck of the femur (top end of the leg bone leading into the hip joint). The bone of the femoral head and neck dies and is gradually resorbed, resulting in collapse of the bone and deformation of the hip joint, leading to degenerative changes in the hip and the development of *arthritis.* Signs include lameness and pain associated with the hip joint. Age of onset is usually five to nine months, and the cause is not precisely known. X rays are needed to confirm the diagnosis, and surgical treatment is recommended. With surgical correction, the prognosis is good. Small breeds and terriers are often susceptible to this disease, particularly American Eskimos, Jack Russells, Miniature Pinschers, and Westies.

**Lens luxation:** The lens of a dog's eye is held in place by fine little fibers that may become weak and torn with age. This allows the lens to move around abnormally inside the eye. If the lens stays in the back part of the eye, it is not a major problem. If, however, it moves to the front part of the eye, it can block the flow of fluid in the eye and lead to *glaucoma* (see page 324). Miniature Bull Terriers and Tibetan Terriers are especially prone to this disorder.

**Liver problems/disease:** Liver disease in dogs is often nonspecific. Just as in humans, liver disease in dogs is characterized by jaundice (yellowing of the mucous membranes) and abdominal distention caused by the accumulation of fluids in the stomach cavity. It is also often accompanied by vomiting, diarrhea, and loss of appetite. Liver disease may progress for a long time with no signs at all until it reaches a critical point. If there is inflammation of the liver cells, it is called a *hepatitis,* but if the inflammation is accompanied with the bile ducts or gallbladder, it is referred to as a *cholangitis.* Dogs can suffer from *cirrhosis of the liver.* This condition is of unknown causes except that there usually has been some kind of chronic inflammatory liver disease, which resulted in the destruction of normal tissues and the formation of scar tissue. We rarely see *infectious canine hepatitis* today because dogs are routinely vaccinated against it. Sometimes we see a condition known as *hepatic encephalopathy*—a condition in which the liver completely fails to eliminate toxic products from a dog's body. This may be a congenital problem. Toxins in the blood will immediately cause a dog with this condition to lapse into a coma or go into a seizure, especially after eating meat proteins. Dietary therapy is important in these cases, with dairy products being substituted for meat and meat-type proteins. Breeds that are susceptible to liver disease are Doberman Pinschers and Papillons.

**Liver shunts/portasystemic shunts/portacaval shunts:** These are abnormal communications between the portal vein coming from the gastrointestinal tract and the posterior vena cava, which carries blood back to the heart. The communications are usually present during fetal life and then close shortly after birth. When these communications do not close properly, the vessels act as shunts so that portal blood flow does not pass through the liver before being delivered to the rest of a dog's body. Signs appear in puppyhood and include neurologic indications of hepatic encephalopathy (liver disease), depression, seizures (see *epilepsy*—page 322), *ataxia* (see page 304), vomiting, excessive thirst, and retarded growth. An ammonia tolerance test is the most reliable way to determine that the signs are caused by a liver abnormality, and the diagnosis can be confirmed by an X-ray imaging study. Most cases can be treated successfully by a partial surgical closure of the shunt. Dietary management will help alleviate signs in dogs that are not operated on. The dog must have an adequate food intake, consisting of proteins from milk and soybean foods that are home-prepared. Cottage cheese or tofu, boiled rice, and a vitamin-mineral mixture with adequate vitamin C, zinc, and a greater than usual amount of vitamin E. Breeds that are susceptible to liver shunts are Cairn Terriers, Doberman Pinschers, Havanese, Irish Wolfhounds, Norfolk Terriers, and Scottish Deerhounds.

**Lupus erythematosus:** There are two kinds of lupus erythematosus: *discoid* and *systemic*. They both affect a dog's skin.

*Discoid lupus erythematosus:* This is a fairly common autoimmune skin disease in dogs. This is a bone disease characterized by a bony overgrowth of the jaw and surrounding skull bones. Onset usually occurs when a dog is between four and eleven months of age. Signs include swelling of the jaw, drooling, inability to open the mouth, and pain if the mouth is manipulated. X rays are needed to confirm the diagnosis, and the cause of the disease is not known. Treatment is symptomatic, and most dogs are more comfortable when they are given steroids or aspirin. The disease is usually self-limiting, and although many dogs may continue to have impaired mouth function, they are usually able to eat. Because it is aggravated by sunlight, the lesions are often more severe in the summer or in areas with high solar intensity. Signs are usually facial and involve a symmetrical pattern of depigmentation (loss of color), reddening of the skin, and scaling, especially on a dog's nose. Loss of the normal "cobblestone" architecture of the tip of the nose may occur. Lesions may also develop on the top of the muzzle, lips, around the eyes and on the ears. They may infrequently occur in the form of mouth ulcers and lesions on the genitals and extremities. Hair loss, crusting, erosions, ulcerations, and scarring may appear in severe cases. Long-standing lesions are fragile and bleed readily. Diagnosis is based on history, clinical signs, and skin biopsy. Treatment consists of restriction of access to sunlight, and the application of sunscreens and topical anti-inflammatory medications. Systemic anti-inflammatory drugs should be given only if absolutely necessary. Collies, Shetland Sheepdogs, German Shepherds and Siberian Huskies are especially prone to this disorder. White German Shepherds are particularly susceptible.

*Systemic lupus erythematosus (SLE):* This is a rare autoimmune disorder that involves many body systems and is characterized by a general derangement of key immune defense mechanisms. In SLE, a variety of immune mechanisms begin to attack structural components of the body, such as DNA. Autoantibodies are directed against these host-cell components and attach to cells in the blood, kidneys, skin, and elsewhere, causing a widespread immunologic assault on the host. Dogs between two and four years old are most often affected. Skin lesions can include erythema (a reddening of the skin), scaling, crusting, loss of pigmentation, and hair loss. Ulcers may appear from ruptured vesicles (a small sac containing liquid) in the skin, in areas where mucous membranes and skin adjoin, such as the lip margins, and on mucous membranes. Common sites include the face, ears, and extremities. Diagnosis is made on the basis of history, clinical signs, and laboratory test, including the ANA test, which detects autoantibodies directed against DNA. Corticosteroids combined with more potent immunosuppressive medications are used. The prognosis is guarded to fair. Canine SLE is prevalent in Collies, German Shepherds, Poodles, Shetland Sheepdogs, and Spitzes.

**Lymphangiectasia:** This is a disease of the intestinal lymph vessels, which causes *malabsorption* (see below). It may be congenital or acquired. Management of malabsorption involves the feeding of a controlled diet consisting of cottage cheese, tofu, boiled rice, and tapioca. This diet must be fed indefinitely and should be supplemented with vitamins and minerals after three weeks.

**Lysosomal storage diseases:** This is a group of progressive multifocal neurologic disorders caused by specific enzyme deficiencies leading to the death of nerve cells and the accumulation of their respective enzyme substrates in cells.

**Malabsorption:** Malabsorption is caused by problems in the small intestinal mucosa that diminish the proper absorption of nutrients. Affected dogs have ravenous appetites but fail to gain weight. They have a huge volume of feces, which contains excess fat, identified by fecal staining and fecal smears. The feces may also be stained by starch granules and muscle fibers if the dog is eating muscle meat. Fecal tests are performed, but there are no reliable, easy tests to indicate that biopsy is the next best step. A measurement of *breath hydrogen* may be used to determine bacterial overgrowth and malabsorption of carbohydrates in the small intestine. An intestinal cancer may be one of the causes. Another is *lymphangiectasia,* a disease of the intestinal lymph vessels. Yet another is *inflammatory bowel disease*. Most important in management is to feed a controlled diet. The cottage cheese, tofu, boiled rice, and tapioca diet can be used and must be fed indefinitely. After three weeks, minerals and vitamins can be added.

**Mast cell tumors:** A mast cell is a granule-containing cell that plays a central role in the development of allergies. Tumors of the mast cell occur frequently in older dogs. They usually appear on a dog's extremities and external body walls. Diagnosis of malignancy requires a biopsy and, whenever possible, surgical removal is the therapy of choice. Prognosis depends on the degree of malignancy. Approximately half these tumors may be curable with surgery alone. More malignant types may also require chemotherapy or radiation to prevent recurrence and spreading. A second form of mast cell tumors, called *systemic mastocytosis,* invades the blood-forming organs of a dog's body, such as the bone marrow and spleen. In this case, prognosis is guarded and chemotherapy is necessary. Breeds that are susceptible to mast cell tumors are Boston Terriers, Boxers, Chinese Shar-Peis, Rhodesian Ridgebacks, and Staffordshire Bull Terriers.

**Megaesophagus:** Enlargement of the esophagus is a fairly common problem that results in paralysis of part or all of the esophagus. This is often congenital in puppies. However, an acquired form can also be seen in adult dogs of any age. Clinical signs include regurgitation that can occur immediately after eating or some time later. Most affected dogs are underweight and have a voracious appetite. Some dogs develop a loss of normal motility (the ability to move spontaneously), but this is reversible. The cause of megaesophagus is not known, but in some cases other neuromuscular problems such as *myasthenia gravis* or some toxicities may be at the root of the acquired form of the disease. Diagnosis is made by X rays of the chest with or without barium. There is no treatment for the congenital form of megaesophagus, other than helping the dog eat by placing his food in an elevated position so that he may stand while eating. Affected dogs are at risk for developing *aspiration pneumonia,* due to the inhalation of food into the lungs. Most young puppies with this congenital condition are euthanized, but if a known treatable cause can be discovered in dogs with the acquired form of the disease, the problem may be treated. In general the prognosis is poor. Large breeds such as Irish Setters, German Shepherds, and Great Danes are most likely to suffer from this condition.

**Microphthalmia:** The condition of undersize eyeballs can be congenital or may develop from an uncontrolled inflammation of the inner structures of the eyes. If the undersize eye still has identifiable internal structures, the shrunken eyeball is said to be *atrophic* (atrophia bulbi) while one that has been so internally scarred as to possess no recognizable structures is said to be *phthisical* (phthisis bulbi). In both cases, opaque corneas may result, partially hidden by passive protrusion of the third eyelid. Sometimes shrunken eyeballs must be surgically removed because of chronic irritation caused by a number of factors due to their diminished size. Eyes that acquire either of these conditions are usually blind. Eyes that are undersize at birth are often sighted with diminished vision.

**Mouth disorders:** Mouth disorders in dogs can range from: *oral papilloma tissues, oral tumors, pharyngeal disease, and poor teeth,* to *soft palate disorders.*

*Dental care/disease:* With the dog's mouth closed, pull back on his lips to expose his gums and teeth. Healthy gums are pink and firm, and the teeth should be firm and free from bad stains. Push gently on the corners of the dog's jaw, open his mouth, and examine his tongue and the insides of his teeth. If a dog's gums are pale or bleed when touched or if there are any swellings or red marks inside a dog's mouth, or any sensitive, loose, or broken teeth, they should be seen by a veterinarian.

It is best to brush, or clean, a dog's teeth regularly to remove tartar and invisible plaque that can cause tooth loss. An adult dog that has never had proper tooth care should be given an initial scaling by a veterinarian. As with all routines, it is easiest to perform tooth care if you start early in a dog's life. Begin by using a rough cloth (a washcloth or gauze square) and rub each tooth from gum to tip. Work up to a rougher cloth and then to a child's toothbrush using a mixture of one-half salt and one-half baking soda, slightly moistened.

Dental disease is very common in older dogs, and an oral examination should be part of every older dog's usual veterinary exam. If an older dog's teeth have not been cleaned regularly, plaque and tarter buildup and cavities can form. If an older dog has bad breath, bleeding gums, eats less, and finds it difficult to chew hard biscuits or toys, one should suspect tooth or gum problems. Sometimes a dog with a painful mouth will approach food, seem to want to eat, and then back away or stand looking sadly at his plate. Sometimes food will fall out of his mouth. This calls for a veterinary exam and a complete scaling and deep cleaning. After that, regular home cleaning will help keep an older dog's mouth free from problems. Older dogs may also develop oral tumors—see below—that will show up in an oral exam.

*Broken teeth:* A dog's tooth may be broken at either the crown or at the root. X-ray evaluation is always used to determine whether the tooth can be salvaged, or should be extracted. A freshly fractured tooth that exposes the pulp is a dental *emergency.* Preferably, the integrity of the pulp can be saved and the tooth will remain alive. A partial *pulpectomy* (removal of the damaged pulp) and protection of the remaining tooth by means of a cap can achieve this. It is controversial how long pulp can be exposed and still be salvaged by capping. General guidelines for the maximum time varies with the age of the dog. Dogs under eighteen months of age can wait for up to two weeks, while older dogs need dental attention within twenty-four to forty-eight hours.

*Oral papilloma tissues (oral papillomatosis):* This is an uncommon canine infectious viral disease of young dogs causing benign but terrible-looking wartlike growths on the tongue and mouth. It is transmitted from dog to dog by direct contact, licking, and shared dishes. It is usually self-limiting and goes away as the dog gets older and gains immunity. Sometime surgery is used to remove these growths.

*Oral tumors:* Masses in a dog's mouth may be benign or malignant. *Malignant melanomas, fibrosarcomas,* and *squamous cell carcinomas* are the three most commonly seen mouth tumors in dogs. Signs of oral tumors are an inability to eat, bad breath, bleeding or discharge from the mouth, and visible masses.

*Malignant melanomas* have a high propensity to spread to other parts of a dog's body, usually to the lungs and regional lymph nodes. Diagnosis can be made only by biopsy of the removed tissue. Treatment consists of surgical removal of the mass and other therapies, depending on the spread, and includes radiation, chemotherapy, and radical surgery. Prognosis depends on the type of cancer, early recognition, and diagnosis.

*Fibrosarcomas* are malignant tumors of fibrous connective tissue cells. They are usually surgically removed. Often, radiation to prevent spreading or chemotherapy is also used.

*Squamous cell carcinomas* are especially common in dogs and are often transformed from *actinic keratoses,* which are danger signs of overexposure to the sun. In dogs, the lesions are usually found on the lower abdomen and inner surface of the thighs in short-coated, white-haired dogs with lightly pigmented skin and thin haircoats. Affected dogs should receive minimal sun exposure and be treated with sunscreen. Diagnosis is based on clinical history, physical exam, and laboratory studies including biopsy. Therapy of extreme lesions is surgery or cryosurgery (removal by local freezing of tissue). Breeds with a predisposition toward actinic keratoses are American Staffordshire Terriers, Basset Hounds, Beagles, Dalmatians, Italian Greyhounds, and Whippets.

*Pharyngeal diseases:* The pharynx is actually the back of the mouth, where a sore throat is usually felt. Signs associated with pharyngeal disease are usually related to eating or drinking. A dog will gag, choke, and have difficulty swallowing. In addition, a gurgling or rasping noise can sometimes be heard when a dog swallows. Problems associated with the pharynx include an overlong *soft palate,* tonsillitis, cysts or masses, and, in rare cases, tonsillar cancer.

*Soft palate disorders:* Cleft palates and overlong soft palates are both congenital canine disorders and most commonly occur in brachycephalic (flat-faced) breeds. The most common sign of an overlong soft palate is excessive snoring and snorting. If this problem is severe, it can be corrected surgically, but is left alone if the palate is only slightly elongated. A puppy born with a cleft palate will pass milk out of his nose while nursing. The problem is corrected surgically as soon as the puppy is old enough, but in the meantime, tube feeding is necessary to support the puppy.

**Obesity:** Up to 44 percent of dogs in the United States are overweight. A dog is considered obese when his body weight exceeds the ideal for his age, sex, and breed by 20 percent. Although obesity by itself may not shorten a dog's life, it does increase the risk of developing certain diseases that can impair the quality of a dog's life. It increases the risk of cancer, diabetes, infections, and skin disease and may also be associated with *hypertension* (elevated blood pressure) and cardiac, neurologic, orthopedic, and reproductive disorders. Obesity is simply the intake of too many calories or decreased energy output, or a combination of the two. It is most often found in neutered females, especially as they get older, due to decreased activity. Other factors can be highly flavorful commercial diets, or table foods that encourage overeating, and diets that are high in fat. A hormonal imbalance, such as *hypothyroidism* (see pages 328–29) can promote obesity by reducing a dog's body's basal metabolism, thereby decreasing energy (caloric) needs.

The onset of obesity can go unnoticed by owners, especially in longhaired dogs. Objective ways to determine an "ideal" weight for a particular dog are not available. Therefore, both owners and veterinarians must rely on a "look and feel" technique to determine if a dog is overweight. A dog is considered to be at his ideal weight if his ribs can easily be felt. His abdomen and chest should form an hourglass shape when seen from above. Signs of obesity include accumulated fat over the hips and at the base of the tail; face, neck, and shoulder broadening; lethargy; a lower capacity for exercise; noisy breathing; and waddling. Some of these signs may indicate other physical conditions or diseases such as heart disease (see pages 324–26), hormonal imbalance, pregnancy, and so forth. Because obesity is caused by the chronic consumption of too many calories, the best way to treat it is to avoid it by providing plenty of exercise, a low-fat diet, and not feeding table food or scraps. Short-legged, long-bodied dogs such as Bassets and Beagles have a particular propensity toward obesity.

**Open fontanel:** This is a soft spot in the skull of a fetus or infant dog that is not covered by skin.

**Optic nerve hypoplasia:** The optic nerve extends from the brain to the back of the eye (retina) and transmits signals from light energy that are translated into a visual image by the brain. In this disorder, there is an underdevelopment or incomplete development of the optic nerve, resulting in distorted or incomplete images. In Collies there is a rare congenital abnormality in which there is a large pit in the head of the optic nerve tissue, which can lead to severe visual problems and, in some cases, a *detached retina* (see page 318). In mild cases there may not be noticeable visual problems, but sometimes *blindness* (see page 308) occurs.

*Optic nerve colobomata* is a rare congenital abnormality most often seen in Collies in which there is a large pit in the head of the optic nerve tissue, which can lead to severe visual problems including a *detached retina* (see page 318) and perhaps *blindness* (see page 308).

**Osteochondritis dissecans (OCD):** This is one of two common congenital joint problems (the other is medial patellar luxation of the knee). It is a defect in the normal development of the articular (joint) cartilage and underlying bone surface. Both transient and permanent lameness can occur. The lesion develops most commonly in the shoulder joint, the knee (stifle), and hock (ankle) joints of dogs. Diagnosis is by orthopedic examination and X rays. Treatment is often by surgical exploration of the joint and removal of the cartilage flap. Prognosis depends on the joint involved and the degree of secondary *degenerative arthritis* (see *arthritis,* pages 302–304).

**Pancreatitis:** Inflammation of the pancreas seems to be the result of several factors and is most commonly seen in obese, middle-aged female dogs. Symptoms may vary from abdominal pain, mild appetite loss, depression, diarrhea, and occasional vomiting to severe gastrointestinal upsets including bloody diarrhea and, eventually, severe shock. Regular ingestion of high-fat foods may be a contributing factor. The inflammation itself is an autodigestive process in which the pancreatic enzymes that are released actually digest the pancreas itself, perpetuating the inflammation. Therapy involves hospitalization, during which a dog is kept off food for a long period, given intravenous fluids, and then given a reduced intake of low-fat foods along with moderate exercise to reduce weight, while supported with intravenous fluids and antibiotics to decrease the pancreatic enzyme flow, and followed by dietary therapy. Pancreatitis is a common cause of *diabetes mellitus* (see page 318) in older dogs, while a more severe, acute form of the disease may result in shock and eventual death. Other complications can include secondary damage to the heart, lungs, kidney, liver, and brain;

blood clotting abnormalities; and infections. In acute pancreatitis, many of these complications lead to death. Diagnosis is difficult because it can manifest itself in so many ways. After recovery, the dog should be fed a low-fat high-quality diet. Commercial dog foods and table scraps should be avoided. German Shepherds are especially susceptible to this disorder.

*Chronic pancreatitis:* Dogs that have recovered from acute pancreatitis may develop a chronic form of the disease. There may be no outward signs, and blood chemistry results may be normal. With ultrasound examination, however, the pancreas will appear abnormal. There is no treatment except the feeding of a low-fat diet. These dogs are at risk for eventually developing complications of diabetes or pancreatic insufficiency, or both.

**Pannus:** This is an eye disease that consists of an ingrowth of blood vessels into the cornea, which appears as a hazy reddish tissue on the corneal surface. It is incurable, but can be well controlled with medication. Left untreated, it may lead to blindness. German Shepherds and German Shepherd crosses are usually affected.

**Paralysis (plegia, paresis):** *Motor plegia* is the complete absence of purposeful movement—the inability of a dog to move a muscle or body part voluntarily. *Sensory plegia* is the complete absence of deep pain sensations. It is often accompanied by depression, lethargy, and obvious pain and may be caused by *arthritis* (see pages 302–304), a bone tumor (see *tumors*, page 351), *invertebral disc disease* (see page 329), muscle disease, or *spinal disease* (see *spinal arthritis, spinal disc problems, spinal meningitis,* or *spinal paralysis*—pages 357–58). *Paresis* involves partial paralysis and possible seizures. It may be the result of *botulism,* which is contracted by eating contaminated food or by contamination of a wound; *cryptoccosis,* which is a fungus that affects the central nervous system and is found in bird droppings and in the soil—in this disease head tilt and ocular disease often accompany the incoordination; *distemper* in puppies; and *neospora cannum,* a recently identified protozoan that is progressive and difficult to diagnose, and for which there is no proven effective therapy—it is often fatal.

**Patellar (knee) luxation:** Luxation, or dislocation, of the kneecap (patella) can be congenital or may be induced by trauma. It is either *medial,* in which the kneecap is displaced from its normal femoral groove to the inner aspect of the leg, or *lateral,* in which the kneecap is displaced toward the outer leg. Signs vary according to the degree of luxation. Some dogs are in intermittent pain and occasionally limp with a rear leg, while others have persistent, severe lameness. Diagnosis is made with an orthopedic examination, and treatment varies according to the severity of the luxation and resulting lameness. Surgery is the primary means of treatment. Prognosis depends on the severity of the luxation, the breed of dog, and the particular surgical technique used. Congenital medial luxation is common in Toy breeds, while congenital lateral luxations occur more often in large and giant breeds. Trauma-induced luxations are seen in every breed. Breeds subject to this problem are Bichon Frises, Boston Terriers, Cairn Terriers, Chihuahuas, French Bulldogs, Great Pyrenees, Papillons, Pharaoh Hounds, and Pugs.

**Patent ductus arteriosus (PDA):** This is an abnormal persistence after birth of the embryonic blood vessel connecting the pulmonary artery to the aorta, causing arterial blood to circulate through the lungs. It is one of the most common canine congenital defects. The *ductus* is a vessel that, during fetal life, allows blood to bypass the lungs, which are not functional at that time. It normally shuts down shortly after birth. In dogs with PDA, the ductus remains open, allowing blood to flow from the arteries through the *patent* (open) ductus and into the side of the lung. To compensate for this "leak," the left ventricle has to pump more blood to maintain normal blood flow to the rest of a dog's body. Diagnosis is made by listening to the heart and finding a continuous heart murmur, and may be confirmed with a chest X ray and an echocardiogram. Left heart failure is a complication of PDA, which results in a pulmonary edema (the accumulation of a lot of fluid in the lungs) followed by breathing difficulty. Dogs with heart failure are first treated with a diuretic (medicine that promotes urination), followed by surgical closure of the patent ductus. It is often congenital in Miniature Poodles, and frequently seen in German Shepherds.

**Pemphigus group:** This is a collective term for certain autoimmune skin diseases in which a dog's body forms antibodies that are directed toward specific skin layers. The disease complex may take many forms and cause a variety of skin problems. There is *bullous pemphagoid, pemphigus foliaceus,* and *pemphigus vulgaris.*

*Bullous pemphagoid* is very rare and is characterized by the formation of autoantibodies (antibodies directed towards the dog's own body), and the development of vesicles (blisters) and bullae (large blisters containing fluid) beneath the skin's surface. The condition may be either acute or chronic. Because of their location, the blisters are often found intact. Dogs with this problem have swollen, distended blisters that develop quickly and then rupture and produce widespread ulceration. Usually the ulcers remain the same size as the blisters. Secondary bacterial infection and scarring are both complications. Most dogs with this condition have lesions in and around their mouths and around their eyes; but lesions are also common in other locations, such as the armpits and groins. Dogs that are badly afflicted with the acute form may also have fever, loss of appetite, lethargy, and depression. Diagnosis is based on the history, clinical signs, skin biopsy, and immunologic testing. Immunosupportive drugs (corticosteroids and other more potent medicines) are used to treat the disease. Prognosis for recovery is poor. This disease is more common in older dogs. Dachshunds and Dobermans seem to have an increased risk of developing the disease.

*Pemphigus foliaceus* is an uncommon autoimmune disease that is characterized by autoantibody production and development of blisters and pustules on the skin surface that occur in waves—the animal may have no disease signs and then suddenly have dozens of pustules, which quickly progress and form thick, adherent crusts with marked peeling. The top of the muzzle and nose, ears, skin around the eyes, and foot pads are the most common sites. Diagnosis is based on history and signs, skin biopsy and immunologic testing. Immunosupportive drug therapy (corticosteroids, and the like) is used to treat the disease, and the prognosis is guarded. Akitas, Bearded Collies, Chow Chows, Doberman Pinschers, Newfoundlands, and Schipperkes are all genetically predisposed toward this disease. In the case of Akitas and Chow Chows, facial lesions predominate.

*Pemphigus vulgaris:* This is also a rare autoimmune disease that is characterized by skin blisters. Fragile, irregularly shaped, fluid-filled blisters develop in small groups. When the blisters break, the resulting erosions are much larger than the original blisters, and secondary bacterial infection results in widespread ulceration. Pemphigus vulgaris most often appears in the mouth (tongue, palate, and gums), and the mucous membranes around the lips, eyelids, nostrils, anus, prepuce (fold of skin enclosing a male's penis), and vulva. At least 90 percent of affected dogs have mouth lesions and thick, ropy, smelly saliva may drip from the dog's mouth. Oral ulceration is often the initial sign of the disease. Diagnosis is based on history, clinical signs, skin biopsy, and immunologic testing. Immunosupportive drugs (corticosteroids and others) are the main treatment. Prognosis for recovery is poor.

**Perianal fistulas:** Perianal fistulas are chronic draining tracts in the tissues surrounding the anus. They are common among German Shepherds and are often surgically removed.

**Progressive retinal atrophy (PRA):** This is an umbrella term under which a number of degenerative retinal diseases are lumped. It is the most common retinal problem seen in dogs. One of two things can happen: either the photoreceptor cells in the retina are improperly formed at birth (congenital PRA); or they do not hold up well and degenerate as a dog ages. The most common first sign is night blindness because the disease first affects the rod photoreceptors. It is a problem that often develops gradually, and an owner may notice it only when a dog is in a new environment. There is no effective treatment for this disorder, which can eventually lead to *blindness.* It can affect all breeds, but most often appears in American Cockers, American Eskimos, Basenjis, Belgian Tervurens, Collies, English Springer Spaniels, Irish Setters, Labrador Retrievers, Norwegian Elkhounds, Papillons, Poodles (often occurs with aging), Samoyeds, Staffordshire Bull Terriers, Schnauzers, and Tibetan Terriers.

*Central progressive retinal atrophy (CPRA):* This is a similar inherited disorder that affects the deepest layer of the retina. It is inherited by Border Collies, English Springer Spaniels, Golden Retrievers, Irish Setters, Labrador Retrievers, and Shetland Sheepdogs. There is no effective therapy.

**Retinal dysplasia:** This can be a congenital or acquired eye problem. If it is not congenital, it may be caused by a viral infection, irradiation, certain drugs, vitamin A deficiency, or trauma. Inherited dysplasias are more common and can be passed on to future generations. In some individuals or breeds, there may be minimal vision disturbance that is virtually undetectable, while in others the condition leads to *blindness*. A retina that develops normally and is healthy at birth can degenerate later in life as the result of either inherited or acquired disease. The inherited forms of retinal dysplasia are varied and complex and affect various breeds at different stages of life. There is no effective treatment. Breeds that are known to have genetic predispositions toward this disorder are American Cocker Spaniels, Australian Shepherds, Bedlington Terriers, English Springer Spaniels, Labrador Retrievers, and Sealyham Terriers.

**Sebaceous adenitis (SA):** This is a rare skin disease in which the sebaceous glands become inflamed and destroyed and the hair follicles may not mature. The cause is unknown; however, some researchers believe both genetic and autoimmune origins are responsible. There is plugging of the hair follicles and subsequent scaling, which occur as complications of reduced sebum flow. Young adult dogs are most often affected with this disease, and severity varies among different breeds. Scaling is the most common sign. Coat quality diminishes as the disease progresses, resulting in dull, dry, brittle, and broken hairs. Diagnosis is made on the basis of history, clinical findings, and skin biopsy. Treatment is symptomatic and involves the use of special shampoos. Secondary bacterial infection of the affected hair follicles is common, and a dog with this disease may have fever, malaise, and weight loss. Dogs with this disease should not be bred. Akitas may have the most severe hair loss. Samoyeds and Standard Poodles have similar lesions, but hair loss is worse in Standard Poodles. Vizslas and other short-coated breeds are apt to have coexisting nodular lesions and plaques, hair loss and scaling on the trunk.

**Shoulder luxation:** See *patellar (knee) luxation,* page 343.

**Splenic torsion:** The spleen is an "immunologic filter" of the blood and contains many important cells of the immune system. In splenic torsion, this organ has twisted, turned, or rotated. Greater Swiss Mountain Dogs are especially apt to display this disorder, which is treated surgically.

**Spinal arthritis (spondylosis):** See *arthritis,* pages 302–304. Spinal arthritis causes severe pain, lethargy, limping, and may result in a refusal to walk at all. Sometimes, fused discs can be repaired surgically.

**Spinal disc problems (invertebral disc disease):** This disease occurs when one or more spinal discs (the cushioning structures positioned between the vertebrae of the spine) lose their shape and over time protrude into the spinal canal, which puts pressure on the spinal cord. Usually, the hind legs are affected. Older, large-breed dogs may also suffer from pressure on the neck and spine caused by a congenital malformation of the ligaments surrounding the cord, or malformation of the neck vertebrae. Breeds most commonly afflicted with this problem are Basset Hounds, Beagles, Clumber Spaniels, Dachshunds, Doberman Pinschers, French Bulldogs, Pekingese, and Skye Terriers.

**Spinal meningitis:** Immune mediated meningitis of the spinal cord is recognized in dogs. The meninges are three membranes that line the spinal cord. Signs of spinal meningitis include cyclical bouts of fever, severe neck pain and rigidity, reluctance to move, and depression. Each attack may last for five to ten days, often with periods of complete or partial recovery that last for a week or so. The cause is not known, is usually self-limiting, and is most often seen in adolescent or young adult dogs. Breeds most often affected are Akitas, Beagles, Boxers, and German Shorthaired Pointers.

A more severe type of immune-mediated spinal meningitis occurs in young Bernese Mountain Dogs, in which the condition is less likely to be self-limiting and may require long-term high doses of glucocorticoids.

**Spinal paralysis:** See *paralysis (plegia, paresis),* page 342.

**Stenotic nares:** This is a congenital defect that occurs commonly in brachycephalic breeds, in which the outside opening of the nose is much too narrow. This condition can lead to problems in the upper respiratory passage. Boston Terriers, Pekingese, and Pugs are especially apt to have this defect, which can be corrected surgically.

**Stroke (or ictus):** This is a sudden, severe blow, seizure, or attack on the ventricles of the heart, which usually involves loss of consciousness. Immediate veterinary help and probably hospitalization are necessary to stabilize the heart.
*Heat stroke/hypothermia* is caused by long, excessive, exposure to heat (or sun), and inadequate drinking water; or it is an appropriate response to an infection, exercise, or confinement in a hot or humid environment. It is characterized by dry skin, elevated body temperature, vertigo, headache, thirst, nausea, muscle cramps, and an elevation of body temperature. Cell damage begins to occur at body temperatures above 108 degrees Fahrenheit. Severe hyperthermia results in kidney and liver failure, blood-clotting disorders, metabolic disorders, gastrointestinal failure, hypoxemia, destruction of skeletal muscle cells, brain dysfunction, and heart failure. Effective cooling, including plenty of drinking water, wetting of the dog with cool water, using a fan, and removal to a cool place, will help. With these steps, a dog will recover fairly quickly. Brachycephalic breeds, with their shortened airways, are especially prone to heatstroke. *Veterinary help should be sought as soon as possible.*
*Heat exhaustion* occurs when a dog is exercised on a particularly hot, humid day. The animal may collapse, lose normal brain activity, feel sick, vomit, and have muscle cramps and abnormally rapid heartbeat and breathing, muscular weakness, and fainting spells. Some of the cooling methods above should help, but *the dog should be seen by a veterinarian for assessment.*

**Torsion:** (See also *bloat.*) Torsion is the act or process of rotating, turning, or twisting around a central axis. In dogs, *gastric torsion* is an acute, quickly progressing abdominal enlargement caused by the distention or twisting of the stomach. It occurs mainly in large-breed dogs, usually after a big meal, and can cause death in a short time. The enlarged stomach interferes with the return of blood flow to the heart, lungs, stomach, and spleen; it can lead to severe tissue damage and death. Gastric torsion is a severe, life-threatening *emergency,* which requires immediate veterinary help; the veterinarian will insert a tube to remove gas from the stomach and then assess whether the stomach has twisted. If the stomach is twisted, surgery must be performed to repair it, and the dog may have to be hospitalized for follow-up observations. Breeds prone to this problem are Akitas, Black and Tan Coonhounds, Bloodhounds, Borzois, Briards, Chow Chows, Collies, English Foxhounds, Gordon Setters, Greater Swiss Mountain Dogs, Greyhounds, Irish Wolfhounds, Komondors, Samoyeds, Scottish Deerhounds, and Weimaraners.

**Thyroid problems/diseases:** The thyroid glands are part of the *endocrine system,* and they exert a major impact on a dog's metabolism and regulate how rapidly a dog's body's metabolic functions occur. The glands are two lobes located on either side of the windpipe. (Because of its two-sided structure, the thyroid gland is often called the "thyroid glands.") It secretes two major hormones, *thyroxine,* and *triiodothyronine,* which together are referred to as *thyroid hormone.* Secretions of thyroid hormones are controlled by the *pituitary gland* via the pituitary hormone known as *thyrotropin or thyroid-stimulating hormone (TSH).*

The thyroid hormone regulates the overall metabolism of almost all body cells. Thyroid problems can affect all organs and can produce many different manifestations. The thyroid gland also produces another important hormone, *calcitonin,* which lowers blood calcium levels. This acts to decrease the *parathyroid hormone (PTH),* produced by the parathyroid glands, which raises blood calcium levels by drawing calcium out of the bones. Akitas, Alaskan Malamutes, Bearded Collies, Belgian Malinois and Tervurens, Borzois, Boxers, Brittany Spaniels, Chow Chows, Clumber Spaniels, Collies, Dalmatians, English Setters, German Shepherds, German Shorthaired Pointers, German Wirehaired Pointers, Great Pyrenees, Irish Setters, Italian Greyhounds, Komondors, Miniature Pinschers, Norwegian Elkhounds, Petit Basset

Griffon Vendéens, Rhodesian Ridgebacks, Scottish Deerhounds, Shetland Sheepdogs, Siberian Huskies, Tibetan Terriers, and Vizslas are particularly susceptible to these diseases.

**Tumors:** (See also *cancer,* page 311): Dogs are susceptible to a large variety of tumor types, and they can appear in a number of body parts. The most common sites for cancer in dogs are the skin, mammary glands, lymph nodes and other blood-forming organs, mouth, and bones; and any site may develop either *benign* (incapable of spreading) or *malignant* (capable of spreading) tumors. The tumor types most often seen in dogs are *adenocarcinomas* (malignant tumors in glandular tissue), malignant *lymphomas* (malignant tumors of the glandular tissue), *lymphomas* (malignant tumors of the lymphocytes), and *osteosarcomas* (malignant bone tumors). There are also many benign and malignant skin tumors. Older dogs are especially susceptible to tumors. Sometimes tumors are also seen during the periods just before and after birth, and others occur early in a dog's life. When tumors appear in a young dog, it is often because of exposure to a cancer-causing agent, or it may be a spontaneous mutation that occurs prior to birth. *Perianal gland* tumors usually affect aging males. Boxers and Scottish Terriers are at risk for malignant *melanomas* (a malignant tumor of pigmented skin cells); large and giant breeds are prone to malignant bone tumors; German Shepherds are prone toward *hemangiosarcomas* (malignant tumors of the blood vessels); Saint Bernards are at risk for osteosarcoma; English Bullmastiffs for malignant lymphoma; rare blood disorders in Bernese Mountain Dogs; while the sporting breeds have an increased chance of mammary gland tumors.

**Urinary stones:** Dogs with urinary stones may have bloody urine, tend to urinate frequently in small quantities, and may have difficulty holding their urine. "Infection stones" are caused by a bacterium in the urinary tract that may cause *struvite* stones, which are, in turn, all caused by *staphylococcal UTI.* Diagnosis is made by a urine culture, direct culture of the stones, identification of the causative bacteria, and antimicrobial susceptibility testing. Management of urinary stones of any type begins with complete surgical removal of the stones themselves. Penicillin is the antibiotic of choice for all UTI caused by staphylococci. The dog's urine should be retested when the stitches are removed. If the urine is negative for bacteria at this time, a six-month treatment with long-term, low-dose antibiotics should be started. If the urinary tract remains bacteria-free, stones should not form again; however, dogs that are susceptible to staphylococcal UTI remain at risk for a further stone-forming episode months to years later. A low-protein, low-ash, high-salt commercial dog food is recommended to help dissolve struvite urinary stones but, because many stones are combinations of struvite and *apatite (calcium-phosphate)*, struvite and *uric acid*, or struvite and *oxalate* (salt of oxalic acid) the components other than struvite are not affected by this diet and some stones may not dissolve at all, or dissolve incompletely. At the same time, antibiotic use is important and should be continued until the stones have either disappeared or it becomes clear that they will not dissolve. Dogs on a stone-dissolving diet must not be supplemented with other foods. X rays should be taken every three weeks to see if the stones are dissolving. Male dogs should not undergo dietary dissolution of urinary calculi because the smaller size calculi may pass into the urethra and cause acute urinary obstruction, which is an *emergency* that requires immediate veterinary care. Dalmatians have a high incidence of *urate* (acid) stones. In these dogs, it is advised to give a high-quality, low-purine prescription diet after surgery. *Allopurinol* is a medicine that helps to decrease the amount of uric acid in a dog's urine, and should be given to affected Dalmatians for life.

**Von Willebrand's disease:** This is an hereditary bleeding disorder in which clotting factors are deficient. It is characterized by hematomas, intermittent lameness caused by bleeding in the joints, and nosebleeds. Puppies bleed excessively when they are teething or if they have ear or tail traumas. Treatment is mainly supportive, and diagnosis is made by a blood test. Basset Hounds, Bearded Collies, Doberman Pinschers, Fox Terriers, German Shorthaired Pointers, Golden Retrievers, Miniature Schnauzers, and Tibetan Terriers all have a propensity for this disease.

# Appendix II

# DIRECTORY OF DOG ORGANIZATIONS

AKC Canine Health Foundation
252 West Garfield Road, Suite #160
Aurora, Ohio 44202-8856
(330) 995-0807
www.akcchf.org
E-mail: akcchf@aol.com

American Kennel Club
260 Madison Avenue
New York, New York 10016
(212) 696-8200
www.akc.org

AVMA, American Veterinary Medical Association
1931 N. Meacham Road, Suite #100
Schaumburg, Illinois 60173
(847) 925-8070
www.avma.org
E-mail: avmaininfo@avma.org

AAHA, American Animal Hospital Association
P.O. Box 150899
Denver, Colorado 80215
(800) 252-2242
www.aaha.org

ASPCA, American Society for the Prevention of Cruelty to Animals
441 East 92nd Street
New York, New York 10028
www.aspca.org

Humane Society of the United States (HSUS)
2100 L Street, NW
Washington, D.C. 20037
(202) 452-1100
www.hsus.org

United Kennel Club, UKC
100 E. Kilgore
Kalamazoo, Michigan 49001
(269) 943-9020
www.ukcdogs.com

Canadian Kennel Club
89 Skyway, Suite #100
Etobicoke, Ontario M9W6R4
Canada
(416) 675-5511
www.ckc.ca
E-mail: information@ckc.ca

Paws Across America
www.pawsacrossamerica.com

Pet Finder
www.petfinder.com

The World Canine Freestyle Organization
P.O. Box 350122
Brooklyn, New York 11235-2525
(718) 332-8336
www.worldcaninefreestyle.org
E-mail: wfcodogs@aol.com

Delta Society
580 Naches Avenue SW Suite 101
Renton, Washington 98055-2297
(425) 226-7357
(425) 235-1076 (fax)
www.deltasociety.org
E-mail: info@deltasociety.org

National Association for Search & Rescue (NASAR)
4500 Southgate Place, Suite 100
Chantilly, Virginia 20151-1714
(703) 222-6277
(703) 222-6283 (fax)
www.nasar.org

Photo by Bruce Plotkin

**Bash Dibra,** organizer of such events as Paws Across America, is the recipient of the New York State Humane Association Award and the New York City Veterinary Medical Association's Unsung Hero Award. A consultant to many organizations, he is also a trainer who has provided services to Martin Scorsese, Sarah Jessica Parker, Jennifer Lopez, and other celebrities. Bash is a member of the Bronx County Kennel Club, the Queensboro Kennel Club, and the Saw Mill Kennel Club, as well as the Animal Behavior Society, the ASPCA, Bide-a-Wee, the Humane Society of New York, and the New York State Humane Association. He lives in New York with six dogs, four cats, and bird. You can contact him at www.pawsacrossamerica.com and at bash@pawsacrossamerican.com.

**Elizabeth Randolph,** a former pet care columnist for *Family Circle* magazine, is the author of more than a dozen books about pets and their care, including (with Bash Dibra) *Dog Training by Bash, Teach Your Dog to Behave,* and *CatSpeak*. She lives in suburban New York with a Norwich Terrier and two British shorthairs.

**Kitty Brown** is a writer and pet columnist whose work has appeared in *USA Today, Forbes, Ms. Magazine, American Kennel Club Gazette, Soap Opera Digest,* and *Soap Opera Weekly*.